MACMILLAN HISTORY OF LITERATURE

ENGLISH GOTHIC LITERATURE

Derek Brewer

First published 1983 by
THE MACMILLAN PRESS LTD
London and Basingstoke
Companies and representatives
throughout the world

ISBN 0 333 27138 6 (hc)
ISBN 0 333 27139 4 (pbk)

Printed and bound in Great Britain by
Antony Rowe Ltd, Chippenham and Eastbourne

Contents

List of Plates

The author and publishers are grateful to the copyright holders listed above for permission to reproduce these plates.

Acknowledgements

I gratefully acknowledge permission from the publishers to quote the passage from Paul Theroux *The Old Pategonian Express* (London: Hamish Hamilton, 1979).

Among many debts for comments and ideas incurred over the years to friends with whom I have discussed medieval English literature I should particularly like to mention those to my Cambridge colleagues, Professor J. E. Stevens, Dr. R. P. Axton, Dr. Jill Mann, Mr. A. C. Spearing and Dr. B. A. Windeatt, and to my wife.

The book itself could not have been produced without the unfailing help and co-operation of Ms. Linda Mitchell and Mrs. R. M. Bruce, to whom my thanks.

The author and publishers are grateful to the Council of the Early English Text Society for permission to reproduce quotations from their publications.

Editor's preface

THE study of literature requires knowledge of contexts as well as of texts. What kind of person wrote the poem, the play, the novel, the essay? What forces acted upon them as they wrote? What was the historical, the political, the philosophical, the economic, the cultural background? Was the writer accepting or rejecting the literary conventions of the time or developing them, or creating entirely new kinds of literary expression? Are there interactions between literature and the art, music or architecture of its period? Was the writer affected by contemporaries or isolated?

Such questions stress the need for students to go beyond the reading of set texts, to extend their knowledge by developing a sense of chronology, of action and reaction, and of the varying relationships between writers and society.

Histories of literature can encourage students to make comparisons, can aid in understanding the purposes of individual authors and in assessing the totality of their achievements. Their development can be better understood and appreciated with some knowledge of the background of their time. And histories of literature, apart from their valuable function as reference books, can demonstrate the great wealth of writing in English that is there to be enjoyed. They can guide the reader who wishes to explore it more fully and to gain in the process deeper insights into the rich diversity not only of literature but of human life itself.

A. NORMAN JEFFARES

Preface

My story is told differently from other histories of earlier English literature already available. I assume no specialist knowledge in the reader and describe in detail a relatively few outstanding or exemplary texts so that the reader may gain some direct feeling of actual medieval works, and not be encumbered with lists or mere opinion. This emphasis inevitably leads to the omission of or only very brief reference to a number of interesting texts. The book is designed as a readable unit and not as a reference manual.

In the medieval period, literacy develops, and even some literalism. There is a strong growth in the concept of the individual as set against the archaic collective social group. Notions of religious and secular love take on special configurations. Medieval works of literary art are based on manuscripts which are intrinsically variable and are related to the nature of what is heard and spoken in a group; they are therefore different in style and attitude from the literature with which the modern world is familiar through the medium of print, for print disperses multiple identical copies of a text to isolated solitary readers largely unknown to each other or the author. Hence the different feeling of medieval literature. Medieval rhetoric, also, though bookish, is more closely related to natural speech, to the devices of folk-tale and traditional narrative, than it is to print-culture. Folk tradition is important, as well as the learned tradition. This historical amalgam, developing from the twelfth to the sixteenth century, is not unreasonably summed up as 'Gothic'.

We are paradoxically now in a more favourable position to understand medieval 'Gothic' literature, than we have been for a long time. Contemporary non-naturalistic developments in literature and the visual arts, the popularity of song and dance on radio and television, enable us to see and respond to many 'Gothic' or traditional, non-realistic oral characteristics in our own culture that were often misunderstood from the seventeenth to the early twentieth centuries. At the same time we can still respond, as all centuries have, to the remarkable continuity of English literature, to the humanity, love, pathos and comedy of many medieval texts.

There is no such thing as 'progress' in works of art. Homer, Chaucer, Shakespeare, Dickens and James Joyce cannot be put on a scale of progressive improvement. On the other hand, there may be progress in general literary *culture*, in the wider spread of literacy, in greater learning, in the range and depth of literary education. The medieval period, besides producing great works of art, was also one of great general progress in literary culture as in society as a whole. The Norman Conquest had dealt an almost mortal blow to English, the most advanced vernacular culture in Europe, at the beginning of our period. By the end of the medieval period the general state of England, and the achievement of English literary culture, were vastly improved. During the medieval period the main structures of the national culture were formed; they maintained themselves for many centuries after and not all are yet passed away. The history of English medieval culture is a remarkable success story which culminates in the sixteenth century.

Part of this story is the history of the English language, whose vicissitudes in the medieval period were crucial to its present supremacy as a world-language and cannot be understood in separation from the facts of language. The passage of time, as with all things, has much changed the language. For this reason the language of medieval English literature is sometimes difficult. Readers may therefore have to exert some energy and patience at first when they explore medieval literature further, though they will not find anything in medieval English as difficult as some modern English texts. Since my story is of literature the history of the language occupies a subsidiary place, but its fundamental importance must not be neglected. The passage of time, the various disasters which occurred, all cause the language of medieval English literature on first acquaintance to appear strange in spelling, vocabulary and, sometimes, grammar. But the strangeness disappears with a little familiarity, and the language soon reveals its special beauty and interest.

In the present book when quoting texts I have as often as possible gone back to the manuscripts or in some cases facsimiles. In order to minimise the apparent quaintness of the first appearance of these texts, which may give a new reader a misleading impression that the literature is quaint or naïve, I have regularly modernised such obsolete letters as 'thorn' (representing *th*), and 'yogh' (which I transcribe as *y* or *gh* or *s* as appropriate). I follow modern usage of i/j, u/v, and modern capitalisation and punctuation. In a few instances spelling is clarified, as for example by transcribing *the* as *thee* where necessary. I have sometimes supplied final *-e* where required by the metre, and made minor emendations without note. These are the conventions of most editions of Chaucer. For quotations from Chaucer I use F. N. Robinson's second edition (London: O.U.P., 1957).

The reader unacquainted with the pronunciation of Middle English can achieve a very rough approximation by pronouncing the vowel letters as in modern Western European languages and by pronouncing all the consonants. A more correct pronunciation is worth attaining since the purity of most Middle English vowels and the strength of the consonants make the language more musical than Modern English.

Verse varies in metre. Alliterative metre broadly speaking follows the normal stress patterns of modern English and is therefore not difficult. Other metrical verse often scans regularly, and Chaucer in particular does so. As in all such metrical verse in English there is an interplay between the underlying regular metrical beat and the normal pattern of speech-stress as dictated by meaning, so that the resultant rhythm is not monotonous. In order to achieve metrical regularity it may be necessary to sound final *-e* at the end of a noun, or inflexions of the plural, as *-es*, or of verbs, as *-eth*. Some verse may be less polished than Chaucer's, partly because of faulty transcription by scribes, but non-alliterative verse normally has an underlying regular metrical beat.

In writing literary history much has to be explained that is only preliminary to literature, and much more of great interest has to be omitted for lack of space. I conclude with Chaucer's Knight's words:

> But al that thyng I moot as now forbere,
> I have, God woot, a largė feeld to ere — plough
> And waykė been the oxen in my plough, — weak
> The remenaunt of the tale is long ynough.
>
> (**Canterbury Tales** I, 885–8)

DEREK BREWER

CAMBRIDGE

1982

1

Continuities and beginnings

Invasion

In 1066 the English people fell for the first and we hope the last time to the ever-eager invader. In the use of their mother-tongue for literature and records, the English were the most advanced people in Europe. England was prosperous and relatively orderly, with a high level of freedom and culture. But prosperity, internal division and ignorance of advanced military technology invited attack from two Continental enemies, from Scandinavians on the north-east coast, and Normans from France on the south-east. Harold of England defeated the Danish Tostig at Stamford Bridge, then to meet the Norman assault rushed by forced marches to the south-east coast near Hastings, where the abbey of Battle, founded by a grateful William, the Bastard of Normandy, Conqueror of England, now stands. On that low hill Harold was defeated by the superior tactics of Norman cavalry and himself killed.

The Normans were far from unknown, for England had many connections with Europe. An earlier visit by Harold to Normandy and a rash promise made in the time of Edward the Confessor had given William the Bastard some legal right to succeed to the throne of the francophile Edward the Confessor. But the English people did not want William. He and some six thousand French-speaking Norman fighting-men came for English loot and came to stay. The result was a savage pruning of a native culture superior in many respects, if not in military power and organisation, to that of the invader. Foreigners ousted the English secular landowners, and almost all the English bishops and the abbots of monasteries, who were the natural leaders of English society. A few English remained, like the long-lived Bishop Wulfstan of Worcester (d. 1095), and the turbulent young English nobleman Hereward, who for years waged a doomed guerrilla war in the Fens. The recalcitrant north of England was laid waste by William, not to recover for a generation.

William had no racialist policy. When the Norman knights seized a man's property, they sometimes married his widow or daughter, and had children who naturally spoke English. English remained the language of the English people. English literary culture seems to have lasted longest in the west, furthest from the origins of invasion and the centres of government, and where the doughty Wulfstan survived longest. But the flourishing of English language and culture was cropped down. Latin was the official language of the Church, which was the only international organisation in Europe and was the driving power of intellectual culture and education. The English language rapidly lost status as the language of government and education. The ruling class spoke French, which became the dominant language of law and of social and literary culture throughout the thirteenth century and half of the fourteenth century. English was temporarily maimed; on it had to be grafted many new words and structures. In the end, disadvantage was turned into benefit. Part of the story of the medieval centuries of England is of the successful struggle to achieve unity of language as part of the unity of the English people (see chapter 14). Yet if in the long run most of the effects of defeat could be turned to advantage, the division of languages, causing among the great majority of the people difficulty of access, and consequently hostility, to the higher levels of culture, seems never to have quite been healed in England. The surrounding Celtic cultures, which never knew such division, have never shown the hostility to education and culture of which traces have survived in England for many subsequent centuries.

The Anglo-Saxon literary achievement

The English have always called themselves the English from their arrival in the fifth century in that part of the island which is named after them, and their language has always been English. It has become a convention to refer to the English people before the Conquest as the Anglo-Saxons, but it is preferable to call their language Old English. They had a rich and varied literature. Some 30,000 lines of verse, including the great poem *Beowulf*, have survived. The prose is even more extensive and varied, including much translation from the Bible and Latin works of learning, many sermons and saints' lives and, amongst other material, a considerable number of charters. Some of the prose religious texts continued to be copied as late as the twelfth century in the west of the country, where Worcester Priory, amongst other places, gave some continuity. The descendants of the rhythmic prose of Aelfric (*fl. c.* 1000) are found in the religious writings of the writings called the Katherine Group in Herefordshire about 1200 (see below, p. 29). Old English verse must have survived the Conquest in looser oral forms. Its metre is a selection of rhythmic stress-patterns from the ordinary spoken language, with four stressed syllables, interspersed with an irregular number of unstressed syllables, making up each line. You can often hear this beat under the regular ten-syllable five-stress lines of later verse, such as that of Shakespeare and Milton, and in modern English verse. In the Old English verse line, three of the four stresses are marked by beginning with the same sound, and it is therefore called alliterative verse, though alliteration is not so crucial as stress-pattern. Alliterative verse of a looser type than the Old English appears in the twelfth and thirteenth centuries and reaches great heights in the fourteenth, but surviving Old English verse itself had almost no influence on later poems. Its artistic practice was lost.

The Anglo-Saxon Chronicle

The most remarkable part of the Old English literary record is the *Anglo-Saxon Chronicle*. It is unique in European literature; in itself it is the main index of Anglo-Saxon cultural consciousness. It arose out of notes made in monasteries to mark the separate years and developed in Alfred's reign (871–99) into a national historical record of major literary importance, various versions being written in a group of monasteries which to some extent circulated their copies and notes. It includes some poems as well as a saga-like passage of prose, together with more usual prose. The Conquest dealt it a fatal blow, though it died a lingering death. The *Chronicle* survived longest at Peterborough Abbey, and though the quality of the post-Conquest entries varies, at their best they make a moving historical record, which lasts until 1154. It gives us the first and a continuous record of the post-Conquest English language, known as Middle English. The manuscript of the surviving version, Bodleian MS Laud Misc 636, comes from Peterborough Abbey and contains various subject matter, but the *Chronicle* was written up to 1121 by one scribe, and was then continued by others, of whom the last wrote, and perhaps composed, about 1155, the unified passage for 1132–54. He gives the famous, moving account for the year 1137 of the Anarchy under King Stephen (1136–54), from which the following sentences are quoted, followed by two more in translation.

> This gaere for the king Stephne ofer sæ to normandi & ther wes underfangen forthi that hi wenden that he sculde ben alsuic the eom wes . . . Tha the suikes undergæton that he milde man was & softe & god & na iustise ne dide tha diden hi alle wunder.
> [J. Hall (ed.), *Selections from Early Middle English* (Oxford: O.U.P., 1920), vol. I, pp. 6–7]

> (This year king Stephen went oversea to Normandy and was welcomed there because they thought that he would be such a man as the uncle [Henry I] was . . . When the traitors saw that he was a gentle soft and good man and gave no punishment then they all committed atrocities.)

We are then told the terrible story of how, under this good weak king, the barons broke their oaths of loyalty and filled the land with castles in which they imprisoned innocent men in order to get their gold and silver, and

> tortured them; indescribable torment, for never were any martyrs so tortured as they were. They were hung up by the feet and smoked with foul smoke. They were hanged by the thumbs or by the head, and armour was hung on their feet. Knotted strings were put round their head and twisted so that it went to the brains. They put them in cells where there were adders and snakes and toads, and so killed them. Some they put in a torture box [*crucethus*], that is, in a chest that was short and narrow and not deep, and they put sharp stones in it, and crushed the man in it, that all his limbs broke . . . They laid taxes on the villages at times and called it protection money [*tenserie*]. When the miserable people had no more to give they robbed them and burnt all the villages, that you might well go a whole day's journey and you would never find anyone staying in a village, or land tilled . . . Wherever one tilled, the earth bore no corn, for the land was all ruined by such deeds, and they said openly that Christ slept, and his saints. Such, and more than we can say, we suffered nineteen winters for our sins.

The style is vivid, personal, emotional, even extravagant. It is passionate but not artless; inversion, parallelism, repetition, metaphor, give emphasis and colour, as Cecily Clark points out (*The Peterborough Chronicle 1070–1154*, 2nd edn., Oxford: Clarendon Press 1970). Many of the characteristics of later English, such as the decay of word-endings, fixed word-order and many spellings, begin to appear in the text, and a number of new words from French have been introduced, like *carited*, 'almsgiving'; *iustise*, 'just punishment'; *tenserie* 'protection money'; (not found elsewhere); *pais*, 'peace'. There is the linguistically curious *crucethus*, from the Latin *cruciatus*, though the ending was probably thought to be *hus*, the Old English word which gives us 'house'.

The development of language is discussed more fully later (pp. 280 ff.) and it is enough here to remark that Standard Old English has been lost, and spelling may vary even from line to line. Modern readers, used to the blessed regularity of print and unused to Middle English, will wish to be on their guard against thinking that because the language is variable it, and its contents, are for that reason inferior, quaint or absurd. The loss of a national written standard was all the same a disadvantage, and its re-creation took centuries of effort, to be achieved by the end of the fifteenth century, when it was then reinforced by the introduction of printing.

Social and religious bases of literature

Though the area around Peterborough, terrorised by the local warlord Geoffrey de Mandeville, may have suffered worse than elsewhere, there was savage banditry in much of the rest of England. In the twelfth century one ill-named Philip Gai who held Bristol Castle had a reputation for inventing new tortures. Robert Fitzhubert of Devizes boasted of burning monks alive in their church, and of his intention of grieving God by destroying Winchester and Malmesbury churches. The plight of the martyrs, the suffering of saints and the horrors of civil war were known in twelfth-century England. A fear of such anarchy still haunts Shakespeare's interpretation of the history of England. In the twelfth century and still, though diminishingly so, in subsequent medieval centuries, the risk to peaceful men and women of horrible and arbitrary suffering caused by both men and nature was great.

In considering medieval literature we must remember its part in the general flow of life. The constant danger of violence and the natural needs of defence and maintenance of order made the power of kingship and the ethos of the soldier the most noble secular ideals. As late as the eighteenth century Dr Johnson could say that every man thinks the worse of himself for not having been a soldier. The tremendous labour involved in an agricultural economy with primitive technology required the vast majority of the population to toil and suffer on the land. Harvest surpluses were small and a bad summer could bring famine, disease and death. The plague, or pestilence, the worst epidemic of which struck in 1348–9, and was called the Black Death, was an intensification of a normally hard life. Infant mortality was prevalent and probably four out of five children born alive died before the age of five. In an era without modern medicine, death could follow a broken arm, or drinking from a well of sparkling water. Everyone knew death at first hand.

Yet happiness and joy were also available, and perhaps more intense. The worse one's position, the smaller an improvement needed to be to bring pleasure and hope. The worse a position men find themselves in, short of absolute powerlessness, the more likely it is that most will struggle for life. Purpose in life is self-evident. Morbidity or even despair may occur, but rarely nihilism. God may sleep, but the universe is not felt to be a purely arbitrary valueless accident. Medieval so-called pessimism is too often exaggerated by modern literary critics; it was rather a grim realistic assessment of likely changes, based on a stoical religious acceptance of the inevitable suffering in this life. (People in modern advanced industrial states should remember how prevalent such conditions still are in the twentieth century in much of the world.) The existence of suffering does not make men in general less religious. The medieval thought-world, like that of all traditional societies, was naturally 'religious'; that is, it perceived a world in which material values and factors were penetrated by spiritual or, if the word is preferred, psychological elements. Christianity is itself based on the suffering of God, who is man in Jesus; he is the Redeemer who will in the end, and in one sense already has, overcome suffering. Robert Fitzhubert and other cruel men like him were not modern atheists or nihilists who did not believe in God; rather, they fought against him. Others, sometimes cruel men who had repented, fought against the Devil, whom they saw in physical shape. Devout recluses like St Wulfric of Haselbury in Somerset, and St Godric of Finchale in Durham, wore real armour, partly as penance but partly in aid of a real battle, as they saw it, against devils. They are good examples of how external to most medieval men was what seems to us mental. For us, such battles are symbolical, metaphorical, psychological, in a word subjective, though they need not be therefore less real. For them, such phenomena seemed largely objective. Hence so many miracles. There was less distinction between religious and non-religious spheres, between physical and mental. The 'mind' of a traditional society is less differentiated and specialised than Western culture has become since the seventeenth century.

The central symbols of Christianity remain largely the same through many centuries, but they were felt differently in the Middle Ages. Since traditional religion has become largely incomprehensible to those of us lapped in the comfort and *angst* of advanced industrial societies, and because a sympathetic understanding of religion is necessary for understanding all traditional cultures including medieval English, it may be helpful to take as an illustration a modern report on a poor traditional culture. The traveller and novelist Paul Theroux has recorded the conversations and attitudes of ignorant modern Western tourists travelling in a train in Peru in the mid-1970s. Their attitudes are sometimes matched by impatient modern readers of medieval literature.

> Those gold altars really get me, said one. I don't understand why they don't melt them down and feed some of these starving people. And the statues, said another: they're so exaggerated, always bloody and skinny. Everyone was shouting and argufying at once: the Christ statues were the worst, really gory; the Mary ones were chubby and dressed up like dolls in lace and velvet; Jesus on the cross looked horrible among the gold carvings, his ribs sticking out; you'd think they'd at least make them look human. It went on: blood, gold, suffering, and people on their knees. Why did they have to exaggerate, said one man, when it only ended up looking vulgar?
>
> I had been hearing quite a lot of this. There was patronizing mockery in the pretense of bafflement and disgust. *I just can't understand it*, they said, but they used their incomprehension to amplify their ignorance. Ignorance licensed them to indulge in this jeering.

I felt my moment had come to speak. I had also seen those churches, and I had reached several conclusions. I cleared my throat.

'It *looks* exaggerated because it *is* exaggerated,' I said. 'It's possible that the churches here have bloodier Christs than those in Spain, and they're certainly a lot bloodier than anything you'd see in the United States. But life is bloodier here, isn't it? In order to believe that Christ suffered you have to know that he suffered more than you. In the United States the Christ statue looks a bit bruised, a few tear-drops, some mild abrasions. But here? How is it possible to suffer more than these Indians? They've seen all sorts of pain. Incas were peace-loving and pious, but if anyone broke the law he got unbelievable punishment – he might be buried alive, clubbed to death, staked out on the ground and ritually trampled, or tortured. High officials who committed an offence had heavy stones dropped on their backs from a high cliff, and virgins caught speaking to a man were hung by their hair. Pain wasn't brought here by the Spanish priests, but a crucified Christ was part of the liturgical scheme. The Indians were taught that Christ suffered, and they had to be persuaded that his suffering was worse than theirs. And by the same token that Mary, the world's mother, was healthier and better dressed than any woman in their society. So, yes, the statues are exaggerations of their lives, because these images represent God and the Holy Mother. Right?'

Convinced I was right, I warmed to my theme. Mary in the Church of San Francisco in Lima, in her spangled cape and brocade gown and holding a silver basket, had to outshine any Inca noble and, at last, any Spanish woman of fashion. These divine figures had to be seen to exceed the Spaniard or Peruvian in suffering or wealth – they had to seem braver, more tortured, richer or bloodier in order to seem blessed. Christ in any church was more battered than the very battered leper in the plaza; he had to be. The lesson of the Peruvian – perhaps Latin American – Church demonstrated the extraordinariness of the Saviour. In the same way, the statues of Buddha as a mendicant showed a man who was hungrier and skinnier than the skinniest Buddhist. In order for you to believe in God it was necessary to see that God had endured a greater torment than you. And Mary had to look more motherly, more fecund and rich, than any other mother. Religion demanded this intensity in order to produce piety. A believer could not venerate someone like himself – he had to be given a reason for the holiness of the God statue. And he responded by praising it in the most appropriate way, by enshrining it in gold.

[Paul Theroux, *The Old Patagonian Express* (London: Hamish Hamilton, 1979) pp. 266–7]

Medieval Europeans and English in a similar way created the intensities of medieval Christianity out of the suffering and the hope of glory in their lives.

The *Anglo-Saxon Chronicle* died in its last flame of passion, and then there is hardly any English recorded until the end of the twelfth century, when a group of works of high quality appear. Also around 1200 we find a beginning of new historical documentation, a spread of literacy, as M. T. Clancy has shown. Songs and spoken tales in English must have continued without break from earlier times, but oral culture perishes with the men on whose lips it lives. Literacy is the key to literary culture. Around 1200 appear Layamon's *Brut, The Ancrene Riwle* (*The Anchoress's Rule*) and *The Owl and the Nightingale*, besides devotional works of various kinds, a collection of proverbs, and some early lyrics. From now on the record is continuous, and the polish of these early works suggests that even they are not the first of their kinds. Yet they are very different from any Old English works.

Layamon's 'Brut': almost an English national epic

The name Layamon is of Scandinavian origin, meaning Lawman, but he tells us he was the son of Leofnath, a not uncommon Old English name. The poem was composed in the late twelfth century in Worcestershire near Areley Kings, as Layamon tells us. Its metre is a loose alliterative line, reminiscent of Old English poetry. It is a history, but for all his historical interest Layamon introduces himself and his poem with a quite novel personal enthusiasm, as different from the tone of any surviving Old English poetry as it is from the prose of the *Anglo-Saxon Chronicle*. His alliterative verse, though derived from Old English, has a less majestic movement, and much internal rhyme.

An preost wes on leoden, Layamon wes ihoten. 1
He wes Leovenathes sone – lithe him beo Drihten.
He wonede at Ernleye, at æthelen are chirechen,
Vppen Sevarne stathe – sel thar him thuhte –
Onfest Radestone. Ther he boc radde.
Hit com him on mode, & on his mern thonke,
Thet he wolde of Engle tha æthelæn tellen,
Wat heo ihoten weoren, & wonene heo comen
Tha Englene londe ærest ahten. . . . 9
Layamon gon lithen wide yond thas leode, 14
& bi-won tha æthela boc tha he to bisne nom.
He nom tha Englisca boc tha makede Seint Beda,
Another he nom on Latin the makede Seinte Albin,
& the feire Austin the fulluht broute hider in.
Boc he nom the thridde, leide ther amidden,

Tha makede a Frenchis clerc,
Wace wes ihoten, the wel couthe writen,
& he hoe yef thare æthelen Ælienor,
The wes Henries quene, thes heyes kinges.
Layamon leide theos boc & tha leaf wende.
He heom leofliche biheold – lithe him beo Drihten.
Fetheren he nom mid fingren & fiede on boc-felle,
& tha sothere word sette to-gadere,
& tha thre boc thrumde to are.

[1–28: Adapted in spelling from MS Cotton Caligula A ix ff. 3r and 3v, ed. G. L. Brook and R. F. Leslie, *Early English Text Society* 250 (1963), and vol. II, *EETS* 277 (1978), from which quotations are taken.]

(There was a priest amongst the people called Layamon. He was the son of Leofnath – to whom may God be gracious. He lived at Areley, at a noble church, on the bank of the Severn by Redstone – delightful it seemed to him there. There he read books [*or* he read the church services]. It came into his heart, into his eager [*literally* splendid] mind that he would tell about the noble English, what they were, and where they came from who had earliest possessed the land of the English . . . Layamon travelled far throughout the land, and obtained the noble books which he took as guides. He took the English book which St Bede made; he took another in Latin made by St Albin and the fair Augustine who brought baptism [i.e. Christianity] here. He took a third book, placed it in the middle, which a French clerk made who was called Wace, who could write well (and he had presented it to the noble Eleanor who was queen of Henry the high king). Layamon laid out these books and turned the page. He looked at them lovingly – may God be gracious to him. He took the quill with fingers and wrote on the parchment and put the truer words together and compressed the three books to one.)

Layamon conveys the primal joy of having an idea, finding books, the sheer pleasure of turning the page, of writing, of elucidating a single narrative from multiple sources. His untiring gusto carries him through 16,000 lines. This is an archaic directness rather than naïvety, and it is not as artless as it may appear. The English Bede must have been the Old English translation; the Latin book is unknown; Layamon's principal and almost single source is Wace, a crisp and lively narrative in French octosyllabic verse, of which more later.

The poem survives in full only in the British Library MS Cotton Caligula A ix, which also contains *The Owl and the Nightingale* and other poems (see below p. 40), and was written in the early thirteenth century. One other text, in

British Library MS Cotton Otho C xiii of the late thirteenth century, is modernised and cut, which indicates that Layamon's mixture of the modern and the archaistic was already giving trouble.

Layamon demonstrates the trilingualism, the knowledge of books as well as of oral tradition, the developing self-awareness and individualism of a new era. His endearing relish for the act of writing, the solitary author eagerly taking up his (quill) pen, with no address to audience or patron, in order to relate the truths of the history of his people for his own people (since it is in English) is modern in spirit. Yet he evokes much that is traditional. His work is at the meeting-place, and margins, of several countries of the mind.

The River Severn near Areley Kings is a big river winding through a broad vale of fresh pastures, old woods and small hills. The ancient waterway has cut beautiful cliffs into the New Red Sandstone of the hills, giving the name of Redstone to the little village nearby. Areley Kings is on a hill, and from it you can see to the east the low green hills of England and to the west the Black Mountains of Wales. It had a little Romanesque (Norman) church in Layamon's time, now replaced by a more modern one of the fifteenth century. From the church you can still see much the same view that Layamon saw, though now with industrial encrustation. In Wales dwelt the earlier, though not the first comers to what is now called England. They were then called the British, and they are the heroes with whom in his narrative Layamon identifies himself and us. 'We' are the landholders, whether British or English, and our fight is against the invader, once we ourselves have possessed the land. In the story the worst villains are actually the 'Saxons', the historical English, who are defeated by Layamon's greatest hero, Arthur.

Story and style

The poem begins with Aeneas's flight from Troy, not, as a monastic chronicle would, with the Creation. We are in the secular world. Aeneas founded Rome, and his grandson Brutus came to Britain, previously called Albion, and to which he was thought (wrongly) then to have given his own name, occupying it with his people and killing the few giants already there. Then proceeds the long sequence of British kings, including Lear and Cymbeline, which is eventually spliced into actual English history of the seventh century.

Layamon is interested in good and bad kings and their effect on the country. He praises the beauty of Britain (a stock theme with medieval historians) (ll. 620 ff.) and the British are always in the right except when misled by bad kings. There is no 'narrator's voice' different from and in ironic relationship to the 'real' poet. Like almost all traditional poets Layamon speaks the action like a whole man, not a puppet, sharing and judging, as he communicates his information, joy and sorrow. He is pious, sententious and moralistic, condemning treachery above all, denouncing traitors and assigning them cruel deaths. Layamon has some sense of motive, of causal connection, of mood, but does not usually give us a richly encrusted realistic narrative. He is more archaic. He retails a somewhat repetitious sequence of the actions of kings both good and bad, their councils, speeches, battles (with more speeches), journeys, feasts; major images of human life that still have powerful appeal, all conveyed in a vigorous style which plays variations on a small but clearly formulated vocabulary. In deploying these images of stirring events he shows clearly his derivation from Old English poetry. For example, he describes fifteen feasts, all of much the same pattern, often introduced with the heart-stirring strains of the trumpet, with plenty of joyous food and drink (*heo drunken heo dremden*, 'they drank, they rejoiced': 1.6719 repeated 1.7024) when gifts were given. This is a note familiar in Old English poetry, especially in *Beowulf*. Brutus is a heathen and as such to be condemned, but the expression of joy in hall, at the feast, with the company of warriors, is common to all. It is both concrete, even materialistic, and highly symbolic and expressive, part of the general pattern of deprivation, suffering, conquest, joy, and it is natural for Layamon to return to these basic constants and high points of human existence. His enthusiasm never flags. It reaches its heights in the fortunately disproportionately long section on Arthur 'the darling of the British' (1.12356). Layamon must have known the medieval expression for King Alfred, 'England's darling', though his story does not come down as far as Alfred, and surely he sees Arthur as an earlier Alfred. In Layamon's Arthurian section the texture is even more enriched with descriptions of battle and festivity. Arthur is wondrously born and crowned, defends the kingdom against invaders, establishes the Round Table of his knights, resists and overcomes the might of Rome, creating a continental British Empire, then is betrayed by Modred and dies. The battles against the Saxon foemen, who are defeated as, we may feel, the Normans *should* have been defeated, have in particular a fierce poetic zest (ll. 9978 ff.). The Saxon leader Colgrim, with his huge army, attacks Arthur *athelest kingen*, 'the noblest of kings', as Layamon often calls him. Colgrim thinks to kill King Arthur with his people, bury them all and take this kingdom for himself, to fell the young Arthur to the ground. They fight by the river Duglas, *feollen tha væie, volden to grunde*, 'the doomed men fell, crumpled to the ground' (l. 10018). There is much bloodshed. Then Arthur says, 'See, my British, on this side, our utter enemies – may Christ strike them dead! – Colgrim the strong, out of Saxland' etc. (ll. 10030 ff.). Arthur raises his shield before his breast and he rushes out like the gray wolf when he comes out of the wood hung with snow, and thinks to devour such animals as he likes. Arthur drives Colgrim and his men into the deep water – there seven thousand Saxons are drowned. Some wander around as does the wild crane in the moorland fen when his power of flight is damaged, and swift hawks hunt after him and hounds meet him among the reeds with cruelty. Then neither land nor water is any good to him, hawks smite him, hounds bite him, then the royal bird lies doomed on his side (ll. 10040–67).

This simile is one of the famous half-dozen occurring in the passage between lines 10000 and 11000 which may derive from a lost Old English poem. The best of these similes is the one of the dead men's armour in the river Avon glinting like steel fishes (ll. 10639–45). Another passage in the same section describes a lake which recalls the deadly pool in *Beowulf*. Exceptional as such passages are in the poem as a whole, they are at one with a style whose plain narrative is continually enlivened with brief comparisons that have an archaic archetypal flavour even though they may be peculiar to Layamon himself. His stern epic enthusiasm derives its strength from the evocation of the ancient language and metre, developing the hammer-like style of such phrases as

Godes withersaka, 'God's enemy' (l. 906); *mid orde and mid egge*, 'with point and edge' (l. 2594). To complain of repetitiousness or ask for realism is to reject the essence of its poetry and of all the, to us, unfamiliar echoes and nuances of an archaic society. The recognition of the atrocities suffered in Britain from the invasion of Childric from Normandy, while Arthur is in the North, is cause both of the fierceness and the pity (ll. 10428 ff.). Notwithstanding the fierceness, there is also compassion. Arthur, for example, having thoroughly beaten the Scots, when appealed to as a Christian king, spares them in their misery (ll. 10944 ff.). The whole poem has a noble vigour of feeling; nothing is mean.

Layamon can also create a calm archaic sense of wonder, without fancifulness, as with the elves who enchanted Arthur at birth (ll. 9608 ff.) and perhaps above all in the superbly elegiac account of Arthur's death after the battle against his treacherous nephew (not, in this version, his bastard) Modred. As he dies Arthur bequeaths his kingdom to Constantine, and says:

> And ich wulle varen to Avalun to vairest alre maidene,
> To Argante there quene, alven swithe sceone
> And heo scal mine wunden makien alle isunde,
> Al hal me makien, mid haleweiye drenchen.
> And seothe ich cumen wulle to mine kineriche
> And wunien mid Brutten, mid muchelere wunne.
>
> [ll. 14277–82]

> (And I will go to Avalon, to the loveliest of all maidens, to Argante the queen, most beautiful of elves, and she shall make my wounds well, and make me whole with healing drinks. And then I will come to my kingdom and live with the Britons with great joy.)

Profound, complex image of the death of the king! It is very archaic, not internalised, nor spiritualised, not even Christian, though not anti-religious. We recognise the image but have no modern words or concepts easily to match it. The modern *elf*, though descended from *alva*, is hopelessly inadequate to convey the image of the beautiful supernatural women in the Happy Land of the dead. So the mysterious boat comes from the sea, and the British still await Arthur's return.

King Arthur

Thus Arthur makes his first and one of his grandest appearances in English literature; the British hero of one of the most English of authors. Layamon gives his Arthurian story an archaic flavour, as so many later English poets have done. But Arthur is a new hero for English. Where does he come from? He is certainly not in that great and sober Anglo-Saxon historian, Bede. Leaving aside much else of interest in the *Brut* we must follow his sources to their potent origin.

Of Layamon's three named sources, he makes no use of Bede, the second may be bogus, and (apart from the possible lost Old English poem) he really uses only Wace's crisp and lively narrative in French octosyllabic rhymed verse, transforming and modifying Wace's tone and sometimes his content.

Wace is more modern in tone though older in time. He was writing, if Layamon is correct, for King Henry II's Queen Eleanor, reference to whom opens up the whole twelfth-century world of the Angevin Empire from the Cheviots to the Pyrenees, Eleanor's own brilliant French court, the new world of troubadours and love and luxury. Wace has touches of French courtly brightness, frivolity and even tenderness. Not so the serious English enthusiast, Layamon. But he was responding, nevertheless, to the newer history to which Wace had responded, for Wace himself was translating and modifying the great secular literary success of the twelfth century, Geoffrey of Monmouth's Latin *History of the Kings of Britain*. Geoffrey was perhaps of Welsh parentage, presumably born or early resident in Monmouth, educated and possibly a teacher at what was still only the pre-university of Oxford. He completed in 1135 his 'history', largely invented or cobbled up from fables, as a scornful contemporary historian, William of Newburgh, remarked. Latin, the language of the Church, of higher culture, and of sober history, is used for a fantasy about 'British' history which not only captivated Europe but was seriously adapted as their own history by most Englishmen from the twelfth to the early seventeenth centuries. (Milton, when he wrote his history of England, abandoned it only with reluctance.) Up to Shakespeare's day Englishmen regarded themselves as 'Trojans', and London was Troynovant, 'New Troy', as in Spenser's *Faerie Queene*.

The success of Geoffrey's *History* undoubtedly depends on the creation of the story of Arthur, to whom Geoffrey devotes about a quarter of the whole book. Wace followed Geoffrey's structure (inventing, amongst other things, the Round Table, which Layamon further elaborates). A fascinating mixture of Latin, French, English and Welsh strands is being woven into a creative tradition in which the old continually begets the new. For all the rivalries and hostilities there is no racial prejudice in our modern sense. Thus, out of this mixture, Arthur, already known as a Welsh folk-hero even in Europe, became the magnetic image of chivalry which has drawn the Western secular imagination from the mid-twelfth century until today. We return to Arthur and his knights later in this book.

Wace himself is a little detached in his narration, occasionally sceptical, as well as inventive. If one thing about the essential Arthurian story is more striking than its drawing power, it is its malleability. Westerners have found it an invaluable secular mythology, providing a host of motifs, from the power and transience of earthly kingdoms (as in these earlier versions), to the richly varied joys and torments of personal relationships which developed later within this frame. For Geoffrey it was almost history; for Wace, almost a courtly romance; for Layamon almost a national epic. Malory will further blend all these elements together in a more modern way, without eclipsing Layamon's remarkable achievement.

2

The inner life

Spiritual instruction as literature

DEVELOPMENTS in the culture of Europe in the twelfth century profoundly influenced modern Western culture. The new religion, science, history, philosophy were in Latin. Englishmen played their part in the sphere of Latin, and some major works in English absorbed the new themes in their own way. One of the most striking is *The Ancrene Riwle*, 'the rule for anchoresses', that is, for women recluses; not at first sight a promising subject for literary treatment. But traditional culture is less specialised than modern. The passage of time turns all documents, even sermons, into fictions, that is, into symbolic verbal structures, which we must first understand literally, but may interpret metaphorically. Thus the highly practical yet spiritual instructions given by a virtually unknown cleric to three well-born sisters who lived near Wigmore in Herefordshire will legitimately claim our attention as a work of literature.

To many nowadays it may seem incomprehensible that three rich healthy girls should shut themselves up for life in the cramped solitude of one or two rooms, in a round of devotions, of reading religious books, of weeping and occasional self-flagellation. But in all periods there is a tiny minority who tire of the superficial changes of sorrow and joy in ordinary life and seek a more intense spiritual reality by limitation of bodily pleasure and freedom. All higher religions recognise the compulsion on a few to follow an ascetic, solitary, meditative life. In England even Anglo-Saxon kings felt the call. A powerful general movement towards the eremitical life of solitary prayer and penance arose in Europe in the eleventh century, with a new intensity of religious feeling. The English seem to have felt it particularly strongly, and the names of many such recluses from the eleventh century onwards are known.

English recluses: Christina and Wulfric

The life of Christina of Markyate is known in such detail from an almost contemporary biography in Latin, C. H. Talbot (ed. and transl.), *The Life of Christina of Markyate* (Oxford: Oxford University Press, 1959), that it offers an excellent example. She was born in the little town of Huntingdon in East Anglia just before 1100 to well-to-do English parents. Their place even in a Norman-dominated society was assured. Christina's aunt Alveva was the mistress and mother of several children of the famous and ruthless Ranulph Flambard, Justiciar (chief law-officer and administrator) of England. When he became Bishop of Durham, whose noble cathedral he was mainly responsible for creating, he set Alveva up in Huntingdon with a husband and used to drop in during his journeys between London and Durham. Her niece Christina on the other hand, when in her early teens on a family visit to the great cathedral church of St Albans some forty miles to the south, took a secret vow of chastity, and wished to become a nun. When she was about sixteen Ranulph on one of his visits attempted to seduce her. The episode, like so much of the biography, is told with vivid realistic detail, and though told with shame is also not without a touch of unintentional comedy. The story must have come from Christina herself. Ranulph inveigled her into his beautifully tapestried room in her own house; she knew it was useless to scream or resist, or she would certainly be raped. She pretended to agree, swore she would not deceive him, asked if she might bolt the door to ensure their privacy, and quick as a flash slipped out of the room. It was the beginning of a long persecution by Ranulph and even by her family. Finally Ranulph out of malice arranged for her to be married to a young nobleman, Burthred (we note again the English name). She resisted because of her desire for chastity; much family bullying followed. Eventually she was forced into betrothal, which was as good as marriage, but she denied Burthred consummation. Her father Autti and mother Beatrix locked her up or as an alternative made her attend their parties, where she was made to act the part of the hostess cup-bearer, with cloak removed and arms bare, taking around the loving-cup. (Hrothgar's queen performs the same function in *Beowulf* and Layamon frequently mentions it as an

Anglo-Saxon custom.) The parents hoped that since Christina had to take a drink with each guest she would get so drunk that her husband-to-be could easily seduce or rape her. Needless to say she held out. At last the parents secretly introduced Burthred into Christina's bedroom at night; but she was dressed and awake, and she told the young man the popular story of St Cecilia (it is also in Chaucer's *Canterbury Tales*) who persuaded her husband on religious grounds not to consummate their marriage; both were martyred. Thus a traditional story, in a traditional society, conveys a message. Christina's story-telling was as successful as Cecilia's own eloquence, and her husband, no match for any member of this strong-minded family, departed leaving her untouched. He was mocked for his decency. After several similar episodes, she was imprisoned at home: then taken to the prior and the bishop who, as sensible practical men, at first tried to persuade her to marry, but were then persuaded by her arguments and fervour that her previous personal vow was good and that the betrothal should be annulled. Her father, equally practical, bribed the bishop, who then reversed his decision. At last, not without secret recourse to the Archbishop of Canterbury, Christina escaped, though worried lest the boy who helped her might be killed. One night she had a vision in which he came and reproached her for her empty fears and told her to trust in God. The next day she learnt he had died, and knew that he was now with the elect in heaven. Heaven and Hell were very near in the twelfth century. The account of such visions, often rich in imagery, with their implicit or explicit messages, is an essential part of the story of this twelfth-century Clarissa Harlowe, who was in the end more fortunate than the heroine of Samuel Richardson's eighteenth-century novel. Though the story is told so realistically it is underpinned by the spiritual dimension. Eventually after many further difficulties and severe devotional practices Christina succeeded in becoming a recluse near St Albans, and the fame of her holiness and wisdom spread. She also became a famous embroidress of the work known as *opus Anglicanum*, and one of the great illuminated manuscripts of the twelfth century, the St Albans Psalter, now at Hildesheim in Germany, is associated with her.

St Wulfric

Not all recluses were women. The most famous twelfth-century recluse was St Wulfric of Haselbury Plucknett in Somerset, who likewise lived an enclosed life of penance, about the first half of the twelfth century, yet was consulted by all from king and pope downward. He had the gift of second sight. His life was also written in Latin, though with more miracles and less realism than that of Christina, by John, Abbot of Ford, about 1185 (M. Bell (ed.), *Wulfric of Haselbury:* Somerset Record Society, XLVII, 1933). Like Christina, Wulfric was also associated with illuminated manuscripts, having a scribe to work for him; he was English in origin and in native speech, but knew French and Latin as well.

'The Ancrene Riwle': manuscripts and author

The classic work in English connected with the life of the recluse is *The Ancrene Riwle*, written about 1200, though like other medieval works somewhat fluid in form, and revised in form at least once. The earlier version, extant in several manuscripts written from the early thirteenth to the fifteenth centuries, was designed mainly for the three young ladies already mentioned, although other anchoresses were often in mind. The British Library MS Cotton Nero A xiv, of the early thirteenth century, may be in the handwriting of the author himself. The author soon slightly expanded his text to refer more specifically to a larger group of recluses, twenty or more, scattered through the country, and perhaps less well-disciplined. The slightly fuller version exists in only one manuscript, the text of which is usually called *Ancrene Wisse*, a title which has the same meaning. This manuscript, in a beautiful regular early thirteenth-century script, is Corpus Christi College Cambridge MS 402. *The Ancrene Riwle* was very influential over a number of later texts, and was also translated into Anglo-Latin and Anglo-French. (As no general edition yet exists references are made to the translation by James Morton, *The Nun's Rule* (London: Chatto & Windus, 1926), to which also are referred the editions of separate manuscripts by the Early English Text Society. The classic edition *Ancrene Wisse: Parts Six and Seven* by G. T. Shepherd,

(Manchester: Manchester U.P., 1959; originally London: Nelson) is referred to where appropriate.) The author was very probably an Augustinian Canon from Wigmore in Herefordshire, named Brian of Lingen, as argued in the impressive study by Professor E. J. Dobson, *The Origins of Ancrene Wisse* (Oxford: O.U.P. 1976).

Noble love and suffering

Good negative reasons can easily be imagined for withdrawing from secular life in the twelfth century, but these devout men and women, though they were seeking a higher way of life, a more internalised, individual, joyous communion with God, were not taking an easy way out. Paradoxically they sought greater suffering and deeper sorrow than the world offered; they plumbed the depths of personal suffering to achieve a more than self-regarding joy. Of course their reasons were complex and conditioned by their own circumstances. In the *Ancrene Riwle*, as is evident elsewhere in Europe, the social ideal of nobility is dominant, with its accompanying characteristics of spendthrift generosity, passionate personal relationships, a desire for privacy, and a longing for the best, which can only be heaven. Moreover, the ascetic life also included reading and meditation. In a word, it was not for peasants. The very fact that it involved conscious self-humiliation further emphasises its aristocratic nature. Much of the eremitical ideal may be summed up in religious aspects of the ideal of love, which may or may not transcend sex, but which, as everyone knows, while it promises joy, inevitably causes suffering.

Anchoresses choose withdrawal which is a form of suffering greater even than living in the world. The paradoxical reward is great. 'Their *bliss* is to be hanged painfully and shamefully with Jesus on his cross' (Shepherd p. 5, l. 38). The author himself asks the question which was as natural in the twelfth as the twentieth century. Why punish oneself so? (Shepherd p. 10, ll. 16–17). How is God the better if I torment myself for his love? (Shepherd p. 11, ll. 30–1). But after bitterness comes sweetness (p. 15, ll. 12–13). God comes in love to the one who pines for him with a pure heart. He will make the soul queen of more than the world, of heaven (Shepherd p. 25, ll. 24–5). Love is the supreme joy. Love is God's chamberlain, his counsellor, his wife, from whom he can conceal nothing (Shepherd p. 30, ll. 15–16). Although the author recognises four loves; between friends, between man and woman, between mother and child, between soul and body (Shepherd p. 23, l. 9), and argues that the love of God subsumes them all, it is not surprising, especially in view of his primary audience of three young ladies, that the sweetness and power, as well as the suffering, of the love between man and woman, dominates his thought as an analogy for the love of God. In this respect he reflects the growing feeling for personal love between the sexes which is found from the late twelfth century onwards everywhere in Europe. (For its secular form, see below p. 93 ff.). He even reflects the superiority attributed to the lady when he says that God, the princely lover of the human soul, figured as a lady, recognises her as his 'master' (Shepherd p. 29, l. 38). The concept of love is enriched by many references from the Bible (especially the Song of Songs) and from many recent devotional Latin treatises, notably those written or inspired by the immensely influential St Bernard (1091–1153).

Structure of The Ancrene Riwle

The meditative life requires self-discipline, knowledge and reading. The *Riwle* advises the first and provides the others in richly imaginative prose. The work is divided into eight sections or chapters. The first and last govern the outer life, and are as servants to the inner six, which are appropriately concerned with the inner life. The first section regulates devotional practices and encourages much prayer for others. It begins, in typical medieval style, with puns (witty, not funny) on *right, rule, righteous*. The structure has a loose general logic in which chapter six on penance and chapter seven on love form a climax, but the method is allusive and associative, with much description, comment and aside. The text is studded with Biblical quotation and vivid, surprising, allegorical interpretation: though highly original as a work of literature all the material is traditional, illustrating the European as well as the English religious imagination.

Temptations and the Seven Deadly Sins

The second section is about controlling the senses which guard the 'wild beast' the heart. The five senses are each dangerous, though the examples concerning sight and speech show that the author has other anchoresses in mind besides the primary three. Some anchoresses are too much at their window, he says of the dangers of sight, though not the sisters. 'I write much for others' (Morton 51). The glances of the eye are like arrows. When someone wishes to speak to her the anchoress should use her maid as intermediary. She should believe secular men little and religious men less (Morton 66). The tongue is slippery, for it wades in the wet. Keep silence. Heresy, lying, backbiting and flattery are poisonous, though there is no heresy in England (Morton 82). Backbiters and flatterers, those two minstrels, are the Devil's lavatory-men. He gives a famous description of back-biters (Morton 57–9) which is based on one of St Bernard's sermons, whose dry and abstract scheme the author has expressed in vivid concrete detail.

The third section is on the custody of the heart. Anger is condemned, for man is mild by nature. Here the implicit dualism of so much of the most advanced religious thought of the twelfth century appears in the contempt for the body, very different from Layamon's archaistic unity of secular and religious. It is a great wonder, says the author, that the soul of man, the highest thing under God, made in his image, should be joined to the flesh, which is only mud and earth, and that the soul should love the flesh so much as to leave her divine nature (the soul being thought of as feminine) and displease God. The flesh is at home in this world and therefore bold, as it is said 'The cock is brave on his own dunghill'. The anchoress is not so, but is likened to a night-raven and, by an obvious pun, an anchor; she is the anchor for the church, to hold it, like a ship, against the Devil's puffs of wind.

The fourth section is about temptations, for, says the author, the better an anchoress's life the more she will be tempted – the higher the hill, the more wind upon it. Temptations, *i.e.* tests, are analysed as either outer, from men, such as praise, or from God, such as sickness, poverty, etc., or inner such as are the vices, the Seven Deadly Sins.

The solitary life is a wilderness inhabited by wild beasts, the deadly sins, the lion of pride, etc. The author describes the grotesque activities of the sinners in Hell (Morton 210–17). The proud are the Devil's trumpeters. The envious are his jesters, of the same kind as those who in this life can only make faces, and twist their mouths, and scowl, in order to make their envious lord laugh in his court. The wrathful man is a knife-thrower before the Devil, and the sharp point of a sword weighs on his tongue, because of the sharp and cutting words he once threw from him. The devils play with such sinners using sharp hooks to toss them about like an old rag. The slothful man lies and sleeps in the Devil's bosom and the Devil whispers to him. The covetous man is the Devil's ash gatherer, and he rakes up piles of ashes, and blinds himself with them, and makes arithmetical figures in them, like accountants. Like ashes is worldly wealth.

> The greedy glutton is the Devil's manciple, for he always sticks in the cellar or in the kitchen. His heart is in the dishes, his mind in the cups, his life in the barrel, his soul in the pot. He comes forth before his lord stained and smeared, a dish in his one hand and a bowl in his other, mispronounces his words, wobbles like a drunken man who is inclined to fall, and looks at his great belly. And the Devil laughs fit to burst . . . Give the toss-pot molten brass to drink, and pour it down his wide throat, that he may ever burn inwardly. For one [that he drank in the world] give him two. Lo, such is God's judgment against the glutton and the drunkard in Revelation.
>
> [p. 95, l. 30–p. 96, l. 12; see Morton 214–16]

In the Devil's court, the lecher has the foulest office, and stinks intolerably.

An anchoress may think that temptations will be worst in her first year. Not so; it is as with a woman in marriage, the first years are easiest for her, and God, like a good husband, corrects her more severely as the years pass. But after the trial comes joy in the end. Furthermore the Devil is subtle in temptations; like a wrestler, he pretends to pull in one direction, and suddenly pulls in another. Thus he may cause an anchoress so to mortify her body as to kill her soul; or to be so merciful as to become worldly. An anchoress may comfort herself in several ways, as by realising that if God hides himself, it is as when a mother plays with 'her young darling, and flees from him, and hides herself, and lets him sit alone, and look eagerly about, and cry Mother! Mother! and weep a little; and then with outspread arms she leaps forth laughing, and embraces and kisses him, and wipes his eyes' (Morton, 230). So does our Lord with us. Prayer was a great help against devils to many Saints, and the three sisters have the account of Margaret repelling the devil Ruffin in their English book of St Margaret (Morton, 244). And just as, when castles or towns are attacked, the defenders pour out boiling water, so when the castle and citadel of the soul is attacked, should an anchoress pour out scalding tears on the Enemy.

The Lateran Council of 1215 and the cultural importance of confession

The fifth section is on Confession. In the twelfth century confession became progressively practised until in the Lateran Council at Rome in 1215 private confession was made obligatory on all Christians at least once a year. Private confession means moral and hence psychological self-examination, increased self-awareness, which is a major index of the modern attitude as against the archaic. Confession requires a subjective, emotional consciousness. It thus contributes to more refined feelings, to a divided self, to the possibility of realising the self as against the crowd, to self-criticism, even, paradoxically, to the Protestantism whose individualism rejects private confession as not necessary. The possibilities of these developments are always present in all cultures and are strong in the Bible, but religious meditation and philosophy in the twelfth century, and the Church's efforts to educate the European peoples in the thirteenth, mark a great strengthening of them. Here in *The Ancreñe Riwle* we are well launched upon the process. Confession is analysed in two branches, many times subdivided, characteristically illustrated and sententiously commented on with examples from the Bible, biblical commentators and ordinary life.

Gothic sensibility in religion

This leads to the sixth section on Penance, of peculiar importance to the anchoresses whose whole life is a penance, crucified with Christ, in order to repay his sacrifice, earn his love, and share his bliss in heaven. Here, with the next section, on Love, is the heart of the book; suffering and love are inextricably twined in this Gothic thought-world. Early in section seven on Love appears a potent image of how God through Christ seeks the soul of man.

> A leafdi wes mid hire fan biset al abuten, hire lond al destruet, & heo al poure inwith an eorthene castel. A mihti kinges luve wes thah biturnd upon hire swa unimete swithe thet he for wohlech sende hire his sonden, an efter other, ofte somet monie; sende hire beawbelez bathe feole & feire, sucurs of liveneth, help of his hehe hird to halden hire castel. Heo underfeng al as on unrecheles, & swa was heord iheortet thet hire luve ne mahte he neauer beo the neorre. Hwet wult tu mare? He com himseolf on ende, schawde hire his feire neb, as the the wes of alle men feherest to bihalden; spec se swithe swoteliche, & wordes se murie, thet ha mahten deade arearen to live, wrahte feole wundres & dude muchele meistries bivoren hire ehsithe, schawde hire his mihte, talde hire of his kinedom, bead to makien hire cwen of al thet he ahte. Al this heold nawt. Nes this hoker wunder? For heo nes neaver wurthe forte beon his thuften. [*The Ancrene Wisse* (Morton 388–90; Shepherd p. 21, ll. 11–25)]

> (A lady was besieged all around by her foes, her land all destroyed, and she quite poor within an earthen castle. A mighty king's love was however turned upon her so immeasurably greatly that in courtship he sent her his messengers, one after another, often many together. He sent her splendid gifts, many and beautiful, help for sustenance, help of his noble army to hold her castle. She received all like someone without thought, and was so hard hearted that he could never be the nearer to her love. What do you want that is greater? He came himself in the end, showed her his beautiful face, as he who was the most beautiful of all men to see. He spoke so very sweetly and words so pleasant that they might raise the dead to life; he performed so many miracles and did great works of power in her sight, showed her his might, told her of his kingdom, offered to make her queen of all that he possessed. All this went for nothing. Isn't this contempt astonishing? For she was never worthy to be his serving-maid.)

The author tells how the king wooed the lady, fought for her, put her foes to flight, was himself killed, and by a miracle rose from the dead. 'The king is Jesus', who woos our soul besieged by devils.

> And he like a noble suitor after many messengers and many good deeds came to prove his love and showed by chivalry that he was worthy of love, as knights were once accustomed to do. He took part in a tournament, and had, for his beloved's love, like a brave knight, his shield, pierced on each side. His shield, which concealed his divinity,

> was his beloved body that was spread on the cross, broad as a shield above, as his stretched-out arms, narrow beneath, with the one foot, as many think, set upon the other. That this shield has no sides is a symbol that his disciples, who should stand by him and have been his sides, all fled from him and left him as a stranger, as the gospel says.
>
> [Morton 390–2]

This translation, as literal as it can be, gives little sense of the subtle interlacing of thought and word, or of the supreme artistry of the placing of words.

The ancient folk-tale theme of King Cophetua and the beggar-maid had been early taken up by Eastern monastic writers but is more widespread in religious writers of the twelfth century. *The Ancrene Riwle* gives it a concrete, personal, feudal embodiment in this *exemplum*, as illustrative stories were called, which was popular up to Langland's equally characteristic adaptation (omitting the lady) of the theme of the Christ-knight. Secular imagery is used for religious purposes. The author's reference to tournaments to win the love of ladies is so early that it probably represents a memory of Geoffrey of Monmouth's *History of the Kings of Britain* rather than actual practice, but such tournaments came to be held in the thirteenth century, for chivalric life was much prone to imitating literature. The reference to Christ crucified with one nail piercing the feet is equally a response to the new Gothic feeling for suffering, pity and love. Such a representation, involving the body in the characteristically sinewy S-curve of Gothic art, is more apparently realistic, and more painful to see, than the preceding Romanesque representation with the feet side by side, which is the only style known before the early thirteenth century. The iconography of the Gothic Christ is a product of the new devotion to the physical suffering and death of Christ, known as his Passion, which developed around 1200, and of which this is by far the earliest vernacular description. The whole devotional movement represents not only a new emotionalism but a new realism, still balanced against a basically non-naturalistic or non-materialistic view of life. The tension between new realism and a fundamentally non-materialistic, a mentalist view of life is characteristic of the general Gothic 'style' of the era. The new emotionalism led to such figures as Francis of Assisi in the thirteenth century, who himself received the *stigmata*, that is, signs of Christ's wounds on his own body, and whose fervent piety exercised a far-flung effect through his order of Franciscan Friars extending to secular feelings and vernacular literature.

The realism of daily life

This section on Love, the seventh chapter of *The Ancrene Riwle*, is rich in material and imagery, representing, as Professor Shepherd shows, many strands of European culture. The following section, the eighth and last, moves easily from the latest European thought to many practical considerations of the outer rule which bring alive for us much of the ordinary detail of life in the twelfth century in Herefordshire. The anchoresses should keep no animals save a cat. If an anchoress keeps a cow, she is concerned for it, and thereby becomes worldly. The sisters should have nothing to do with buying or selling goods, or looking after other people's goods for them. They should be clothed warmly but coarsely, and wear no hair shirt nor iron fetters, nor adornments such as rings, nor gloves. They should never be idle, but they should not sew purses or silken bands for gifts to make friends; they should sew and mend church vestments and poor men's clothes. They should not teach children, though the maid may teach little girls if necessary. They should not write or receive letters without permission, and should have their hair cut, and be let blood, four times a year. When they let blood they are to do nothing for three days but talk with their maidens and amuse themselves together with instructive tales, as they may also often do when sick, or dispirited, or sorry about some worldly matter. They should also rest when ill, for it is foolish for the sake of one day to lose ten or twelve. They are to wash whenever necessary, as often as they will. Each anchoress should have two maidservants, and the author refers to Slurry the cook's boy – *slurry* means dirty water, and this nickname is doubtless a shared joke. At the end we are again reminded that this strenuous effort towards the inner life is not a voyage into mere personal subjectivity. The sisters are urged to read the book, and to pray for the author and for other people. As for him, he would rather make the toilsome journey to Rome again than have the book to do again.

Other devotional texts

The Ancrene Riwle is part of a whole group of English devotional texts, not by the same author, but also in excellent prose. These are called the Katherine Group after *The Life of St Katherine* which is one of them. The group includes *The Life of St Margaret*, other saints' lives, an alliterative prose tract entitled *Holy Maidenhood*, giving a gruesome picture of the pains of marriage for women, a prose allegory called *The Guardian of the Soul*: (*Sawles Warde*) and some enthusiastically devotional pieces to the Virgin Mary and to Christ. The sermons of Lambeth Palace Library MS 487, the only surviving portion of a much larger collection, may be by the author of *The Ancrene Riwle* himself. The only manuscript of *The Ancrene Wisse*, which is remarkably regularly written and spelt, is virtually identical in spelling and language with a manuscript which contains many Katherine Group texts, Bodleian MS 34. This suggests the existence of a regular *scriptorium*, where scribes could preserve 'a living literary language which retained many features of the traditional vocabulary, syntax and idiom of OE homiletic prose' (Shepherd, p. xv). This in turn reflects a unified organised society of local gentry, from the family of one of whom the sisters must have come. They are clearly continuous (as Christina's family were) with Anglo-Saxon society, yet fully in touch with modern European movements. The very language of *The Ancrene Riwle*, though closely related to Old English, has nevertheless many new French words. It has nothing naïve or clumsy in it. Its influence continued amongst religious people until the fifteenth century, although new currents of written prose developed. The vast majority of people would never seek such heroic heights of devotion as these texts represent. Even for the devout it was normally enough, as in the case of the rich neighbour of the three sisters of *The Ancrene Riwle* (perhaps their father), simply to support with alms or other assistance those 'athletes of God' as they were sometimes called. But the texts represent the high skyline of divine aspiration: sources of beauty, terror and help for many more ordinary lives.

3
The question of song

'The Owl and the Nightingale'

STILL about 1200, we move from the epic struggle of a nation, and from the individual's cosmic drama of eternal salvation or damnation, from love of country and love of God in the West Midlands, to an out-of-the-way corner of a valley in summer on the south coast of England, where in the person of a poet we overhear, among the blossoms, green leaves and branches, the song of a nightingale singing so vigorously that it might have come from harp or pipe. Nature is seen in terms of man. The poet is hearing a debate between a nightingale and an owl:

> That playd wes stif and starc and strong! — debate
> [l. 5]

The pleasing absurdity is calmly announced and sets the tone. The light bright metre also makes us prick up our ears. This four-stress rhyming verse, with its basis of regularly stressed and unstressed syllables (final *-e* being usually pronounced) is something genuinely new in English, quite different from the syllabically irregular four-stress alliterative verse without rhyme of Old English, which Layamon still hankered after even when seduced by rhyme.

Beside the thick hedge, from whose security the Nightingale pours out her mellifluous abuse, is an old tree-stump overgrown with ivy where the Owl, whom many people think so disgusting, is perched. The Nightingale is the attacker:

> 'Vnwyht', heo seyde, 'awey thu fleo.
> Me is the wurs that ich thee iseo.
> Iwis for thinċ wlc lete
> Wel oftė ich my song furlete.
> Min heorte atflyhth and falt my tunge

Hwenne thu art to me ithrunge.
Me lustė bet speten than singe
Of thinė fowlė howelynge.

[ll. 33–40, Jesus College Oxford MS 29 f. 156 r. Cf. ed. E. G. Stanley, Manchester: Manchester U.P. (originally London: Nelson) 1960, p. 50]

('Monster', she said, 'Fly away. It is the worse for me that I see you. For sure, because of your foul appearance I often have to leave off my song. My heart flies away and my tongue fails when you are close to me. It is more pleasure for me to spit than to sing at your foul howling [*pun on* owl].)

The Owl replies with equal acerbity – could she only hold the Nightingale in her claws, she'd make her sing another tune. The Nightingale describes the loathesomeness of the Owl, her small body and big head; her nature is like the frogs, mice and other disgusting creatures which are her food. She soils her own nest as proverbs and stories show. She cannot deny her nature – as the proverb says, 'However far the apple rolls from its tree, it shows from which tree it comes' (135–8). The Nightingale is so pleased with herself at this stream of abuse that she again bursts out in song as loud as a harp, while the Owl swells with anger as if she has swallowed a frog. But who, asks the Owl, will judge between us? That wise clerk Master Nicholas of Guildford, replies the Nightingale, and the Owl agrees, for though Nicholas used to love the Nightingale and other creatures that are gentle and slim, he is now much cooled down and will not misjudge because of his former love. Such unique agreement between such extravagant quarrellers leads the reader to suppose that the ingenious and, as it later appears, insufficiently paid Master Nicholas, may well be the poet himself.

Symbolism of Owl and Nightingale

The Nightingale then resumes her abuse of the dismal Owl and they both invoke all the long-accumulated learned and popular lore about the Owl's largely disagreeable nature. In a traditional thought-world creatures have attributed to them a multiple set of symbolic meanings; they become part of the system of communication by which men frame their understanding of the nature of things. The poem's greatness consists of the way it gathers up so much of current attitudes, both secular and religious, and arranges them in a typically medieval pattern of contrarieties which are nevertheless held within an overall unity. The Owl represents a whole set of characteristics, attitudes and functions associated with each other through real similarities or historical coincidence. The Owl's ugliness and especially her dismal shriek have caused her for many centuries to be associated with forebodings, expectations of death, solemnity. The poet expands on the difference between the Owl's song and the Nightingale's to make it one of the dominant themes. He associates the Owl's song with church services, and so with traditional plainsong chant. He gives the Owl various defences, including an attack on the Nightingale's trivial cheerfulness (317–44). Above all the Owl claims to be useful to men. The Nightingale inwardly accepts this but nevertheless ingeniously puts it in the worst light, and makes a counter-claim for the joy she expresses (433–57). The debate is between songs of joy that disregard human sorrow, and songs of sorrow that disregard human joy; between summer and winter; fecklessness and prudence; care for the body, and taking no thought for it to the extent of dirtiness; taking no thought for the morrow, fleeting the time carelessly, and careful foresight; all in connection with the real or supposed attitudes of each bird. Each quality is seen in favourable or unfavourable terms, each argument is supported by abuse, proverbs, illustrations, examples, folklore and traditional fables of various kinds. Although not an 'imitation of life', a vivid sense of life emerges, both in concrete particulars and in popular (or learned) traditional wisdom. On the subject of whether one absolutely certain trick is worth a hundred devices that may fail:

> If twey men go to w[r]astlinge,
> And eyther other vastė thringe,
> And the one can swengės swithė fele,
> And the other ne can sweng bute anne,
> And th[at] is god with echė manne,
> And myd than one leyth to [the] grunde
> Anne after othe[r] a liitle stunde,
> Hwat tharf he recche of a mo[rė] swenge,
> Hwenne the on him is so genge?.
>
> [ll. 795–804, f. 161v.]

> (If two men go to wrestling, and each presses the other hard, and the one knows many tricks, and the other knows only one, and that is good against every man, and with that one he lays to the ground one [man] after another, in little while, what need he care for a better [*literally*: bigger] trick, when the one is so convenient to him?)

The sports and occupations of the countryside are as much the material as the problems of foreseeing the future.

Although the Owl is associated with traditional, perhaps monastic church services and plainsong, the Nightingale by no means attacks religion. On the contrary she claims that her joyous song is more likely to bring men to heaven's gate. This aspect of the argument is associated with a debate that began in the twelfth century and went echoing down the medieval centuries and beyond about the appropriate nature of religious music, whether it should be solemn or joyous, simple or elaborate. The Nightingale is associated with the new modes of 'cracking' the note, elaborating the music by giving many notes to one syllable, and thus, as some argued, devaluing the words. The Nightingale implicitly denies that religion should be all penitence and penance. The author of *The Ancrene Riwle* would here have been on the Owl's side, though he knew the Nightingale's arguments.

Secular romantic love

The Owl does not simply represent asceticism any more than the Nightingale represents (as the Owl accuses her) lechery. A most interesting section of the debate centres on secular romantic love. The Owl has boasted of her book-learning and powers of foretelling the future by astrology (1207 ff.), to which the Nightingale replies that 'an ape can look at a book, but know no more for it, and yet you have the nerve to accuse me of encouraging adultery!' (1325 ff.). (Connections in the argument are not organic but associative.) But it is true, the Nightingale agrees, that she sings of love to maidens and wives, for a good wife may better love her own husband in marriage than some boyfriend out of it. And maidens may love with 'right love' without losing honour. If some women are foolish, the Nightingale cannot be blamed, for though love is good there is nothing, however good, that may not be misused. The Nightingale was traditionally associated with romantic love and thus with love songs. She gives a tender picture of women, and 'may the Holy Cross become angry with those who pervert natural instincts!' (1382–3). The concept of the Cross as becoming angry is not a personification in the later abstract sense of the word, but is an archaic concept, often unexpectedly present even in modern minds, of the living nature of all objects; or rather, it is the concept that there are no mere 'objects' which are purely objective, material and lifeless, any more than there are birds with no significance beyond themselves, but that the whole world, animate and inanimate as *we* now see it, is in fact a vibrant web of personal beings, qualities and relationships. It is from these deep wells, easily missed by the modern reader, that much of the poetry derives.

The Nightingale takes a compassionate view of fallen women (1387–94). She is much harder on the sins of the spirit, as ruthlessness in making money or in getting to the top, and such like. As to girls who 'luveth dernliche' ('secretly', 1423), whose young blood leads them astray, they can make all well by marriage. The Nightingale cannot but pity girls made sad for love, for love soon passes, like her song itself. As to adultery, to lie with another man's wife is disgusting for each partner.

The Owl accuses the Nightingale of being sympathetic only to girls, while it is the Owl whom ladies turn to. The Owl is particularly sympathetic to ladies whose husbands are unfaithful, and she draws a genuinely affecting picture of an ill-treated wife (1559–61). Nevertheless, she says, many a merchant, many a knight and many a bondman loves and treats his wife properly and she treats him with care and affection. When such a man goes away his wife is sad and then the Owl goes to sing to her and she is comforted. After much argument on many topics the birds agree to go to arbitration by Master Nicholas, who lives at Portisham in Dorset, doing wonders in judgement and writing many pieces of wisdom, though it is a shame to bishops that he has but one dwelling.

And so we are left without a victor, or a solution. The poem is humane, open-ended and amusing in its very refusal to conclude. The light manner handles serious problems without trivialising them. At the heart of our experience is a real paradox, and it is possible to classify many problems according to this Gothic binary scheme, either putting one thing in straight opposition to another or, more subtly, as the poet often does, seeking two quite different and apparently incompatible aspects of the same thing. The poetic effect is a richness of ambivalence, of meanings connected by association (that is, metonymy not metaphor), a wealth of puzzles and jokes, laced with the derisive abuse of popular comedy. The style is as popular as it is learned, for word-play, proverb, repetition and hyperbole (exaggeration) are both recommended by medieval authorities on rhetoric and are the natural stuff of popular heightened speech and song. The vocabulary similarly spans the learned and the popular. The poet has a mind well stored with the concepts and parables of learned discourse and yet has a true feeling for ordinary life. Religious and secular interests are similarly united, with an emotional bias towards the secular and perhaps an intellectual bias towards the religious.

The audience for learned yet popular English poems

The poet of *The Owl and the Nightingale* may stand, effectively unknown as he is, for many quite unknown poets of medieval England, who filled the land, we may suppose, with songs now largely vanished. Master Nicholas, if he was the poet, was a cleric and surely a mature man, learned, experienced and tolerant, if insufficiently appreciated and perhaps rather boastful. From around 1200 we begin to hear of other men whom we may suppose he in general resembled, and from whom we can deduce the kind of society which valued literature in English. One of Thomas Beckett's biographers, William Fitz Stephen, had been a clerk in Beckett's office (his chancery, where there were fifty-two clerks), a subdeacon (a grade below priest) in his chapel, a reader in his law court, and sometimes a judge in the court. He would have been familiar with different kinds of writing, official documents, literature and law pleas, in French and Latin. Thomas Beckett himself, the martyred Archbishop of Canterbury, had started life as an accountant to a London merchant before entering Archbishop Theobald's service. A little later Matthew Paris, the famous historian of St Albans, not only wrote his histories in Latin but composed lives of English saints in French verse for aristocratic ladies (Clancy, *op. cit.* p. 61). These men would have been native speakers of English: by 1200 French had not acquired the literary prestige of the mid thirteenth century. The dialect of *The Owl and the Nightingale* is south-eastern, not the south-western of Dorset, and the poet may have been of such a brilliant circle around an Archbishop of Canterbury as Beckett attracted, but it is hard to imagine such a poet existing in a social group quite bereft of the presence of ladies. Although the poem is learned it would have been very suitable for reading aloud in a social group comprising ladies as well as knights and clerics.

There must have been other poems like, if probably not as great as, *The Owl and the Nightingale.* One that survives, perhaps influenced by it, is the charming *The Thrush and the Nightingale*, of about the mid thirteenth century, but recorded later in the Auchinleck manuscript (incompletely) and complete in 192 lines in the Bodleian Library MS Digby 86. Its opening lines are similar to 'Lenten ys come with Love to Town' (see below, p. 56), and in form and matter *The Thrush and the Nightingale* represents much medieval thought on the ever-interesting subject of women. The scene is a beautiful May morning. A Thrush and a Nightingale debate, the Thrush attacking and the Nightingale defending women. When the Nightingale reminds the Thrush that Christ was born of Mary, the Thrush immediately concedes defeat. Debates about love flourished, especially in French and Anglo-Norman, becoming more secular in the fourteenth century, and often concerning the rivalry between clerks and knights, which, since clerks wrote them, tended to give clerks the victory. The climax in English, far surpassing all such debates, is Chaucer's *Parliament of Fowls.* A graceful pendant to that is Sir John Clanvowe's debate *The Boke of Cupide*, sometimes called *The Cuckoo and the Nightingale*, written about 1390.

'The Bestiary' as an example of the archaic world-view[1]

Another poem, possibly from the early thirteenth century and one which is strange at first sight to the modern reader, but still of instant appeal, as modernised versions show, is *The Bestiary*. It is an example of the use of animal images to convey an archaic, moralised view of the totality of experience. While no nineteenth-century concepts of poetry could contain these strange descriptions of fox, lion, panther, elephant, whale, etc., with moral applications, which go back to the second century in Alexandria, and which would appear no more than charmingly absurd in summary, they sometimes represent both true facts (e.g. the way foxes pretend to be dead), and true perceptions about the nature of life, e.g. the account of the whale. The whale, who is mistaken by seamen for an island in the sea, and who plunges with them on his back to their destruction, is described in poems from Old English to as late as Milton's *Paradise Lost*. It symbolises the wonder and uncertainty of the world. The concepts of *The Bestiary* were very popular and constituted the symbolism of much medieval art. The English version of 802 lines mixes alliterative verse with rhyme in a plain direct style whose simplicity presents the image without fuss.

Anecdotal didactic poems and the Church's educational effort

The four-stress mainly octosyllabic couplet of *The Owl and the Nightingale*, besides being used for romances, was turned in the fourteenth century to practical use in a number of very long poems devoted to straightforward instruction. These are part of that large movement of education and self-realisation promoted by the Church, especially following the Lateran Council of 1215, whose effects hardly reached Britain and the English language until the fourteenth century. One of the most entertaining, and meant to be so, is the promisingly entitled *Handlyng Synne* by Robert Manning of Brunne, that is, Bourn in Lincolnshire. He was a Cambridge graduate and a canon of the Gilbertine Order, the only religious order founded by an Englishman. He illustrates his individualism by telling us who he is in his Prologue, and that he began the work in 1303. His poem is a translation with a perhaps deliberately equivocal title from an Anglo-Norman poem perhaps by William of Waddington called *Manuel de Pechiez*. He tells us in his Prologue that he wrote it in competition with secular works for ignorant English men, who enjoy hearing stories and tend to waste their time on rubbish. A similar aim is expressed in his *Chronicle of England* (finished 1338) written in the same direct easy style, not for *'disours, seggers, no harpours'* ('tale-tellers nor harpers' 75–6), but for the love of simple men. *Handlyng Synne* is a series of entertaining stories, remodelled from the source, which give a vivid account of the England of his day, often satirical, but without rancour.

Another roughly contemporary poem written with the same aim is the vast *Cursor Mundi*, an encyclopaedic poem which gathers together much of the popular religious material of the period. It is written mainly in the short couplet form, originating somewhere in the north of England. The Prologue lists romances and condemns the popular ideal of secular love in favour of a poem written in honour of the Virgin. The poem's aims are well realised and there are over ten manuscripts, though several are only fragments.

With this we move into more directly religious material, such as the Northern Homily Cycle, a well-written collection of sermons and saints' lives, deriving perhaps from Durham, certainly from the north, of about 1300. The stories and their allegories were frequently added to in many manuscripts.

Most popular of all medieval English poems, and now amongst the least read was *The Pricke of Conscience* in 4812 couplets, again a compendium of religious knowledge, and of interest in urging the need for knowledge of the self. It is, however, a dry work and its popularity was probably due to its practical utility for ecclesiastics.

More interesting are the various collections of saints' lives, a vast body of material in prose and verse, in which the habit of traditional literature of expanding and embroidering a given narrative is seen at its most extensive. They are best understood as religious folk-tales, and the earlier ones are the better. Verse narratives were collected in *The South English Legendary* originating in the thirteenth century but amplified later. In the mid fifteenth century Osbern Bokenham's *Lives of Saints* was written for a group of gentry in Suffolk which must represent many such groups in all the medieval centuries. The wit and liveliness of *The Owl and the Nightingale*, the combination of secular and religious inspiration in an individual poet, are rarely found, but we have the genuine interests of the whole people represented in many affecting narratives, portraying a whole range of human feelings, and many an incidental insight and comment on ordinary life. The most modern historians, those most deeply interested in historical 'mentality', are increasingly aware of the riches of this vast body of medieval writings, technically known as hagiography, extending from 500 to 1500 and later. The later versions, gathered together in *The Golden Legend* (see below, p. 258), are mostly in prose, but verse continued to be used. Verse or prose, they make little direct appeal now, but sympathetically yet analytically read they can speak vividly from a lost and very human world.

Note

1. A fuller account of my slightly specialised use of the concept of the 'archaic' will be found below (p. 125), in my chapter 'The Archaic and the Modern' in *Tradition and Innovation in Chaucer* (London: Macmillan, 1982), pp. 1–21, and my 'Malory: the Traditional Writer and the Archaic Mind', in *Arthurian Literature I,* Richard Barber and D. S. Brewer (eds.), (Cambridge: Rowman and Littlefield, Totowa; 1981), pp. 94–120.

4

The question of song – lyrics, short poems, ballads

Early poems: men speaking plainly to men

MANY shorter poems were written during the medieval centuries, sometimes recorded regularly in manuscript anthologies, sometimes recorded as snatches in sermons or other serious works, sometimes scribbled in a margin or on a flyleaf, agreeable witness to a haunting refrain or poignant thought amongst the heavier business of the day. These poems are of great variety and many remain no more than versified remarks and instructions. Even these may be of literary interest and unsuspected merit if we are not too concerned with post-medieval notions of *genre* and 'art-lyric' and especially of poetic subject-matter, for they speak often in a homely direct way, men speaking to men in the traditional sententious style of proverb, pun and hyperbole, about ordinary human concerns. They make a large record of what many English people wanted to say, or sometimes sing, in their own language, though the dominance of clerical influence in writing has caused a surely disproportionate amount of routine religious verse to survive. Secular or religious, there were no Neoclassical notions about subject-matter especially appropriate, or inappropriate, for verse, and a heartfelt appeal may sometimes ring across the centuries as with the plain sharp beginning, 'Tax has teened [ruined] us alle', though it is a learned poem, with lines in Latin alternating with English, in the manner known as macaronic. (Corpus Christi College Cambridge MS 369, f. 46b. See C. Sisam (ed.), *The Oxford Book of Medieval English Verse*, Oxford: Clarendon Press, 1970, p. 558.)

The Owl and the Nightingale was composed about 1200, but it is recorded in only two manuscripts each of the thirteenth century, one in the British Library, Cotton Caligula A ix, parchment of 518 pages, roughly 8½ inches by 6, and one in

Jesus College Oxford, MS 29, of parchment and paper, roughly 5½ inches by 7 inches. The contents of these manuscripts show a mixture of texts both religious and secular, in Latin, French and English. The Cotton manuscript begins with one of the two versions of Layamon's *Brut*. This is the later of the two versions extant of that poem and the scribe has modernised the text, substituting new words, sometimes French, for those that presumably had become incomprehensible, thus frustrating part of Layamon's archaising intent, but making another bridge between old and new. The Cotton manuscript continues with two religious poems in Anglo-Norman by a poet called Chardry, followed by an account in Anglo-Norman of the Anglo-Saxon and Norman kings down to the accession of Henry III. Then comes *The Owl and the Nightingale*. Seven religious poems in English follow and the last item is another devout poem in Anglo-French by Chardry. The Jesus College manuscript is partly made up with another manuscript of the fifteenth century in mixed paper and parchment containing an English chronicle, written in Latin, but the thirteenth-century portion in parchment begins with a poem in couplets in English on the Passion of our Lord, continues with *The Owl and the Nightingale*, follows with *Poema Morale* and other religious poems, *The Proverbs of Alfred*, then an account of the shires and hundreds of England, and finally the same French poems (apart from a missing leaf) by Chardry.

Taking both of these obviously related manuscripts together, we see the pattern of association already in *The Owl and the Nightingale* extended further, to history both poetic, as it were, in *Brut*, and then primarily factual, as in the chronicles. The Owl's interests are expressed in *Poema Morale*:

> Ich am eldre than ich wes, a winter and ek on.
> Ich welde more than ich dude. My wit auhte beo more lore.
> [l. 1–2, f. 169]

(I am older than I was [by] a winter and also one. I control more than I did. My mind ought to be more learned.)

The gravity in this fine poem merges into the 'sententious' style which was characteristic in the Middle Ages of both learned and popular verse on serious matters. Poems have a concern for the good behaviour and well-being of men. They are didactic by virtue of the subject-matter, not by virtue of being art, as the Neoclassical view maintains. Medieval art was mostly applied art. Verbal art was not thought of, as Sidney, Shelley, D. H. Lawrence and others thought of it, as by nature virtuous and superior, but as rhetoric, as a skill in communication which could be learned.

Poema Morale is distinguished by being the first English poem in the 'septenary' line, of seven beats often printed in two lines of four and three beats, and the poem was influential for at least two centuries. It appears in six other manuscripts and in its varying forms illustrates the fluidity of text of most traditional literature, from serious prose to folk tales and ballads. The central core of meaning or idea is given varying verbal realisation in different texts.

The sententious style

The sententious style reaches its full effect and natural subject matter in collections of proverbs, at this period, as in *The Owl and the Nightingale*, often attributed to Alfred, 'the shepherd, the darling of the English', England's most successful and best-loved king:

> He wes king and he wes clerek,
> Wel he luvede Godes werk,

to quote from the Jesus manuscript (f. 189). The collection of proverbs appears in three other manuscripts in varied form.

Thus queth Alvred:	
If thu havest seorewe	If you have sorrow
Ne seye thus hit than arewe	Do not tell it to a traitor,
Seye hit thinė sadelbowe,	Tell it to your saddlebow,
And ryd thee singinde forth.	And ride singing forth.
	[Jesus MS 29, f. 190v.]

This is popular wisdom at its best, brave, unsentimental and humane, conveyed in a pregnant, memorable, rhythmic style.

Proverbs have been despised (along with such other characteristics of the popular style as puns and hyperbole), by Neoclassical theory from the seventeenth century onwards and still today. Proverbs, like any other good thing (as the

Nightingale observes), can be misused, but they are part of the sententious style readily employed by great traditional writers from Homer to Shakespeare. They express the pragmatic wisdom of many generations in crisply patterned form – 'what oft was thought but ne'er so well expressed' to take Pope's definition of poetry. That they sometimes contradict each other allows them in totality to convey the contradictory truths of ordinary human experience, for they exist as a body, a vast incremental anonymous poem of multiple authorship, like so much traditional literature. Both Owl and Nightingale can draw on the proverbs of Alfred to support their case.

The variety of poems

The Jesus and Cotton manuscripts have considerable variety even if the English poems alone are considered. Besides such religious poems as addresses to the Virgin, in whose ardour and joy both Owl and Nightingale could join, there is a piquant outburst in the course of a poem in the Jesus manuscript beginning 'Weole, thu art a waried thing' ('Wellbeing, you are a cursed thing, because you come to the unworthy; freemen have plenty, the poor none (f. 179v. *Cf.* Carleton Brown (ed.), *English Lyrics of the XIIIth Century* (Oxford: Clarendon Press, 1932), p. 65). In the same manuscript is what may be the earliest of recorded English songs, a poem to St Thomas Beckett, the Archbishop of Canterbury martyred by knights of Henry II. The poet says:

Thu ert help in Engėlaunde,
Ure stephnė understande. you understand our speech
[f. 125v. *Cf.* Carleton Brown, *op. cit.* p. 67]

A list of the shires and 'hundreds' (smaller districts) in England touches a note of locality found elsewhere, as in Layamon's *Brut* and *The Owl and the Nightingale* and several lyrics, but touched more fully in a fifteenth-century list of the characteristics of the shires (Herefordshire: shield and spear; Worcestershire: pear, etc. (C. Sisam, *op. cit.* no. 235)). You can still get perry brewed in Worcestershire, and the same English note is not forgotten in some of Philip Larkin's poems.

'The Love Rune' and religious love

One of the poems in the Jesus manuscript is *The Love Rune* by the Franciscan Friar Thomas of Hailes in Gloucestershire, where there was a fine abbey whose noble ruins are still to be seen. Friars, unlike monks, were not enclosed, but in preaching and seeking alms worked a district from a base in a friary. The Franciscan Friars (called Grey Friars from the colour of their robes) were an order which arose from the life of St Francis of Assisi, whose passionate devotion to Christ, care for the poor, and almost incredible self-mortification probably did more to change the European sensibility than that of any other medieval man. The aim of the Franciscans, who came to England in 1224, was to practise poverty (collecting alms to live by) and to preach to the people. They were very popular in the medieval centuries, though also savagely satirised by most literary intellectuals. St Francis wished his friars to be 'minstrels of God'; they were influential in the spread of a popular emotional religious devotion and the accompanying literature. Friar Thomas's *Love Rune* is an early example of Franciscan poetry; a beautiful poem written in stanzas of eight lines, each with four beats and rhyming. In it he tells us he wrote it for a girl who had dedicated herself to God, and had asked him for a love poem. While praising heavenly love against earthly he uses the language of earthly love to express divine love, re-creating the traditional commonplaces in fresh words: life is short, the world transitory, man's love unreliable, his wealth a source of anxiety. Where are Paris and Helen, who were so bright and fair to see? Where the heroes and heroines of romance, Amadas and Tristram? Where the warrior Hector and the emperor Cæsar? It is as if they had never been born. Though a man were as rich as Henry our King, it would not be worth, in the end, a herring. Jesus is the most beautiful truest and richest – King Henry is only his vassal. Jesus has given you the best of gems, while you retain it, which is chastity: it is full of *fyn amur*, 'refined love'. He is the lover you should seek.

This poem is more extreme in its attitudes than either Owl or Nightingale, but neither would have disagreed with it, and it shows how powers of feeling were developing. Both secular and religious love are becoming more intense, more opposed, yet they are inextricably entangled with each other, always borrowing each from the other. Both illustrate together a new subjective intensity of personalised feeling, based on, but sublimating, sexuality. The English poems in these manuscripts are thus very varied, both old and new. They are the same kind of thing as the French poems, not surprisingly, since both are destined for the same audience, of which at least some members also knew Latin, since they must have been clerics.

Other Gothic manuscript miscellanies and various poems

Another great manuscript collection of the mid-thirteenth century gathers up earlier poems in all three languages, two of them sometimes in the same poem. English and Latin alternatively have a strange effectiveness. This macaronic poetry is a characteristically Gothic mixture. Trinity College, Cambridge MS 323, in parchment about 7 inches by 5½ inches, was probably compiled in a religious house, perhaps of friars, around the middle of the thirteenth century, and it has many pieces designed for the instruction of laymen. It has incidentally one of the earliest references to drama in English contained in a sermon on St Nicholas in which reference is made to a play to follow. This time the friars may have been that other great contemporary order, the Dominicans (Black Friars), founded by St Dominic specifically for theological study and preaching. They first came to England in 1221.

Trinity College, Cambridge MS 323 has many poems in common with other manuscripts in variant versions and is a similar Gothic miscellany which defies classification by genre. It contains the unique text of the poem entitled by Carleton Brown *The Bargain of Judas*, which is pure folk-tale. This tells how Judas lost thirty pieces of silver (given him by Jesus to buy food for their company) through the wiles of his sister. She lulled him to sleep with his head in her lap so that he could be robbed. He felt so distressed that he accepted the offer from 'the rich Jew Pilate' of thirty pieces of silver, no more, no less, to betray Jesus. The poem shows a stagggering ignorance of the Gospel story from which it ultimately derives, but conveys some profound paradoxes of betrayal in a terse, vigorous, impersonal style. This rapid presentation of the essentials of a powerful personal drama allows the poem to be called the first English ballad, though typical ballads are much later, even post-medieval (see the Appendix to this chapter).

In medieval 'manuscript culture', halfway between a purely oral tradition and the mechanical repetition of 'print culture', we find many poems repeated in different manuscripts with variations. There is often no single authoritative text. All the writings in a traditional culture such as this are to some extent the product of multiple authorship. The Trinity manuscript has a number of poems which appear in other manuscripts, some of them in the Cotton and Jesus manuscripts, others in British Library Egerton 613. Egerton 613 has poems in common with British Library Harley 2253, and that has a poem in common with the Bodleian Library Oxford Digby 2, and others in common with Digby 86 (both Digby manuscripts being probably Franciscan). Digby 86 has a major collection, and is clearly associated with Worcestershire. Harley 2253 is perhaps to be associated with Leominster in adjoining Herefordshire, though the lyrics themselves, which occasionally name such places as Lincoln in the east of the country,, and are written in various dialects, come from all over England. Both Digby 86 and much of Harley 2253 were written in the fourteenth century. Many such manuscripts were written by several scribes and compiled over a long period of years.

Digby 86, on parchment, about 6 inches by 8 inches, has a fine mixture of pieces. Several are in French, not all devotional, and in English it includes two rarities, the comic beast fable of the Fox and the Wolf, and the even more absurdly comic story of a clerk's seduction of a married woman, with lively dialogue, called *Dame Sirith*, which is the only true example in English of those comic tales in verse called in French *fabliaux*. (See also below, p. 77.) Chaucer's bawdy poems in *The Canterbury Tales* may also be called *fabliaux* but they are much more elaborate, rhetorical and humane than those in French.

The development of affective religious lyric

It is typical of English Gothic manuscripts that Digby 86 also contains a valuable collection of devotional lyrics from the last quarter of the thirteenth century, illustrating the growth of that emotional religious meditation which marks later medieval English devotional verse. A moving dialogue between the crucified Jesus and Mary at the foot of the cross has no concern with realism but in representing the emotional situation identifies all mourning mothers with Mary. Jesus is represented as speaking first.

> 'Stond wel moder ounder rode — cross
> Bihold thi childe with gladė mode. — heart
> Moder blithė might thou be.'
> 'Sone, hou may ich blithė stonde?
> Ich se thine fet, and thinė honde
> Inayled to the hardė tre'.
>
> 'Moder do wey thi wepinge.
> Ich tholie deth for monnės kuinde. — mankind
> Wor mine gultes ne tholie I non,' — for my (own) guilts I do not suffer
>
> 'Sone, ich fele the dethės stounde. — death's state
> That swerd is at mine herte grounde
>
> That me byheytė Simeon.' — that Simeon promised me
>
> [f. 127v. *Cf.* Luke ii. 35]

The many lyrics of this type of affective devotion arise from widespread Latin meditations on the Passion of Christ, and often evoke the very popular image of late medieval art in which the Virgin Mother is displayed with the dead Christ taken down from the Cross and spread on her lap, which is called a *pietà* ('piety' and 'pity' are closely related). This is a poignant evocation of the love that is suffering, though some late poems become so emotional as to be sentimental, in so far as such a word can be used of such a situation. On this subject, as so often, the apparently simpler earlier version is the more powerful. One of the greatest poems on this topic is the shortest and earliest.

> Nou goth sonnė under wod — sun; wood
> Me reweth, Marie, thi faire rode, — it grieves me; face
> Non goth sonnė under tre
> Me reweth Marie thi sone and thee.
>
> [*Cf.* Carleton Brown, *Thirteenth Century*, p. 1]

The two images of the sun setting behind the wood and the mother mourning the Divine Son (and the pun must be intentional) are conflated into a complex whole. Another piece of serious wordplay is the double meaning of *rode*, both 'cross' and 'colour of face'. *Tree*, the word so often used for the Cross, also evokes the wood of trees. Conflation of imagery out of time, a kind of implicit metaphor that yokes together material images of a different kind with wordplay or serious puns that achieve a similar multiplicity of reference, are characteristic of archaic traditional and Gothic literature.

Even more striking and successful in the same mode and on the same subject is the great poem composed in the late fourteenth century which is a variant version of one of several poems of around 1400 written with the Latin refrain *Quia amore langueo* (*amore* is pronounced with three syllables) meaning 'Because I am ill with love'. The phrase comes from that beautiful 'love book' of the Old Testament, the Song of Songs, whose richly erotic imagery colours so much devotional writing. It was early interpreted allegorically as the expression of God's, that is, Christ's, love for the Church, but developing Gothic individualism represented the beloved more and more frequently as the individual soul. The first line of the poem gives a remarkable image of yearning search for true love within one's own mind;

In the vaile of restles mynde
I sowght in mownteyn & in mede
Trustyng a treulofe for to fynd.
Upon an hyll than toke I hede
A voise I herd (and nere I yede) nearer went
In grete dolour complaynyng tho
'See dere soule, my sydės blede
Quia amore langueo'.

The poem describes a wounded man, (actually Christ, of course), sitting under a tree. He describes his wounds in traditional 'metaphysical' but vividly ironic similitudes. Then he invites the soul to respond to his love, for example, in the eleventh stanza,

My swetė spouse, will we goo play?
Apples ben rype in my gardine.
I shall clothe thee in new array;
Thy mete shall be mylk, honye & wyne. food
Now derė soule, latt us go dyne.

Thy sustenance is in my skrypp, loo! bag; lo
Tary not now, fayre spousė myne
Quia amore langueo.

The last but one of the sixteen stanzas of this version has the most complex and daring imagery, in which bride, mother and child are conflated, and Christ is lover, husband, mother to the soul. (For the Gothic notion of Christ as mother see Julian of Norwich, writing about the same time, see below, p. 252). This stanza has a plain affecting style, though the underlying images slide into each other with rich and complex implication.

My spouse is in chambre. Hald yowr pease!
Make no noyse but lat hyr slepe!
My babe shalle sofre no disease suffer no discomfort
I may not here my dere childe wepe,
For with my pappe I shall hyr kepe. breast
No wonder thowgh I tender hyr to: I look after her
Thys hoole in my syde had never ben so depe
But *Quia amore langueo.*

This version comes from the University Library, Cambridge MS Hh.iv.12, ff. 44v.–46v. It is a small manuscript of about 200 pages written probably in the middle of the fifteenth century in several different hands, containing a variety of poems, didactic, practical, lighthearted, devotional, by Lydgate and others. It has lost a number of pages at beginning and end, and concludes with Chaucer's *Parliament of Fowls*, of which the last third is lost. A scribble on f. 47v. declares that the book is owned by 'John Peter the minstrel', and lower down the same hand refers to the twenty-second year of the reign of 'kyng harre the eyght', that is April 1530 to April 1531.

Few lyrics achieve such amazing conflations of imagery, but the achievement is inherent in the style of mind of the period. It is the same kind of 'violent yoking together of opposites' as that of the Metaphysical poets of the seventeenth century, which our great Neoclassical critic, Samuel Johnson, in his celebrated attack on them in the life of Cowley, objected to as indecorous and unnatural, but which modern taste can now appreciate. In certain respects the so-called Metaphysical poets were the last in the medieval tradition. The Bodleian MS Digby 86 shares with Trinity College, Cambridge MS 323 a poem on the Debate of the Body and Soul, which is also the subject of a fine poem by Marvell, the last of the Metaphysical poets, and probably the last English poet to treat this popular medieval subject.

Affective devotion finds another supreme expression in a poem of the early fifteenth century in British Library Sloane 2593. This poem derives in a most interesting way from a thirteenth-century poem in Trinity College, Cambridge MS 323.

TRINITY COLLEGE CAMBRIDGE MS 323 *Exemplum de beata virgine & gaudiis eius*	SLOANE MS 2593
Nu this fules singet hand maket hure blisse And that gres up thringet and leved the ris, Of on ic wille singen that is makeles; The king of halle kinges to moder he hire ches.	 I syng of a myden that is makeles Kyng of alle kynges to here sone che ches.
Heo his wituten sunne and wituten hore, I cumen of kinges cunne of gesses more. The loverd of monkinne of hire was yboren To bringen us hut of sunne, elles wue weren forloren.	 He cam also stylle ther his moder was, As dew in Aprylle, that fallyt on the gras.
Gabriel hire grette and saide hire 'Ave! Marie ful of grace, ure loverd be uit thee; The frut of thire wombe, ibleset mot id be. Thu sal go wit chide, for sout ic suget thee'.	He cam also stylle to his moderes bowr As dew in Aprille, that fallyt on the flour.
And thare gretinke that angle havede ibrout He gon to bithenchen and meinde hire thout. He said to then angle, 'Hu may tiden this? Of monnes ymone nout y nout iuis'.	He cam also stylle ther his moder lay As dew in Aprille, that fallyt on the spray.
Mayden heo was uid childe & maiden her biforen, & maiden ar sothent hire chid was iboren. Maiden and moder nas never non wimon boten he: Wel mitte he berigge of Godes sune be.	 Moder & mayden was never non but che Wel may swych a lady Godes moder be.
I blessed beo that suete chid & the moder ec, & the suete broste that hire sone sec;	

I hered ibe the time that such chid uas iboren,
That lesed al of pine that arre was forloren.

[*Cf.* Carleton Brown, *Thirteenth Century*, p. 55 (text slightly emended)]

[*Cf.* Carleton Brown, *Religious Lyrics of the Fifteenth Century* (Oxford: Clarendon Press, 1939), p.119]

The thirteenth-century poem is an admirable devotional account of the Annunciation to Mary by the Angel Gabriel (*cf.* Luke i. 26–38). It is fresh and joyful, clear, with some dramatic force and sympathy; an unaffected evocation of joy at the promise of the Divine Child. Out of this is carved the second poem with subtle changes, well discussed by Professor D. Gray in his *Themes and Images in the Medieval English Lyric* (London: Routledge & Kegan Paul, 1972). The first and last two lines are the framework, taken from the earlier poem. But now it is Mary who chooses; humanity creates divinity. The three central pairs of rhyming lines meditate on and evoke by simple images from nature with incremental repetition, the still, secret, process of fertilisation, in which it is now the child who comes to the mother, divinity coming in weakness and humility to humanity. The final couplet embodies the unique paradox already foreshadowed, with the climactic words, 'lady' and 'God's mother'. It is a triumphant reconciliation of the simple and sublime in a true Christian spirit. Though paradoxical and supernatural it is seen in terms of the annual re-birth of 'ordinary' nature. Natural and simple, for all the profoundly moving paradox that it conveys, the poem genuinely is; yet the style and the subject matter contain wit and learning, a little of which derive from the earlier poem. The word '*makeles*' is a pun and means both without a mate, and without a peer, probably with a further pun on *maskeles*, 'without a stain', referring to the sinless, because non-sexual, Incarnation. 'King of all kings', deriving from the ringing biblical superlative 'King of Kings', comes from the earlier poem, but the surrounding words have been pruned away; it is in splendid contrast with the simple 'maiden', 'mother', 'son'. As object not subject of the word 'choose' it is yet more paradoxical – it is the supreme king who obeys his mother. The word 'still', so quiet in itself, has undertones of secrecy and even of erotic stealth, coming to the lady's bower. The dew, flower and leafy spray are enchanting images, and evoke also the traditional iconography of the Annunciation, in which the Virgin is always shown with a lily, her especial emblem. Both learned and popular traditions believed in the fructifying power of dew, and even in modern times, though we have dissociated nature from our natural feelings, and know that dew does not fall, it is impossible to go out into field or garden early on a bright spring morning in England without sharing the sense of fresh life and fertility. As Professor Gray points out, the power of such imagery here lies in delicacy and restraint. The falling dew was also a common traditional *learned* image of the Incarnation, repeated in the liturgy for Advent, the season before Christmas celebrating Christ's coming, using the Old Testament story of Gideon's fleece (Judges vi). Gideon put out his fleece overnight and on it alone the dew fell. This was interpreted as a 'type', that is an earlier 'example', of the Incarnation (on 'types', see below, p. 212). This apparently simple poem has an astonishing weight of significance lightly carried, in an easy vigorous metre and perfect wording.

The same manuscript, Sloan 2593, has like the others considerable variety. It is a small book, some 6 inches by 4½ inches. It may have been a minstrel's book, since it is of a size convenient to carry. It even has copies of two ballads (F. J. Child, *The English and Scottish Popular Ballads*, Harvard 1882–98, nos. 22 and 115). The seventy-four items include not only many religious poems but several highly secular poems, often with a sexual *double entendre*. One is the charming riddling poem 'I have a yong suster, Far be-yondyn the se' (R. H. Robbins (ed.), *Secular Lyrics of the XIV and XV Centuries*, 2nd edn., Oxford: Clarendon Press, 1955, no. 45) and the broader comic puns and grotesque fantasy of 'I have a gentle cock' (Robbins 46). The poem 'I have a newe gardyn' (Robbins 21) from the same world of domestic nature makes a most curious comparison and contrast with 'I sing of a maiden', though no parody or blasphemy is intended. There is a delightful carol, 'As I went on Yol day, in owre prosessyoun' (R. L. Greene (ed.), *The Early English Carols*, 2nd edn., Oxford: Clarendon Press, 1977, no. 457) which is a cheerful irreverent parody of church-going, with its refrain from the service, 'Kyrieleyson' rhyming with 'Aleyson' (Alison), the typical name for a wanton girl. Jankyn in the song is the parish clerk, presumably, and we cannot but be reminded of Chaucer's *Miller's Tale*, with its Alison and clerk Absalon, and of The Wife of Bath, whose own name is also Alison, and whose fifth husband is a clerk called Jankyn. This is the popular derisive sexual comedy of village and small town, the tragic elements of sex disregarded:

Jankyn at the Sanctus crakit a merie note,
And yyt me thinkyt it dos me good: I payid for his cote.
  Kyrieleyson.

Jankyn crakit notes, an hunderid on a knot,
And yyt he hakkyt hem smallere than wortes to the pot.
  Kyrieleyson.

Jankyn at the Angnus beryt the pax-brede;
He twynkelid but sayd nowt, and on myn fot he trede.
  Kyrieleyson,

Benedicamus Domino: Cryst fro schame me schylde;
Deo gracias thereto; alas I go with hylde.
  Kyrieleyson [Greene 457]

('Hacking' and 'cracking' notes is singing them short and fast, which many moralists disapproved of.) Another carol in the same manuscript unfairly warns men against hasty marriage, with the refrain

Man bewar of thin wowyng
For weddyng is the longė wo. [Greene 403]

Both Owl and Nightingale were more sympathetic to women.

Carols

A special word must be said here about carols. The word denotes a particular form of which there are about five hundred examples, magisterially edited by Professor R. L. Greene. The variety of subject matter, attitudes and social setting makes them representative of the whole body of medieval English lyric poetry. A carol is a poem for singing, on whatever subject, in uniform stanzas and provided with a burden, a choral element which is sung at the beginning of the piece and repeated after every stanza (see Greene, p.

xxxii). Many are found in variant versions and about a quarter are provided with written music. The modern Christmas carol is the limited descendant of the more varied medieval carols. The medieval carol (the word is derived from the French *carole*) was often accompanied by dancing in a ring, and 'carole' denotes a ring-dance with song, an amusement popular in the Middle Ages with high and low, and frequently referred to. It is the subject of a famous anecdote 'The Dancers of Colbek' told by Robert Manning of Brunne in his long poem of edifying anecdotes, *Handlyng Synne* of about 1300 (see p. 37 above). This story shows how the popularity of the carol, with its sexual and fertility associations, was sensibly enough censured by the earlier Church, which disapproved of lewd songs and wanton dancings and leapings, especially in the churchyard where they often took place. (The medieval churchyard was a clear and open yet 'sacred' place, very attractive for all sorts of local gatherings, including quarrelling.) But from early in the thirteenth century at least there was also an attempt, associated particularly with the Franciscans, in all countries in Western Europe, to replace lewd songs with enjoyable but pious ones, for the Church repudiated Gothic variety as vigorously as it did Neoclassical theory, each being equally keen on edification. The most prolific of all known carol-writers is Friar James Ryman of Canterbury, who lived at the end of the fifteenth century. Since even the clergy are only human, the Church often had to reprove its own members for taking part in dances and singing. Yet by the beginning of the sixteenth century the account books of William More, the last prior of Worcester Abbey, show that at the feasts regularly given by the abbey to the city of Worcester there were entertainments given by minstrels and carol-singers of a kind well appreciated by both secular and religious authorities and people. A delightful impression of merry social life in medieval times is received from these accounts books and those of other places, such as Durham Priory, Winchester College (that is, the great school at Winchester) and Magdalen College, Oxford. The carols also remind us that many other short medieval English poems were meant to be sung, though far less music has survived in England than in France.

The carols are social rather than personal, joyous rather than sad, and a counterweight to the serious affective devotion which develops the individual's power to contemplate the world's suffering and sin before rejoicing that they can, in principle, if accepted, be overcome. Yet one late carol, less typical in this as in other respects, evokes strange images of sorrow and beauty. This is the famous 'Corpus Christi Carol' beginning with the refrain

> Lulley, lulley; lulley, lulley;
> The fawcon hath born my mak away. [Greene 322A]

It is close to folksong, with several variant versions found later, and its interpretation has been vigorously argued by scholars, but all agree on its haunting power.

Nature imagery in lyrics

These enigmatic images of romantic mystery are rare in English Gothic literature but may draw on half-forgotten folksong themes, such as, perhaps, that evoked by the equally celebrated and beautiful fourteenth-century lyric, not a carol, but certainly a secular song, possibly associated with a dance:

> Maiden in the mor lay –
> in the mor lay –
> Sevenyst fulle, sevenist fulle. seven nights
> Maiden in the mor lay –
> in the mor lay –
> Sevenistes fulle ant a day
>
> Welle was hire mete. food
> Wat was hir mete?
> The primerole ant the – primrose
> The primerole ant the –
>
> Welle was hire mete
> Wat was hire mete?
> The primerole and the violet etc.
> [R. H. Robbins, *op. cit.* 18]

The names of the flowers are concrete, not abstract; thus they are simple and direct, but they are also general, not particularised, and thus are characteristic of the manner of early poetry. The flowers are the familiar early spring flowers of the English countryside, small, delicate and sweet, yet transformed strangely by being conceived of as food – food for what kind of maiden? – and conveyed in such powerful haunting rhythms.

The imagery of nature is used to create meaning; it is not contemplated for its own sake. Such imagery is part of the poet's normal experience and he is hardly self-conscious about it, or artistically detached. Natural objects which to us are externalised are still for him part of his 'mental furniture', part of his normal symbol-system, the structure of his thought about the nature of experience. The poet is not yet fully withdrawn into his own purely mental world, though the new insistence on the 'I' of both devotional and secular love lyrics, and the act of writing, show that this complex process of withdrawal into the inner world has already begun. Medieval lyrics assume a consciousness at one with nature, and natural imagery expresses of itself a general feeling of unity with nature, not creating a conceit, a 'pathetic fallacy' even though to be able to express such sympathy in writing is evidence of the beginning of a self-conscious separation from nature.

Another beautiful example of natural imagery expressing human feeling is this famous love poem:

Lenten ys come with love to toune	spring (season of lent)
With blosmen & with briddes roune	speech
That al this blissė bryngeth.	
Dayės-eyės in this dales	daisies; these
Notės suete of nyhtegales	
Uch foul song singeth.	Each bird
The threstelcoc him threteth oo,	thrush threatens; continuously
Away is hiere wynter wo	their
When woderove springeth.	woodruff (a plant)
This foulės singeth ferly fele	these birds sing wonderfully much
And wlyteth on huere wynne wele	sing about their wealth of joy
That al the wodė ryngeth	

[British Library Harley MS 2253 f. 71v.]

British Library MS Harley 2253

This is written in British Library Harley 2253, parchment, about $11\frac{1}{2}$ inches by $7\frac{1}{2}$, already mentioned, and perhaps the most representative and yet varied collection of all the manuscript miscellanies. It has poems in Latin, French and English, sometimes in two, occasionally in all three languages at once, with no obvious arrangement of items. In all three languages there are secular and religious poems. The religious poems are of a type already discussed and include one of the best poems on that dominant theme, the Passion of Christ, 'Iesu suete is the love of thee', deriving from the Latin *Jesu Dulcis Memoria*, of which a version is still sung in Anglican churches 'Jesus sweet is the love of thee'. Poems on the Harrowing of Hell, the Sayings of St Bernard, old age, a collection of proverbs, here attributed to 'Hending', are shared with Digby 86.

The love-lyrics are delightfully fresh, with a touch of provincial simplicity which is mocked by Chaucer in the diction of *The Miller's Tale*, as in the use of such words as *gent* and *hende*. The courtly and Europeanised Chaucer wrote much of love, but never so simply. Chaucer's own lyrics are so good and so unlike other medieval lyrics, that they are better discussed with his own work. He is as different from the friars, monks and schoolmasters who wrote the poems of the general tradition represented by Harley 2253 as from the courtiers who succeeded him.

In Harley 2253 where much variety is found, there is a good example of that ancient clerical commonplace, the follies of (female) fashion, amusingly scornful, but also a less usual Marian poem which expresses another poet's regret for scorning women because of Mary. The rousing political song which celebrates with confident jeering the victory of the battle of Lewes in 1264 probably represents many similar songs through the medieval centuries, but not many were thought by monks and friars to be worth recording. The poems by a poet called Minot, of the first half of the fourteenth century, are the best of these energetic expressions of patriotic sentiment. Although such sentiment has become as unfashionable among Western literary intellectuals as with medieval monks, it is not necessarily the basis for bad poetry. The best example is the Agincourt carol with surviving music, 'Owre kynge went forth to Normandy', (Greene 426) celebrating Henry V's famous victory, in which the glory is given to God. To believe that God is on one's side is an 'archaic' sentiment, expressive of a total vision of life, confident in its own values.

Harley 2253 has yet more variety. It includes the amusing sketch of clerical seduction usually given its Latin title *De Clerico et Puella* ('Of the Clerk and the Girl'), as much a 'play' as a lyric (see p. 216), which ends with the girl enthusiastically proclaiming:

Fader, moder, al my kun ne shal me hold so stille,	kin
That y nam thyn and thou art myn,	am not
To don al thi wille	do

Quite different is the delightful poem 'The Man in the Moon', clearly the product of a sophisticated, amused writer who picks up the folklore notion, itself obviously comic, of the man in the moon. The poem, which is linguistically quite difficult, is as if spoken by some drunken reveller on his way home late, describing and arguing with the Man, who pays no attention. It may be compared with the exasperated little poem on noisy blacksmiths who work at night and destroy sleep, in alliterative verse of the early fifteenth century, in British Library MS Arundel 292. Not 'poetical' in a romantic fashion, such poems are a precious glimpse into a human work-a-day world, full of interest and with a touch of humour, expressing constant human emotions, lively, graceful, wittily written. From the fourteenth century onwards there is a considerable spread of such poems, which shade off in one direction into 'practical verse', such as charms, notes of ownership, riddles, medical verses, 'wise sayings', much religious instruction, and in another direction into drinking songs, pleas for drink, praise of women, complaints of girls seduced and abandoned, satires on money, marriage, women in general. Difficult to generalise about, many are only competent and some dull, but if read with imaginative sympathy they are seen to be the speech and feelings of forgotten generations not so very different from ours.

The Vernon MS and a representative Gothic poem

In the fifteenth century the number of manuscripts becomes too great to describe in detail, and only one more can be mentioned. The Bodleian Library's Vernon MS, of parchment, written about 1400, is an immense book, 15 inches by 12 weighing about 20 lbs., with a huge collection of pieces, all religious, though of kinds mostly already mentioned. Unlike the other manuscripts it is a glorious book of 412 leaves, beautifully copied, with initials picked out in gold and in blue and red paint, with decorated margins on most pages, and some pictures. Of the great variety one poem is particularly valuable, not as poetry, but as illustrating both the style of Gothic poetry and the way poetry was thought about. It is composed of forty rhyming stanzas with much alliteration 'reporting' the Disputation between Mary and the Cross. The Cross's speech is full of traditional 'conceits', often to modern feeling tasteless, which would not surprise us in the seventeenth century Metaphysical poets. The Cross says Christ died to save the world which was dying under the devil's sword; the Cross is the wine-press, Christ the grape, the red wine his blood; the Cross carves God's fruit; the Cross is the plate on which the Lamb is roasted in the sun, and our sorrow is the sour sauce needed; Christ's body is our pardon, written on and bound in blood; the Cross carries a bridge on which angels sit. Mary reproaches the Cross for being so ready to tear her son. Finally, 'The queen acordet with the cros' and gave it a kiss (ll. 478–80). Then the poet says (ll. 491 ff.), 'The clerk that fourmed this figour' – this figure of speech – himself spoke those hard words when God's arms were torn about. In other words, the poet explains in the poem that he has invented the dialogue. The Cross is a 'cold creature' in reality, he says, and has always been deaf and dumb. Though this tale is adorned with fair flowers (of rhetoric), the poet says, I prove it 'on Apocrafum' that no witness was ever found to say that Christ's cross spoke. Our Lady never blamed it. But we now tell how Christ was hurt to drive the devil back. The poet's self-conscious explanation is most interesting. That he feels the need to explain that of course the Cross was never alive reveals the incipient literalism of the end of the fourteenth century. It became part of the Gothic tension when such literalism was set against the archaistic wholeness of ancient tradition in which the Cross might, in one sense, speak, because the whole universe was felt to be a living entity. The feeling that the Cross was 'alive', active, is most vividly conveyed by the great Old English poem, *The Dream of the Rood* ('The Vision of the Cross'), where the poet feels no need to divide literalistic truth from what is, in the modern sense, a metaphor. The fourteenth-century poet, by contrast, is obviously close to the modern sense of metaphor as complementary to literalistic truth, yet he is not quite there; he still seems to feel the Cross might be thought of as speaking, hence his explanation. That he puts his explanation *inside* the poem is another example of the Gothic mixture of modern and ancient. The 'frame of the picture' is so to speak broken because the poet is both 'outside' and 'inside' the picture. It would be quite wrong to regard the poet 'inside' as a 'Narrator' who is in ironic relationship to the real poet 'outside'. It is the same poet 'inside' and 'outside', relying on the traditional sense of social context which is implied in the nature of manuscript, if only by memory. Finally the poet is consciously using an artificial rhetoric, inventing speeches, etc., yet is entirely 'sincere', since this is a practical poem to bring home to the reader Christ's saving power as God, attained through his own self-sacrifice. Because the poem is not confessional in a literal way does not matter, and the degree of sincerity does not make any difference to the quality of the poem, (printed in F. J. Furnivall (ed.), *Minor Poems of the Vernon MS*, Part II, EETS Old Series 117, 1901, pp. 612 ff.).

Fifteenth-century religious and secular poems

The stream of short poems broadens in the fifteenth century, but towards the end of the period there are some signs that verse was becoming more restricted to imaginative writing and that prose was taking over some practical instruction. There are more names to be mentioned. Charles d'Orleans, the French prince so long a prisoner in England, and completely bilingual, wrote many courtly lyrics which in subject matter and social context deserve comparison with those of Sir Thomas Wyatt. His 'Confession of Love' has a charming lightness; more typical is this rather flat lyric:

Go forth myn hert wyth my lady,
    Loke that ye spar no besynes
To serve hyr wyth seche lowlynes
    That ye get hyr grace and mercy.
[R. H. Robbins, *op. cit.* 183]

This is a typical courtly attitude of humility towards the lady, and a typical conceit of sending the heart from the body. Such love poetry developed with vigorous conventionalism which can be attractive. These poems are 'counters in a game of love', rather remote from the less sophisticated but fresher love poems of the earlier centuries, and needing a strong effort of the historical imagination to recreate their social setting, their music, and the tensions of courtly society, in order to appreciate their civilised restraint, the decorative marginality of the lace-work, as it were, both of words and feeling. Another such author was the Duke of Suffolk, William de la Pole, husband of Chaucer's granddaughter, who came to a grisly end when his head was chopped off at sea in 1450. We note the large output of religious verse at the end of the century by the Franciscan friar, James Ryman, including many carols. It is symptomatic of developing individualisation to have a named poet and his own holograph text, but the poems themselves are routine.

Meditation through visualisation

Much better is the famous anonymous lyric once ascribed to Skelton, 'Wofully araide'. In MS Harley 4012 a hundred years of pardon are promised for saying this prayer, of which a few lines are quoted here. Versions appear in several other manuscripts.

Wofully araide,
My blode, man, for thee ran,
Hit may not be naide — denied
My body blo and wanne — livid and pale
  Wofully araide.

Beholde me, I pray thee, with all thyne hole reson
And be not hard-hertid, for this encheson . . . — reason

Thus nakid am I nailid, O man, for thi sake.
I love thee, thenne love me. Why slepist thu? Awake! . . .

So rubbid, so bobbid, so rufulle, so red,
Sore payned, so strayned, and for thi love ded.
Unfayned, not demed, my blod for thee shed,
My fete and handis sore,
With sturdė naylis bore,

What myght I suffer more
Then I have sufferde man for thee?
Com when thu wilt, and welcome to me.

Dere brother, non other thing I desire
But geve me thi hert fre, to reward myne hire.
I am he that made the erth, water and fire.
[Adapted from Carleton Brown, *Fifteenth Century*, pp. 156–7]

This poem represents several characteristics of the later medieval devotional lyric. It shows how men extended their sympathy and above all pity by dramatic imitation (as in the Vernon lyric), imagining speech on the part of the sufferer. It illustrates the originally Franciscan religious practice of meditation through visualisation of the details of the Passion. It is thus part of a developing realism. At the same time there is no attempt at historical accuracy, no effort to achieve an objective, naturalistic, coherent image external to the self in the modern manner. The superficial Gothic realism is on a non-naturalistic, archaic base. The time is an eternal present, not a separable past; the object contemplated is assimilated to him who contemplates. Wholeness or unity of being in time, person, place, is the mind's achievement. The style is admirably artful; it is not realistically dramatic as if it were to be imitating the speech of a man dying in horrible agony. (Shakespeare's dramatic speeches are still non-naturalistic in this way.) Sometimes such poems are set out in a pattern. This poem is accompanied, like a number of religious poems, by a small drawing which is also schematic, clarifying the points to think about, not attempting a realistic portrayal. Such illustrations are in the Gothic style, unconstricted by the frame, with no attempt at naturalistic scale and perspective. Most of them are also very rough and inartistic, though sometimes powerful. And finally the poem was set to music.

The affective devotion of religious lyrics did not survive

There is no weakening of force here, yet one must be struck by the way medieval English religious poems, with rare exceptions, were forgotten after the Reformation. Some devotional attitudes persisted and the devotional practices which had developed were even to some extent incorporated into the Anglican Book of Common Prayer. Some of the violently metaphorical characteristics of Metaphysical poetry continue a medieval tradition: but these emotionally contemplative poems themselves dropped out of use, like the bare ruined choirs in which so many of them had once been known. Their lesson had been learnt and newer forms took over.

Continuation of the secular lyric into the sixteenth century

The secular poems were part of a different continuity, though its main force lay in the supremacy of Chaucer, Lydgate and Gower, recognised in the sixteenth century as the great Engish poets. The style and the subject matter of the shorter love lyrics continued into the sixteenth century. Such poems as

O mestres, whye
Owtecaste am I
All utterly
From your plesaunce?

[R. H. Robbins, *op. cit.* 137]

or

I must go walke the woed so wyld
And wander here and there
In dred and dedly ffere,
For where I trusted I am begyld
and all ffor one.

[R. H. Robbins, *op. cit.* 20]

might be minor Wyatt (1503?–42). Wyatt's songs in both style and in the subject matter of love are clearly medieval. His true innovations are in his sonnets translated from Petrarch, his versified psalms and satires, all translations. Even in them, though there is much that is fresh, there is a basic continuity of theme and attitude with the general medieval tradition. The real break does not come till late in the seventeenth century.

Appendix: the ballads

The ballads provide many delightful poems and problems. Their dates, nature and relationship to oral tradition and literacy have all been the subject of impassioned controversy. It is even a question how far they are medieval. Ballads are narrative folksong in stanzaic verse or couplets. The stories are characteristic of folk-tale, that is, of the oral tradition, which allows re-creation of the essential idea of the story by different singers in varying versions according to the ability of the singer and the social circumstances of the recital. The music is similarly capable of variation, which is not to be thought of as error in reproducing one authentic tune. The music is in the traditional form of 'modes', like plain-song, as may be sometimes heard from genuine traditional folk singers even today. It has different criteria from the art-song and harmonic music that developed, in conjunction with Neoclassical literature, from the sixteenth century onwards, to give us the 'Classical' and 'Romantic' music that was dominant in Europe until Stravinsky and others broke the mould in the early twentieth century. The 'modes' are somewhat similar in effect to the traditional non-harmonic music of Eastern countries, without the clockwork regularity of beat, or the need to maintain a 'pure' note. For this reason folk music, like the poetry of the ballads, may give a false impression of crudity or lack of art to ears and minds trained in a culture of literacy and 'classical' music which demands precision and exact reproduction of notes on an harmonic scale.

The essential body of ballads comprises the 305 ballads collected in many variant versions by the great American scholar F. J. Child, first published 1882–98, though since then many more recent ballads have been collected, and the definition has been widened by some to include various popular narrative poems published from the sixteenth century onwards. Such as may be medieval are in the Child collection.

Actual medieval ballads

'Judas' (Child 28) has already been discussed above (p. 45). It is a folk-tale narrative in couplets and may perhaps count as a ballad, though not a typical one. Another folk-tale narrative is that of 'St Stephen and Herod' from Sloane 2593 of the early fifteenth century (Child 22). In this, in astounding fulfilment of Herod's sceptical oath, a cooked cock crows from his dish *'Christus natus est'* ('Christ is born'). This is not apparently meant to be funny, and Stephen for his faithfulness is stoned (Child 22). The style has the repeated formulas characteristic of other ballads and, though not typical in subject, the poem may reasonably be called a ballad. Also from the Sloane manuscript comes the story of 'Robyn and Gandelyn' in which Robyn is killed in the forest but avenged by his faithful servant Gandelyn (Child 115). From manuscripts written about 1450 came two others, Child 1A, 'Riddles Wisely Expounded', which is a riddling contest between the devil and a girl which she wins, and the story of 'Robin Hood and the Monk' (Child 119) the earliest and longest (nearly 3000 lines) of Robin Hood poems. The riddles hardly make a true narrative, though they are traditional enough. The Robin Hood poem is as much a romance as a ballad, and is unlikely to have been sung. But it comes close to the general nature of the best ballads, with their archetypal situations, and rapid impersonal concrete style. It has an attractive typical beginning:

In somer, when the shawes be sheyne
and leves be large and long,
Hit is full mery in feyre foreste
To here the foulys song

The familiar figures are already there, Little John, Much the Miller's son, Will Scarlet and the always beguiled Sheriff of Nottingham. Robin in his anxiety to worship the Virgin in church in Nottingham is captured because a monk recognises him. Little John, though he has quarrelled with Robin, is faithful, kills the monk and his little page ruthlessly, tricks the king, and rescues Robin. It is genuinely popular, harsh, cheerful, knock-about stuff, evoking the deep masculine pieties of faithfulness to one's lord in danger, death to the enemy, and the fantasy of a life untroubled by property and women in the fair greenwood. (Maid Marian appears in the sixteenth century.) 'Robin Hood and the Monk' must have been stirring to hear when sung amongst a group of friends. We easily identify with the young and free who are against authority but are good-hearted, dashing, brave and successful. Langland's idler Sloth in Piers Plowman knew 'rymes of Robyn Hood and Randolf Erl of Chestre' though nothing of Our Lord or of our Lady (*Piers Plowman*, B-text v 396–7, ed. A. V. C. Schmidt, dated 1377–79.). This is unfair to the popular piety of 'Robin Hood and the Monk', but represents the contempt of a minor cleric who is a major poet for these popular pieces. There are several references in the fourteenth and fifteenth centuries to Robin Hood and his companions. A cluster of poems about them, probably dating in their present form from the latter part of the fifteenth century, but perhaps originating in the fourteenth, and certainly continuing in the sixteenth, relates their adventures and rescues. We can easily enjoy these attractively naive narratives of faithfulness and bravery, fun and freedom, in rattling metre and simple concrete vocabulary. They are well constructed with occasional vivid detail. Their cruelties are never sadistic or unprovoked, and they reflect a sturdy response to a harsh world. Very similar are the ballads about the battle of Otterburn which was fought in 1388. The several versions, both English and Scottish, called 'The Battle of Otterburn' or 'The Hunting of the Cheviot' (Child 161 and 162) date from the sixteenth century and are often weaker in style than the medieval Robin Hood ballads, reflecting the deterioration that a true oral tradition undergoes when it turns into low-level literacy. Copies circulated, cheaply printed on large single sheets known as broadsides, up to the eighteenth century. It is salutary to remember that our first great Neoclassical theorist, Sir Philip Sidney, and our first genuinely Neoclassical practitioner, Ben Jonson, each expressed admiration for the Otterburn ballad, sometimes known as 'Chevy Chase', as did Addison. Though their own concepts of literature were very different, their breadth of sympathy and patriotic feeling made an exception of this poem, and Addison declared it to be the favourite ballad of the people of England.

These are the only ballads that can be called medieval for which we have evidence in England, and a similar picture can be seen in Scotland, though the 'medieval' evidence is even later. A reference in the work *The Complaynte of Scotland*, of 1549, refers to the subject of the Otterburn ballads and to the battle of Harlaw (1411), for which a Scottish ballad exists of later date (Child 163), but probably reflecting earlier tradition.

Thus the essence of the verse form of the medieval ballad is first found in the thirteenth century. Scholars have derived it from the French carole which began to be known from about 1200, in which words and song and dance were combined. The form of narrative may have derived from the needs of oral, non-literate tradition, which created a stock of formulaic phrases and concepts structured in twos and threes, allowing of considerable elaboration. The stories arise from various sources. It must be said that as far as direct medieval evidence is concerned, the ballad, though interesting, is a late and minor form.

Later ballads

There is nevertheless more to come of a most interesting kind, though doubtfully medieval in a strict historical sense. There are nearly 300 more Child ballads, including some that are great poems by any standards and many that are very good. The best are a Scottish group of ballads of the late eighteenth century, several of them associated with Mrs Brown of Falkland, some with Sir Walter Scott, most of them deriving from the north-eastern part of Scotland, and the subject of a fine study by Professor David Buchan, *The Ballad and the Folk* (London: Routledge & Kegan Paul, 1972). Their themes are usually those of fatally seductive young men and women, or young lovers hindered by other members of the family, jealous mothers or brothers, or other similar complications. Amongst them are 'Lady Isabel and the Elf-knight', an enigmatically gruesome tale in which the Lady kills a kind of Bluebeard elfin-knight (Child 4); 'Gil Brenton', with a more fortunate outcome of a somewhat similar tale, one of Mrs Brown's ballads (Child 5); 'Willie's Lady', also in a version from Mrs Brown, with many dead and an unhappy ending, like most, and closely similar to 'Erlinton' (Child 8); 'The Cruel Brother', in many versions, including one by Mrs Brown, with a self-explanatory title (Child 11); 'Lord Randal', in early nineteenth-century versions, poisoned by his true love (Child 12); 'Edward', perhaps the best of all, apparently poisoned by his mother (Child 13); 'Babylon' with a brother offering his three sisters, unknown to him, the choice of marriage or death; when after two are dead the third's defiance reveals their relationship he kills himself (Child 14).

Very many ballads are based on powerful psychological dramas involving sex and death within family relationships, usually provoked by the advent of a lover from outside the family. These themes and situations are of such common humanity that they are found in the folklore of many nations, and there are many analogues to these Scottish ballads, especially in Scandinavia. The persons are archetypal; young men or women, and parents, but they are often named as kings, earls, knights, ladies. The stories, like the tunes, exist rather as 'inner ideas', to be re-created anew in each rendition or 'verbal realisation' by a practised singer versed in the tradition. They have a characteristic style created by their oral tradition. The rhythm is powerful, with repeated refrains and set phrases (referred to as the formulaic style), as in a ballad, 'The Elfin Knight' recorded exceptionally early in a broadside of about 1670:

> My plaid awa, my plaid awa,
> And ore the hill and far awa,
> And far awa to Norrowa,
> My plaid shall not be blown awa.
>
> [Child 2]

The vocabulary, like the persons, is limited to concrete generalisations, man, maid, flower, water, sword, blood, ship, with a few general adjectives such as 'fair', as in the refrain to many of the thirty five stanzas of 'The Fair Flower of Northumberland' (first recorded in 1597):

> And she the faire flower of Northumberland,

It is varied by 'And I . . .' or, 'And you . . .' or, 'Even by the good Earle of Northumberland' (Child 9). Most of the trappings are medieval in the simple sense that swords and knights are medieval. Their numbers are stylised; the folklore numbers of three and seven and fifteen are frequent.

Oral culture

Such poems, the product of an oral culture, have quite a different effect, and need to be read differently, from those of a literate culture. They are closely context-bound, and to be appreciated properly should be met, as is of course now almost impossible, in their immediate setting. We have to appreciate repetition, sententiousness, non-sequential structures, non-realistic but psychologically significant situations, all the literary qualities Neoclassicism repudiated. It is a rare good fortune when someone versed in the oral culture is also educated in the culture of high literacy and able to maintain the two together, as Mrs Brown and Scott could, and cherish them both equally. The qualities of Neoclassicism, by invoking the enormous intellectual powers of literacy, thus opening and retaining so many sources of knowledge with the artificial memory of script and print, and freeing poems from their immediate social context, destroy the non-literate creative memory. They thus introduce a class distinction between oral and literate culture, for oral culture no longer represents the whole of society but only the less privileged and less educated. It is with the domination in England of Neoclassicism by around 1700 that we first get the concept of 'the folk', who are by definition not the educated. It seems that it was easier in Scotland, which had not inherited the profound social cleavage of the Norman Conquest, to maintain a sense of unity even in a society with a strong hierarchical structure, so that literate and illiterate were still able to share the same oral tradition, which was not despised.

In so far as the ballads are the products of an oral tradition, and may be classified along with folk-tale, they have important relationships with medieval literature. They represent the substratum of many medieval stories and songs, now for ever lost. Their qualities are different from the preferred qualities of the print-culture which supported Neoclassicism. Ballads are closer to, though not identical with, the qualities of a manuscript culture. To this extent the ballads though the vast majority are post-medieval, may be said to be medieval; they are highly traditional. Medieval English literature itself, however, was also heavily committed to literacy. Some of the tensions of English Gothic literature are due to the interplay between the traditional and the literate, even the literalistic.

5

Adventure and love: romances in rhyme

'King Horn': An archetypal romance

THE shorter poems of the medieval centuries express feelings also found in stories, which like so much else in English first begin to be written down in the thirteenth century. Of uncertain date, but one of the best, is *King Horn* (1,650 lines), written in a spare formulaic style reminiscent of the ballads.

Alle beon he blithe	Let all be glad
That to my song lithe.	listen
A sang ihc schal you singe	
Of Murry the kinge.	
King he was bi weste	
So long so hit laste.	
Godhild het his quen;	was called
Fairė ne mighte non ben.	fairer

[University Library Cambridge, Gg IV.27 (ii), 1–8]

The fundamental images are given in bare essentials. King and queen live by the sea and hạve a child Horn, but Saracens invade, who kill the parents, and send Horn with other children to sea, all terrified:

The se bigan to flowe,	rise
And Horn child to rowe.	[127–8]

They land and Horn tells the others,

Ihc here foweles singe	I hear
And that grass him springe.	grass grows
Blithe beo we on live,	
Ure shup is on rive.	shore
	[139–42]

They have landed in Westernesse, where the king befriends

Horn, has him well educated in skills of wood and river bank, in carving before the lord and serving his cup, and in harping and singing (231–44). He is so beautiful that the king's daughter Rymenhild falls in love with him, has him to her bower, kisses him often, and asks him to marry her. He says he is too low a servant, but if she will help him to become a knight, he loves her and will marry her. Her father knights him, but then he insists on going away to achieve knightly deeds. He kills some Saracens and brings their leader's head in on the point of a sword. Rymenhild has a symbolic foreboding dream. A treacherous friend tells the king that Horn is seducing Rymenhild and the king finds them in each other's arms, though they are innocent. Horn is banished, and tells his darling Rymenhild she may marry if he does not return in seven years, while she swoons with sorrow. He goes across the sea to Ireland, calling himself Cutberd (Godmod in another manuscript), and kills three knights who, it turns out, have been some of the Saracens who killed his father. He declines to marry the grateful king's daughter and inherit the kingdom, but stays for seven years. Meanwhile a king comes to marry Rymenhild. On hearing this Horn goes back, arrives at the wedding feast disguised as a filthy pilgrim, and demands drink from Rymenhild, who is serving the company in the traditional manner. She offers him beer. He insists on wine, and speaks riddlingly. It is a fine archetypal scene. He puts the ring she had given to him in the horn in which she has just served him wine, and thus makes himself known to her. He and his knights slaughter his rival. He then departs again and succeeds in winning back his own land of Suddene from the Saracens who have captured it, restoring the Christian faith, and bringing his mother with rejoicing from the hermitage in a rock to which she has retreated. While he triumphantly feasts, his treacherous friend Fikenhild back in Westernesse is about to marry Rymenhild. Horn has a warning dream, rushes back, and this time is only able to obtain entrance to the feast by disguising himself as a minstrel. When in,

> Hit smot to Hornès herte
> So bitere that it smerte.
> He lokede on the ringe,
> And thoghte on Rymenhilde.

He yede up to borde;	went; table
With godė swerdės orde,	edge
Fikenhildes crune	head
Ther i-fulde adune;	was felled
And al his men arowe	in turn
Hi dude adun throwe.	threw down
	[1601–10]

All then is well and Horn brings Rymenhild home as queen. They live in true love ever after and love well God's law.

The style is splendidly spare and vigorous. Formulaic phrases are used, but meaningfully and concretely. There is absolutely no sense of a narrator different from the poet. There is no irony. The absence of metaphor, the rarity of repetition except at heightened moments, the equal restraint in the use of hyperbole, create a disciplined 'transparency' of style through which the larger literal, yet symbolic, structures of event work powerfully on the receptive imagination.

Symbolic images and patterns of romance

This popular story is composed of the archetypal images of romance – the growing youth, the absences, voyages, battles, feasts and last-minute returns to save the beloved from marriage to a hated rival. It is full of journeys and coastal images, ships, seaside castles, strangers from the sea. Today swords and cups of horn, knights and armour, pilgrims and voyages in open boats on pathless seas, no longer part of our ordinary lives, are even more obvious symbols for the loves and separations, conflicts and reconciliations, which are still the essence of our personal relationships. Traditional stories such as this have to be read not as novels imitating ordinary appearances and motivations, following causal sequences, but as myths, fairy tales, ballads. Their incidents and settings are romantic and exciting at a literal level, and the story also works at an unconscious or symbolic level, in an 'archaic' timeless present. All is to be interpreted in connection with the hero, with whom we identify. The story is of the fairy-tale type, in which the hero or heroine grows up, disengages from parent-figures, seeks the beloved. All of us as children, as in so many fairy tales, feel ourselves to be in a sense 'royal children'. All are opposed by hostile parental images, by the dragons and monsters of our own inhibitions. We all feel ourselves, though really 'royal', to be also unappreciated, degraded, used as a servant, dirty, like Cinderella or Horn. This psychological dilemma has to be worked out in all our lives, and imaginative participation in narratives is one way of doing it. There is further the special need for boys, as in countless folk-tales, to leave home, kill giants and enemies, find appreciative father-figures as well as hostile ones, avoid too much mothering or too motherly a beloved, come and go, and establish independence at home by going abroad.

Though the pattern is general, ways of working it out are manifold. *King Horn* is one very effective version; other romances, far too many to describe in detail here, give other specific versions.

The audience of King Horn

Who are we to imagine listening to or reading *King Horn*? The common assumption that the audience was rough, naive, lower-class, is quite unfounded. Of the three manuscripts the first is from about 1250 and being a manuscript at all implies at this date an educated audience. The two other manuscripts are both early fourteenth century and one is none other than Harley 2253, that classic Gothic miscellany. Chaucer at the end of *Sir Thopas* refers derisively to a number of very popular romances including *Horn Child* (*Canterbury Tales* VII, 898). Since Horn is never in this poem referred to as 'King Horn', which is only the modern title, but several times as 'Horn child', it is almost as likely that Chaucer refers to the present poem as to the much less good rehandling of the story in the fourteenth century in tail-rhyme stanzas (for which, see below, p. 83), now entitled *Horn Childe and Maiden Rimnild*. Chaucer's satire of the English romances arises out of his own early knowledge of and indebtedness to them. Absurd as Chaucer himself in his maturity thought the tail-rhyme romances to be, he knows very well that his courtly and learned audience will all recognise the poems he mocks. His courtly audience has been the audience of the romances. The readers of Harley 2253, which was written early on in the fourteenth century, were trilingual and by no means unsophisticated in their tastes. Their taste in lyric and romance was oldfashioned and provincial to Chaucer, but he lived some seventy or more years later. The dialect of *King Horn* is thought to be south-western, say Dorset or Somerset. We may easily imagine the thirteenth-century audience of *King Horn* as English-speaking country gentry in their houses, descendants of St Wulfric's patrons in Somerset, or men like Master Nicholas of Portisham, clerics relaxing in house or ecclesiastical college. The story was an old folk-tale in England. It had been picked up by an Anglo-Norman writer called (like most twelfth-century Anglo-Norman writers) Thomas, of whose poem three manuscripts survive, and which was certainly courtly. The general directness and the formulaic style of the English poem also suggest, as for the ballads, that it arises from an oral tradition not yet fractured and degraded by the separating processes of literacy. It could interest all groups within a community which had still not been divided by literacy. In the lord's hall, where we may imagine it chanted or told, were lord and lady, squire and chaplain, steward, servants, ploughmen, men-at-arms. The anonymous poet of terse genius might have been the chaplain, or one of the small gentry round about, who knew how to entertain people with his traditional poetic narratives and songs.

'Havelok' and Grimsby

One of the early-fourteenth-century manuscripts that contains *King Horn*, Bodleian MS Laud misc. 108 part ii, contains, besides many saints' lives, *The Lay of Havelok*, which also survives in four other fragments and in two French versions. *Havelok*, which has 3001 four-stress lines, mostly in couplets, is an excellent poem, in some ways similar to *King Horn* but showing some of the progress of literacy, and probably written (the operative word) half a century later.

> Herknet to me godė men
> Wivės, maydnes and allė men,
> Of a tale that ich you wile telle,
> Wo-so it wile here and ther-to dwelle. Who-so
> [Bodleian MS Laud misc. 108(ii), f. 204, 1–4]

This is not as good an opening as *King Horn*. The first rhyme is feeble, the tone aggressive yet insecure. Perhaps the writer, being literate, was imitating the traditional call to listen by traditional singers or tellers of tales. The story is good folk-tale, probably based on local legends in Lincolnshire, for Havelok was associated from very early on with the fishing port of Grimsby on the north-east coast, which knew the Danes well. Havelok himself is a Dane, whose father the king dies while he is young. His guardian attempts to have him murdered – a good folk-tale motif – but he is saved by Grim, the fisherman commissioned to murder him, because Havelok when asleep has a bright flame issuing from his mouth, which denotes his royal birth. Grim flees to England with his family and Havelok where they live in hard work and poverty, while Havelok grows very strong. The king of England has also died, leaving a daughter, and her wicked guardian forcibly marries her to the low-class Havelok to humiliate her. However the bright light from his mouth when asleep cheers her. Eventually after winning some splendid fights, in which Havelok is greatly outnumbered, he becomes king of England and a feast is celebrated with

The mostė joyė that mouhte be;
Butting with [the] sharpė sperės,
Skirming with talevales that men berės, — bucklers
Wrastling with laddės, putting of ston,
Harping and piping, ful god won, — plenty
Leyk of mine, of hazard ok, — play of dice; hazard
Romanz reding on the bok.
Ther mouthe men here the gestes singe, — stories
The gleu-men on the tabur dinge. — drum beat
Ther mouhte men se the boles beyte — bulls baited
And the hares with hundes teyte. — hounds eager
The mouhte men se everil gleu — sport
Ther mouhte men se hw grim greu. — excitement increased
Was never yete joyė more
In al this werd than tho was thore. — world; then; there
Ther was so mikle yeft of clothės — great gift
That thou i-swore thou gretė othės
I ne wore nou the theroffe trod — believed
That may I ful wel swere bi God.
There was swithė godė metes
And of wyn that men fer fetes — fetch from far
With al so mikel and gret plentė
So it were water of the se.
The feste fourti dawes sat,
So riche was never non so that. — as

[2322–45. *Cf. The Lay of Havelok the Dane*, W. W. Skeat (ed.), rev. K. Sisam (Oxford: Clarendon Press, 1915)]

The basis of the poem is fantasy of a familiar kind, as found in films about cowboys in the West and samurai in Japan, though there is a cheerful lack of obsession with sex or love which is refreshing. The poem reveals a pattern of general (not personal) psychological development, but it is less deep than in *King Horn*. To make up for this the poem has an elaborate narrative structure and in particular a delightful realism, or apparent realism, about lower-class life, that is fresh and original and very much the product of a sharply observant literate mind. The homeliness of descriptions, the concern for the poor, for proper laws, the admirably cheerful stalwart hero, the noble chaste heroine, the absence of courtliness, resemble the good qualities of the nineteenth-century novel. It is not surprising that critics who can make nothing of *King Horn* praise the realism of *Havelok*; but we ought to be able to pay both poems their due.

For once the concept of a bourgeois, that is, town-dwelling, audience or readers seems satisfactory, though English towns were so few and small, the *bourgeoisie* and the gentry were so intermingled, that the distinction is even here not very significant. We may, however, imagine the substantial house of a merchant, with his family and friends present, as a typical setting for the poem, especially with its association with Grimsby. But there is no sign of the influence of arithmetic or accounting as there seems to be with Chaucer, and we should not exclude from the audience the gentry and smaller nobility, whose tastes were wide, yet not necessarily very courtly. The author would probably have been some kind of cleric.

'Floris and Blancheflur' and romantic love

A more courtly, or at least romantic, interest in love is evoked by the charming poem *Floris and Blancheflur*, in its English version first written in the latter part of the thirteenth century and thus our earliest story of romantic love. The story originated in France and spread to all European countries. There are two versions in French which suggest how traditional tales often developed in complexity. The earlier French version concentrates on the love affair between the two young people which though full of incident is in itself uncomplicated; the second introduces feats of knight-errantry for the hero, which would appear to be an attempt, in this case unsuccessful, to render the complexities of internal conflict that normally attend the processes of growing up. The simpler English story (incomplete in all three manuscripts) is not without complications, though there is no villain. The heroine is sold into slavery. The hero has to find her and deceive her owner the Sultan. There is a delightful episode when he is conveyed hidden in a basket of flowers into the impregnable tower in which his beloved is kept with the Sultan's harem. The Sultan is understandably annoyed, when he discovers them sleeping together, but is reconciled by their beauty. The poem is written in a vein of idealised realism and lacks the psychological depth of apparently cruder and more absurd stories. Though it appears in the famous mid-fourteenth-century Auchinleck manuscript, containing many romances, which Chaucer may have known, he does not satirise it.

Fabliau and beast fable

It might have been expected that as romances begin to appear in English – and there must have been more than these three in the thirteenth century – so there might also have appeared, as in France, the complementary form, the bawdy story or *fabliau*. Romances are idealistic in moral tone and physical setting; they are usually about noble love and brave adventure concerning knights and ladies in exotic settings and culminating in marriage; and they are often elaborately written. A natural, even proper, cynicism tells us, and in particular told the French in the thirteenth century, that life is not all like that. *Fabliaux* emphasise the opposite point of view. They are stories about sex, not love, concerning adultery mostly between lower-class people and clerics, who are all treated with French aristocratic comic scorn. The adventures are absurd mishaps, often squalid and brutal, and the style is plain and direct, sometimes blunt to the point of coarseness. In a purely literary sense, however, the *fabliaux* do idealise, that is, they do select and emphasise their material; they are, from this point of view, just as much fantasies as the romances. But they are comic and denigratory. There are one hundred and fifty such tales in French, though curiously almost all limited to the thirteenth century: apart from Chaucer, our sophisticated European, who has his own brand, there is only one in English, *Dame Sirith*, some 450 lines of irregular tail-rhyme written in the thirteenth century, originally probably in three-stress couplets. It shares some lines with *De Clerico et Puella* (see above, p. 58) but is itself an expansion of a well-known comic anecdote recorded earlier in a brief Latin note. A clerk, Wilekin, seduces a wife, Margeri, by getting an old woman to make her dog weep by the copious application of mustard and to tell the wife that the dog is the old woman's daughter, bewitched for not letting herself be seduced by the clerk. Margeri rapidly finds the required inclination. It is an amusing coarse clerical anecdote told in a sprightly manner, and not courtly.

In the same manuscript, which we have met before, Digby 86, is another unique example of thirteenth-century narrative, *The Fox and the Wolf*, in 295 four-stress couplets. The beast-fable is an ancient and widespread form, but the home of the medieval beast-fable seems to have been England, where several collections seem to have been written in Latin and Anglo-Norman in the twelfth century which survive in a number of manuscripts. The popularity of such fables is shown by the frequency with which references to them were included in sermons and they appear in the collections of those brief stories with a moral point called *exempla*, which were used by preachers and others. *The Owl and the Nightingale* is an example of how writers used these neat short stories in longer works. Unfortunately, apart from *The Fox and the Wolf* no beast-fable has survived independently in English until we come to Chaucer's *Nun's Priest's Tale*. Lydgate in the early fifteenth century is the first to make a collection (of seven), after which we wait for Henryson and Caxton's collections towards the end of the century. The scarcity in a popular type of story reminds us how precarious and arbitrary is our knowledge of Middle English literature. How much we would have lost if only three more manuscripts had disappeared, Digby 86, Harley 2253 and Cotton Nero A x, which last alone contains the poems of the great *Gawain*-poet. The most popular works and thus, being most copied, those that have the best chance of survival are not necessarily the best as art, as we may judge from the 114 manuscripts of *The Pricke of Conscience*, far exceeding even those of *The Canterbury Tales*.

The Fox and the Wolf well displays the characteristic piquancy of the beast-fable, which selects a general human characteristic for the nub of the story, and combines the human-like characteristics of animals with the animal-like characteristics of human beings in a series of amusing and illuminating, if not always edifying, episodes. In the way that human and animal are seen as part of a single world, and a totally non-realistic action conveys a real human truth, the beast-fable clearly belongs to the unified traditional archaic world. Its evident humour has preserved it from the assault of literalism and we can still easily enjoy it. Yet our equally basic sense of actual difference between human and animal and thus our sense of the absurdity, is equally necessary for understanding and enjoyment.

'Sir Orfeo' and the Auchinleck Manuscript

To these several early examples of fantasy, romance, fabliau, beast-fable, we may add another, descended from myth and not yet quite fairy-tale, the medieval English version of the classical Greek story of Orpheus and of his unsuccessful attempt to rescue his wife Eurydice from the underworld. Like almost all of these early narratives it is in rhyming couplets of four-stress lines. We come again to another crucial fourteenth-century manuscript, though its texts are not normally unique, the Auchinleck manuscript (National Library of Scotland Advocates MS 19. 2. 1.), which provides so many representative romances and a bridge to Chaucer's work. The Auchinleck manuscript is about 9½ ins by 7¼ ins, of vellum, with nearly 700 pages. It was probably produced in a London bookshop about 1345 and its existence allows us to suppose that there were others like it. It is an archetypal Gothic miscellany with a bias towards tail-rhyme romances, and either this book or one very similar to it was known to Chaucer and to his circle. We may imagine that it was made for some rich merchant like Chaucer's father, or a lawyer, or a minor courtier.

The Auchinleck manuscript has the best text of *Sir Orfeo*, though unfortunately most of the first fifty lines are missing and must be supplied from other manuscripts of the fifteenth century. *Sir Orfeo* begins:

We redeth oft & findeth ywrite,
& this clerkės wel it wite — these; know
Layės that ben in harping
Ben yfounde of ferli thing: — found wondrous things
Sum bethe of wer & sum of wo, — war
& sum of joye & mirthe also,
& sum of trecherie & of gile,
Of old aventours that fel while — happened in the past
& sum of bourdes & ribaudry — jokes and ribaldry
& mani ther beth of fairy.
Of allė thingės that men seth — see
Mest o love, for sothe, thai be. — most of
In Breteyne this layes werė wrought.
[*Cf.* A. V. C. Schmidt and N. Jacobs (eds.), *Medieval English Romances*, 2 vols (London: Hodder & Stoughton, 1980), vol. 1, p. 151]

This is a so-called 'Breton lay', a vague medieval English concept for a story of a problem of love. We note the emphasis on writing, but also, typically of manuscript culture, a reminiscence or imitation of the oral tradition and the group-setting for a story, for the poet soon writes, or says,

Thai token an harp in gle & game
& maked a lay & yaf it name. [19–20]

The poet avoids the pitfall of turning the evocative formulaic phrases of the oral tradition into the clichés of literacy by hardly using set phrases in the strict sense at all. He aims at a simple direct style which allows him to keep close to his subject.

King Orfeo is described in the archetypal terms of kingship: stalwart, hardy, generous, courteous, and he most of all loves harping. His beloved queen, Dame Heurodis, is taken away by fairy knights and he is forlorn. In seeking her he lives wild in the woods for seven years, exercising his power of music over the creatures there. Occasionally he catches a glimpse of the King of Fairies riding by,

Com to hunt him al about
With dim cri & bloweing — faint
& houndes also with him bearking [283–5]

and of his own wife, who cannot speak to him. At last he follows the king through a rock to a fair country and a castle to which he claims entry as a minstrel. He plays so well that the king offers him whatever he wills, and he asks for his lady. 'A sorry couple you would make,' says the king, 'you so thin, rough and black, she so beautiful.' But Orfeo makes him keep to his word. They return with his harp, to his own court where the steward treats Orfeo well, as he says, for love of his lost king, king Orfeo the harper, and Orfeo plays so entrancingly that he is known and all ends happily.

It is a poem about faithful love being superior even over death. The images are simple, coherent, clear and we do not ask for rational causation of the mystery of death, the waste land of mourning, the ambivalent attractions of the fairy land of the dead, faith in the re-creative power of art (as music), and in human goodness and loyalty. The poem celebrates faith and love in a beautiful tribute to gentleness and humanity. The poet sees clearly the essence of his story and of the images, both contemporary and poetic, of king and queen, castle and wild wood, through which he creates it, and he does not encumber them with realistic detail. The image of the sorrowing king, become so dirty and unkempt, but so miraculous a musician, is particularly profound. It is an image of the creative mind. The plain style of the poem, which is capable of unaffected expression of feeling, yet is never mawkish, is part of the same capacity to seize the essential element. Though concrete it is still general. Irrelevant particularisation, individual characterisation, motivation, realism, are never attempted. Though literate the style is never literalistic. The poem is purely secular, never confused either with religion or its absence, though we can, perhaps must, now read it 'existentially' in its symbolism; and it ultimately lacks something of the stark power of the confrontation with and conquest over death of the Christian story; but it is not incompatible with that.

Breton lays and folk-tale

There are about eight so-called Breton lays: *Lai le freine* and *Sir Degaré* (if included) are both in the Auchinleck manuscript. Another, *Emaré*, is a story containing incidents similar to those in Chaucer's *Man of Law's Tale* of Constance, and in other romances. Other lays are *Sir Eglamour, Sir Torrent, Octovian* and *Sir Triamour*. The relationships between such stories, which could be pursued for every romance and perhaps every medieval story, is a characteristic of folk-tale, with which romances have close connections, and of traditional literature generally. Traditional stories, like traditional pictures, are symbolic, non-naturalistic, in essence like myths, or the stories of ballads. The stories exist as inherent general 'ideas' of stories, which may be realised in a variety of images, motifs and events, issuing finally in a 'verbal realisation' which may attach specific names, local realistic detail, even character and motivation, to events that are already known in their general outline from tradition and from the habitual workings and expectations of our own minds even today. Thus we all know that in a fairy-tale, it is always the third and youngest son who is the hero, never, for example, the middle son. There is no prejudice against second sons here, but simply the fact that we ourselves identify with the youngest and apparently the weakest, when we read such stories, in order the more satisfyingly to succeed.

The interlocking nature of traditional stories, with the possibility of varying incidents characters, styles, may also remind us that the notion of 'kinds' of writing, *genres*, is so fluid in the Middle Ages as to be of little use, and to some extent misleading. Medieval authors call their works variously fables, *fabliaux*, lays, stories, tales, with no clear or fixed concepts of any except the most general kind. It is useful for this chapter to deal with 'romances', particularly rhyming romances, but many a work in the Middle Ages is called a romance that we cannot recognise as such. Robert Thornton in the fifteenth century, for example, copied out in English 'the romance of the life of Jesus Christ' (British Library Additional 31042). He meant what we call 'history', but the word 'history' is often used to mean just 'story'.

Romances and minstrels

The Auchinleck manuscript has two of the most popular romances ever written in England, *Guy of Warwick* and *Sir Bevis of Hampton*. Each appears in a number of manuscripts in French and English, were often printed in the sixteenth century, and were known to Marlowe and Shakespeare. Many medieval stories were not forgotten even in the eighteenth century, when they appeared in such reduced form as the tiny pamphlets for reading by children and the lower classes, costing a penny or twopence, which were sold by 'chapmen' (pedlars) and hence known as chapbooks – the final repository of much popular medieval literature, secular and pious. The romances evoke the grand popular images – heroes lowly or obscure in birth, scorned in youth, but who make good, overcome giants, dragons, foes and traitors, are patriotic (Guy fights 'for England's sake'), pious (Guy becomes a pilgrim and manages to die both as a hermit and in his wife's arms), win glory, marry great ladies, make good ends. The images are both symbolic and practical. Love, bravery, faithfulness, social and religious duty are commended; who are we to despise such virtues? Life is represented as a significant process, full of expectation, effort, desire and, for the good, reward. Nothing is won without being worked for. The narrative style of *Guy* and *Bevis* is a good example of popular verbal realisation, clothing and dilating upon the inner structure with a multiplicity of incidents, much description and local realism, repetition, sententiousness and cliché. The verbal realisation varies in detail in various manuscript versions. It has all the virtues and faults of relatively low-level but competent literacy, which nowadays cannot but emphasise the lack of ordinary everyday reality in the sequence of events, without enhancing their symbolic significance. Furthermore, the metre is for the most part that peculiarly unhappy stanza known as tail-rhyme, with twelve lines usually of four stresses, and four or five rhyming endings, of which the final line is often shorter, like a hiccup. Chaucer parodied it mercilessly and hilariously in *Sir Thopas*, basing himself mostly on *Sir Bevis*, and it seems to have been one of the chief reasons why he found such romances absurd. There are other extremely popular romances in the Auchinleck manuscript. The story of *Amis and Amiloun* evokes potent images of guilt and restitution, with a dual hero of a type not uncommon in folklore, realised in terms of masculine friendship more common in a warrior society than nowadays. Though the style is not distinguished the tail-rhyme stanza is smooth. *Sir Amadace* also in tail-rhyme stanza has again a folkloric theme, this time of the grateful dead man, interestingly rendered in terms both of chivalry and of knightly poverty (like the Breton lay, *Sir Launfal*, by

Chaucer's contemporary, Thomas Chester). Equally folkloric, and an excellent treatment of 'the family drama', is *Sir Degaré*, though this is written in couplets. (I have discussed it at length in my *Symbolic Stories* (Cambridge: D. S. Brewer, 1980) pp. 66 ff.)

Such romances are sometimes thought of as 'minstrel work', and it is quite likely that the wandering entertainers known as 'gestours' and 'disours' (tellers of tales) knew versions of them and rendered them in hall and even, perhaps, in tavern. Minstrels themselves were primarily and often solely musicians and were usually in the employ of some great man. But these poems were written by poets, probably not themselves minstrels, who were fully literate but were imitating oral delivery. Thus in *Emaré*, a poem composed about 1380 but preserved in a manuscript containing several romances, British Library Cotton Caligula A ii copied in the fifteenth century, the first stanza is a typically pious beginning and the second continues,

Menstrelles that walken fer and wyde,
Her and ther in every a syde,
  In mony a diverse londe,
Sholde at her bygynnyng — their
Speke of that ryghtwes kyng
  That made bothe see and sonde.
Whoso wyll a stoundė dwelle — while
Of mykyll myrght Y may you telle — mirth
  And mornynge theramonge: — mourning mingled
Of a lady fayr and fre
Her name was callėd Emaré,
  As I here synge in songe.

[13–24 M. Mills (ed.), *Six Middle English Romances* (London: Dent, 1973), p. 46]

Literacy and rhetoric

This is too self-conscious to be the product of genuine oral tradition and the formulas sound like clichés. We come closer and closer to full literacy, with all its powers and dangers. The oral tradition no longer provides the sources of creative verbal realisation and the individual work of art depends more and more on the genius of the individual author. It is still possible, perhaps necessary, for writers (the word is used advisedly) to take known stories and adapt them, as Chaucer and Shakespeare do, with supreme success. They may still imitate, invoke or hint at the circumstances of oral delivery and the 'archaic' social group of a total literary experience. They still have some resources from the sententious style of popular delivery. But poets in the later fourteenth century begin to conceive their tasks differently and more self-consciously. They consciously use the devices of rhetoric. Medieval rhetoric is the direct descendant of Classical Latin rhetoric and there were a number of handbooks of instruction, the most famous being the early thirteenth-century *Nova Poetria* of Geoffrey of Vinsauf, written (like them all) in Latin, and referred to by Chaucer. The handbooks are concerned mainly to teach devices of verbal style, and offer a highly artificial classification of what are really the natural turns of elaborate but popular speech – word-play, repetition with variation, hyperbole and much else. They are really handbooks for creative writing, though not of an original kind. Least of all are they, as too often they are assumed to be, handbooks of literary criticism. Valuable as they were, in a limited way, in the recovery of literary style, they only provided an instrument which might be well or badly used, like all instruments. The fundamental association of rhetoric with speech (one of its main uses in classical antiquity being to train lawyers to persuasive oratory) means that it is mainly effective for literature that presupposes an oral basis, as poems often and plays almost always do. Its greatest power is in stirring feeling and imagination in an audience by sympathy, by evocative, emotive language – hence its sententious reliance on the traditional wisdom of proverbs, its pleasure in repetition, in exaggeration, in word-play. It is weak in logic and close description. As literacy, and especially printing develops, rhetoric becomes less useful. The book, especially the printed book, is freed from the social context and does not need repetition or exaggeration. Words become more precise, logic stronger and description more detailed. The reader can measure the times and distances mentioned in the text and compare them with each other as a hearer cannot. Thus literacy brings language as it were closer to its own specific meaning, further from personal social immediate communication. Literacy is in essence opposed to rhetoric.

Changes do not take place immediately. It is long before people read without sounding the words internally. Cultural habits are slow to change. There is always an oral and social residue in language. But it is not surprising that Chaucer, who tells us in *The House of Fame* (l. 656) that he reads 'as dumb as any stone', which very few people in England and in the fourteenth century can have done, shows himself to be very critical of the earlier English romances, which are so clear an example, and for the most part at a rather low level, of an essentially oral type of poetry, merely imitated in writing. It is even less surprising that modern readers, brought up almost exclusively in a print culture, should find orally-conditioned literature strange and hard to take, especially in romances.

Chaucer is remarkable because although so characteristic a product in so many ways of medieval culture he was also extremely *avant garde*. His reading ability and scientific, numerical, interests provide the clue. In these respects he was astonishingly close to Neoclassical assumptions and he displays many Neoclassical attitudes at the height of his achievement, before at his end conclusively rejecting them. Thus, in the case of the romances, the diction and some of the attitudes of medieval romances, are plain to see in Chaucer's earliest surviving poem, *The Book of the Duchess*; but in *The Canterbury Tales*, *The Tale of Sir Thopas* is a hilarious parody of the tail-rhyme romances, and *The Nun's Priest's Tale*, though it uses rhetoric, also satirises both rhetoric and Geoffrey of Vinsauf, whose name was synonymous with the teaching of rhetoric.

Fourteenth-century Arthurian rhyming romances

Chaucer's scepticism in *The Nun's Priest's Tale* extends to Arthurian legend – this story is as true, he says, as that of Launcelot de Lake 'That wommen holde in ful greet reverence' (*CT* VII, 3211–3). This is a bit of gentle male chauvinism about women's credulity. But the English in general seem not to have attained the sophistication of European Arthurian romance, except in the masterpieces of the alliterative *Morte Arthure*, the *Gawain*-poet, and Malory, all discussed elsewhere in this book. *Ywain and Gawain* of the early fourteenth century, from the north, in four-stress couplets, reduces Chrétien de Troyes's great romance *Yvain* of 6800 lines to about 4000 lines by concentrating on the story line and omitting sentiment and commentary. The poem is fluent and direct, with many well-realised passages, not overburdened with cliché, but it is a much less great work.

Sir Perceval of Galles, also of the early fourteenth century, survives only in the Lincoln Cathedral Thornton manuscript of about 1440. It is 2,286 lines long in tail-rhyme, concentrating on the essence of the traditional tale of Perceval's remote upbringing in the forest, his ignorance and fierceness. He wins a bride and returns to his mother. This has no direct relationship to the great complex Perceval romances begun by Chrétien on the Continent, but is given a little chivalric dressing-up and is told with a romping sense of simple comedy and grotesquerie. There is no Grail story here. But Chaucer at the end of *Sir Thopas* shows that he expected his courtly audience to know this *Sir Percevell* 'who drank water from the well'. Another marginally Arthurian story in even more simple style is *Sir Tristrem*, preserved in the Auchinleck manuscript. This is a stylistically crude and jerky version of the Tristram story, although it contains all the incidents of this powerful version of 'the family drama', together with the bizarre addition that Tristrem's dog also drinks the magic love potion, which presumably accounts for his faithfulness.

The best of the Arthurian rhyming romances is also the most central to the story, the stanzaic *Morte Arthur*, almost 4000 lines long in an eight-line stanza, written about 1400. It tells the story of the Fair Maid of Ascolot, who dies for love of Lancelot; of Lancelot's rescue of Queen Guinivere and elopement with her; the fight with Arthur, reconcilement and renewed battle; Modred's treachery; and at last Arthur's death. This is essentially the structure that Malory was to work upon (see below, p. 264). The poet has a strong narrative sense and the capacity to create affecting scenes, though Malory was able to improve on them. The style is undistinguished, as the opening address to 'Lordingis that are leff and dere' leads us to expect. 'Lordings' is never a courtly form of address, as we can see from *The Canterbury Tales*. Chaucer never uses it in his own poetic person or that of the knight, but puts it in the mouth of the Host, Pardoner, Wife of Bath, Friar, etc.

Fifteenth-century romances

Romances in general continued vigorously into the fifteenth and sixteenth centuries until they could influence Marlowe and Shakespeare. Some continued in original verse forms, as *Guy* and *Bevis* did, but these and many others were also turned into prose by Caxton and others, and were joined by the flood of translations of French, Italian and Spanish romances. No amount of literary contempt can deny their historical human importance even for literature. Even a selective list should mention *Ipomadoun* and *Parthonope of Blois*, which in a social and literary way are more ambitious than earlier rhyming romances, and the immensely long verse-translations by Henry Lovelich in the early fifteenth century of *The Holy Grail* and *Merlin*. *The Squyr of Lowe Degre* activates the venerable commonplaces with charm, and the name reappears in Spenser's *Faerie Queen*. A number of romances about Gawain, such as *The Marriage of Sir Gawaine* and *The Carle of Carlile* re-handle popular stories without much art. *The Tournament of Tottenham* is a cheerful chivalric burlesque. Altogether the range is considerable and the achievement modest, like most fifteenth century narrative verse. It was a period of consolidation, of broadening of literacy, rather than of high achievement.

6

Chaucer

'The Book of the Duchess' and the English and European literary traditions

THE English rhyming romances, especially the tail-rhyme romances, lead us straight to Chaucer's work, the greatest, the most delightful, the most idiosyncratic body of all English Gothic literature. If our ideas of what heights medieval English literary culture could reach must be formed by Chaucer, we must also recognise how untypical he is. The exceptional reveals what is potential in the ordinary.

> I have gret wonder *be this lyght*
> How that I lyve, for *day ne nyght*
> I may nat slepė *wel nygh noght.*
> I have so many an ydel thoght
> *Purely* for defaute of slep
> That *by my trouthe I take no kep*
> Of nothing, how hyt *cometh or gooth,*
> Ne me nys nothyng *leef nor looth.*
>
> [1–8 (my italics)]

These are the first lines of *The Book of the Duchess*, marking an exciting new development in English poetry. First we note the continuity of style with the rhyming romances, illustrated by the italicised phrases, common to many romances especially in the Auchinleck Manuscript. The metre is the lightly moving four-stress, roughly octosyllabic, rhyming couplet, long naturalised since *The Owl and the Nightingale*. The italicised phrases are the formulas-become-clichés of the style of the rhyming romances, conversational, even chatty, lively, with doublets and alternatives, assertions and mild expletives; in appearance rather slack. The language is historic English. Only *purely* and *defaute* are not of Old English origin and they had been taken from French around 1300. Chaucer is following the general romance style which at least imitates, and probably envisages, oral delivery, defers somewhat in the *persona* of a minstrel to an audience, yet treats the audience with an almost casual familiarity.

There are notable differences. The 'minstrel' *persona* is confessedly the poet's own and he strikes the personal note of the love-lyric, as in one of the poems of Harley 2253: 'Icham for wowyng al forwake' ('I cannot sleep for loving') (*Cf.* G. L. Brook (ed.), *The Harley Lyrics*, (Manchester: M. U. P., 1948) p. 33.) No minstrel does this. The poem will be a narrative, but far more personalised and lyrical than any earlier romance. The peculiarly personal note is reinforced by the story, in which the poet himself plays an important part, and this is entirely new in English literature.

Novelty increases as the poem continues. The vocabulary of *The Book of the Duchess* introduces some new French words, or new meanings for French words already borrowed, as *ymaginacioun* (1.14). Even more than vocabulary the subject matter is enriched by the stores of European learning never before deployed in English. We are soon given a story from Ovid, and beyond that there is a new richness of comment and information channelled through the *persona* of the poet. Since the Norman Conquest religious writing had always shared in the European cultural stream. Secular writing had only done so to the extent of taking traditional themes and stories, as well as the French and Latin elements of the language, from the Continent. It had never achieved this personal familiarity of knowledge.

The first fifteen lines of *The Book of the Duchess*, so English in appearance, are in close relationship with the first twelve lines of a French poem by Froissart, *Le Paradys d'Amours*. Chaucer probably translated them from the French, but it is just possible that Froissart himself translated from Chaucer. One of Froissart's later poems, *Le Bleu Chevalier*, seems to be influenced by *The Book of the Duchess*. Whichever way translation and influence went, what is most significant is that we find Chaucer as one of a group of courtly poets like Froissart, Deschamps and various courtiers, all of them writing in French. They were all deeply indebted to a French predecessor, Machaut.

Machaut (*c.* 1300–77) was a court poet, who travelled widely, was patronised by various princes, and became a cleric and canon of Reims. He was a great musical composer and a less great, but nonetheless influential, and immensely copious, poet. He developed the long poems of courtly meditation about love and its problems, in which the poet himself is questioner and seeker though not lover, and which showed Chaucer how to modify his provincial English material to find his own characteristic voice and style, though there is no evidence that Chaucer ever composed in French.

If Machaut opened the gate, many others also contributed seed to the fertile English garden of Chaucer's genius. After the poet's self-introduction as so sorrowful and sleepless (we assume, for love), he tells how he read 'a book of romance', written in old time of the lives of kings and queens. It is the tale of 'Ceyx and Alcyone' found in Ovid's *Metamorphoses*. Ovid, with his sensational stories, mostly of love, his flippancy, pathos, richness of material and language, was the favourite secular Latin author from classical antiquity to be read in the Middle Ages by anyone who could at least struggle with Latin. His *Ars Amatoria* ('Art of Love') which gives advice on seduction, and is so sexually outspoken and amusingly cynical, was equally popular, and even his *Remedia Amoris*, a sort of recantation, had its success in medieval culture, which tended to oscillate between theoretical extremes.

Story, purpose and date

The story of Ceyx and Alcyone tells of the death by drowning of King Ceyx, and his queen's death from sorrow soon after. Ovid has them metamorphosed into loving sea birds; Chaucer leaves this out. He then tells how he slept and dreamt he met a man in black in the middle of a forest, and by questioning, elicited from him that his beloved had died. The poem is 1,334 lines long and the narrative is richly, though sometimes diffusely, lyrical, informative, meditative, dramatic. The poet presents himself in his own person in the poem, ignorant, questioning, literalistic, unable to understand the man in black's fairly obvious metaphor from chess about the death of his beloved, but sympathetically listening to the man's account of his courtship. The manners of both are impeccable and the poem has a wonderful delicacy of sensibility. It seems that in so to speak gently forcing the mourner both to recapitulate the joy of his love and to say outright 'She ys ded!' (1.1309) the poet does not so much offer consolation as cause the man in black to realise it for himself, and to face up to the sad truth. A comparison with the *Gawain*-poet's poem *Pearl* is inevitable, and the differences fascinating. Amongst others, Chaucer does not offer a word of religious consolation, and though the whole poem is in effect a consolation, the poet's *persona* in the poem offers only the briefest respectful pity. *The Book of the Duchess* has a death at its centre, but it is an elegy in the form of a celebration of what has been.

The poem ends in a series of references to a long castle with white walls, with an oath to St John, on a rich hill (ll. 1318–19), which are obviously non-comic puns, referring to the castle of Richmond (Richemont) in Yorkshire belonging to John of Gaunt, i.e. John of Lancaster (Longcastel). The lady whose death is mourned is called in the poem at the end of a long description of her, 'goode faire White'. The poem thus delicately and obliquely commemorates and offers sympathy for the death of John of Gaunt's beloved first wife Blanche who died in 1368 (not 1369 as used to be thought), at the age of 28, and mother of five children.

This long poem was written in a fortnight or three weeks from late September to early October 1368. Chaucer might have had the Ceyx and Alcyone passage already composed; for the rest, as with the first few lines, much is very close indeed to French poems, mainly by Machaut. The speed of composition is a product partly of genius, partly of a convention that did not seek superficial originality, and partly of the profound appeal that the situation made in the courtly environment. Joyous life and sorrowful death make a very Chaucerian and Gothic juxtaposition.

Love and loss in Chaucer

Chaucer is a great poet of love and loss. The love that interests him is sexual, rather than religious. He does not here represent secular sexual love even as marital, let alone with religious sanction. One would not guess from the poem that John and Blanche had been married, with five children.

It is true that the hero Troilus in the later poem *Troilus and Criseyde* conceives his love for Criseyde in religious and marital terms, but the course of events in the story and the drift of significance of the poem, suggest he may be confused. Secular sexual love, like religious love, brings joy and suffering, that Gothic antinomy, where each side of the contradiction is as necessary to the other as the chicken and the egg, or sunlight and shadow. The pain of love is as interesting, at least to read about, as the joy, and certainly as real. In this poem the joy rewards, and though it does not cancel, it compensates for the pain. Loss and death (they are almost synonymous) evoke a sombre power in their own right in medieval literature which may be morbid in lesser works but which can bring an unsentimental healing sense of reality and of truth. Thus it is in *The Book of the Duchess*, *Pearl*, Langland's *Harrowing of Hell* and some lyrics. They accept but in so doing triumph over death. They make an affirmation of superiority over the indignities which Fortune inflicts on us, that 'goddess' whom Chaucer's man in black at first ineffectually reproaches, and who presides over so many medieval tragedies.

Medieval romantic love in English

The Book of the Duchess introduces a more elaborate, European, concept of love than had so far been seen in English, and it is appropriate to examine here the medieval English idea of secular sexual love. All societies impose upon the expression of sexual love certain patterns and constraints, both co-operating with and attempting to control 'nature'. Of all our complex experiences in complex civilisations perhaps that of 'love' contains most self-contradictory elements. Sexual love between young persons of opposite sexes focuses our most intense experience of union and conflict with others. Since the technological revolution of the twentieth century, which has largely separated sex from procreation, and thus from necessary long-term personal responsibilities it is much harder for many, especially younger readers, to imagine for themselves the once apparently unbreakable links between sex and life, between sex, integrity and responsibility. The explosive forces, whose inhibition required so much fear or moral self-control, whose legitimate release could inspire such transcendent joy, have in modern culture for many people been simply channelled into a safely sterile physical overflow. But in medieval society, so often uncontrollably fierce and cruel, sexuality could be a torment and a monster, or a representative of all the significance and beauty that life could have; either a wheel, or a chariot, of fire.

In medieval literary culture the mutuality of love, the yearning desire to melt in union, was paradoxically most readily invoked metaphorically by mystics such as Rolle, who used the imagery of love and marriage to celebrate the soul's union with God. They only made themselves free to employ such power by repudiating ordinary human sexual love with what seems to us a morbid contempt or even hatred. There was a beautiful monastic ideal of mutual friendship between equals expressed in Latin, as in the *De Amicitia* of St Ailred (1109–67). The author of *The Ancrene Riwle* knew it. It derived much from Cicero's *De Amicitia* and both works were influential, but they lacked the excitement of sex.

The image of the lady

The chief image of sexual love came to be expressed in secular literature as men's love of women, figured in the knight's desire for the lady, always golden-haired, beautiful, good, kindly and not merely chaste but also not experiencing sexual desire. It took some time for this image to develop. Rimenhild in *King Horn*, Blancheflor, and William of Palerne's beloved, are not quite like this. Their love is spontaneous and either precedes or is mutually experienced with the hero's. As an emotion their love is equal to that of the hero, not a condescension, though it is faithful and tender. Many other romances and lyrics have variants in the forms that love takes. The nearer to folk-tale, the more likely the woman is to take a positive part. Nevertheless it is true of Chaucer, and broadly true of the more sophisticated poems and stories in English from the fourteenth century even up to Shakespeare, that love is characteristically the young man's love for the lady, who is a young girl, beautiful, good, sexually passive and chaste. She is an eminently civilising image of pity, gentleness, restraint, and enduring love – everything indeed that 'natural' sex is not. Rightly is she worshipped before marriage, because a powerful part of her charm is that as a virgin she is not fully known, but may become so. The love she attracts is essentially pre-marital. Because she is bright, joyous, serene, morally superior, the effort to win her evokes in those who love her a spirit of genuine aspiration. She arouses those qualities of tenderness and faithfulness which she represents. Since it is natural that several lovers should love the same lady she also arouses emulation between men, which may issue in aggressiveness to each other; and since men wish to prove their own worth in order to deserve the lady's love, and masculine worth in a chivalric world is honour, which is founded on bravery, the tenderness of the lady may evoke in the knight a paradoxical fierceness towards others. Love based on sexual desire is so powerful an emotion in a man that it was an easy development of the structure of feeling to make love the organising principle, in theory at least, of all good secular activity, including social and intellectual prowess. Secular love created thus a morality much influenced by contemporary Christian teaching. Though secular, the passion for the lady ran parallel with, was influenced by, and influenced, the worship of the Blessed Virgin, Mother of Christ. It is in this religious field that the filial aspect of medieval romantic love, and the paradoxical maternal superiority attributed to the beloved virgin-lady (a truly Gothic paradox of mutually related contradictions), finds its fullest expression.

Love as service

In secular terms, the sweet pain of desire, the wish to prove worthy, the natural modesty of the young, allowed an element of real humility to be developed in the psychological and social pattern of the knight's love. This became so well established, partly because of the parallel feudal model of a man's service to his lord, that 'to serve' became a real synonym for 'to love', and the knight could call himself his lady's 'man', just as he was his lord's 'man'. Since he was also God's 'man', the Lady might take on a religious as well as social superiority as an image in the knight's mind. Since love was service, was regard for the superior Other, it was naturally regulated by the rules of courtesy, which determined how a man should behave in relation to others, from table-manners to inner attitudes, in a hierarchical society. Courtesy became the ritual of consideration for others, originating in the monastic need to regulate the behaviour of a tight, enclosed community, but soon widely influential in the somewhat similar conditions of courts. Love therefore also became courteous, unlike the inherently predatory nature of sex.

Love and marriage

In most romances, French or English, the natural aim of such sexual love was marriage, as had been the case in life with John of Gaunt and Blanche the Duchess. In both literature and life it was customary to obtain the lady's consent to marriage. The wooing, or persuading, might be open, or if the young man, as is often the case in Chaucer, was shy, concealed. *The Book of the Duchess* gives a charming account of the love-suffering of the shy youth, and the way he struggles with infinite embarrassment, shame and nervousness to make his stumbling declaration. Bold lovers in Chaucer are always scoundrels. The young man asks for 'mercy'. Eventually the lady concedes it, that is, grants him her love. Love is much more volitional for the lady than for the young knight, who is fated to fall in love as the sight of the lady pierces his eyes and reaches his heart. But the young knight must earn the reward of the lady's gift of herself. He must first be faithful for ever. This concept of truth in love, which connects with faithfulness in marriage, is again one of those cultural heightenings of a natural but not universal characteristic which nowadays seems to have become for many almost incomprehensible. In medieval culture it was crucial. Like all these cultural patterns it had a practical basis in social arrangements, for the woman was vulnerable and needed all the security she could get. Security itself was a rare commodity in the Middle Ages and consequently, under the name 'stability', highly valued.

The young lover must be brave, honest, honourable. He must promise life-long 'service' and he must, to the lady, be humble. He will feel himself unworthy of her, and will be able to ask only for her 'mercy' on his sufferings, to save his life. Although all this easily becomes the hyperbole of an artificial convention it has a real basis in the natural feelings of modesty that go with intense desire in young men of some sensibility.

Pre-marital love

The absence of reference in *The Book of the Duchess* to marriage indicates that the imaginative emphasis is on pre-marital love. Marriage, though even in romance it is important both as an end and as a symbolic reintegration into society, is not imaginatively the centre. True love, whose course never did run smooth, is that centre, and wooing under social or emotional constraint may easily include the wooing of someone else's wife. It has been argued by some of those who have examined the history of the sentiment of romantic love that in our era it began with the troubadours of Provence in the late eleventh century, partly under Arabian influence, and that the beloved lady was almost always, for social reasons, the wife of the troubadour's lord, was the lady of the castle. In such circumstances romantic love would inevitably be adulterous. That would be too simple an account, but life and literature being what they are, it cannot but be that love will sometimes be adulterous, and that the least smooth-running course of true love is likely to be that which is impeded by a husband. Thus the most famous stories of love are those of Lancelot, in love with his king Arthur's queen Guinivere, and Tristan, in love with his uncle king Mark's wife, Isolde. In these cases love becomes tragic. The superiority of the lady always risks turning her into a version of the mother-figure, and the story becomes a tragic example of 'the family drama', which may trap the lover into a sterile relationship. (The more usual but less striking pattern of non-adulterous love avoids the trap and achieves a happy ending by marriage.) At a less fundamentally psychological level, medieval society, lacking in privacy and rich in social ceremony, often put difficulties in the way of lovers. Moreover the sentiment of personal love is part of the general drive towards a sense of private personal identity, of discrimination of the individual as apart from the collective. All these factors joined to make the sentiment of love intensely private in most cases even when not adulterous, and it was in consequence 'secret'. We meet this 'secret' love, *derne love*, in the English lyrics and romances often enough.

Love is felt by knights

Romantic love in English Gothic literature therefore is a sentiment felt by men (strictly, gentlemen, not 'churls') as courtly service, intensely private, faithful to the one lady to death. The lady is complimented by having attributed to her no feelings but kindliness, friendship to all who are worthy, and reluctance to abandon her virginity. The knight's love is the motive force. The lady's love is given first as 'mercy'. The knight's love precedes sexual intercourse; the lady's follows. A man's honour essentially resides in his bravery, woman's in her chastity. She gives up virginity reluctantly and needs the guarantee of faithfulness for the sacrifice – faithfulness best expressed in marriage. If she is married her honour resides in faithfulness to her husband; if after losing her virginity she has no husband she has no honour, and to lose honour is to be thrust out of society. Moreover the loss of virginity means for her the mortal dangers of childbirth and the sorrows of a mother's tender heart. Both life and love are hard on women in such a society and they deserve all the care that chivalry can offer.

Sex comedy and satire

All this is at the highest social and moral level, mainly in Chaucer, but it is the core of the sentiment of romantic love as it was developing in England, and part of a large European movement of the heart still inadequately described despite many books of analysis. This pattern is the imaginative basis of European romantic love and indeed of marriage as they lasted up until the mid-twentieth century. Below this high level are less strict versions, seductive clerks, easily-won girls. Below that again, as compensation for the idealised lady, we have the images of such a man-eating female as the Wife of Bath, product of centuries of both popular and ecclesiastical anti-feminism; or dangerously seductive beauties as in some Arthurian romances; or the unstable unfaithful heroine Criseyde. Further off is popular coarse comedy of sexual trickery and misadventure which has nothing to do with love and all to do with natural lust of a kind that has always aroused laughter, except in the victims, since the beginning of recorded time in the earliest dirty jokes, the so-called Milesian stories.

Chaucer's works will be found to run the whole gamut of love and sex, but in order to understand the variety we must first give full imaginative sympathy to the controlled passions and now unfamiliar delicacies of the idealised story of love as it should be, as presented in *The Book of the Duchess*. The account of the development of his feelings by the man in black, and the long formal description of the beautiful lady that he gives, provide the stylised basis for the progressively more realistic exploration of love and sex in Chaucer's later poetry.

'Le Roman de la Rose': Guillaume

About the same time that he wrote *The Book of the Duchess*, or even before, Chaucer began to translate the immense French poem *Le Roman de la Rose* written by two authors in the thirteenth century. The thirteenth century was the period of the great flowering of French medieval culture, the age of the supreme Gothic cathedrals, crusades, the great intellectual summaries of the scholastic philosophers, the creation of the wealth of Arthurian and other romances, and of other poetry, including *fabliaux*. The first author of *Le Roman de la Rose* was Guillaume de Lorris who composed about 1230 the archetypal dream-vision poem. The poet tells us that in his twentieth year, when love was dominant, five years ago, he dreamt he wandered on a bright May morning along a river bank and came to a beautiful garden. Outside were paintings on the wall of people representing disagreeable things like Hate and Felony and Old Age. A beautiful girl called Idleness kept the gate and let him into the garden where he saw beautiful people such as Mirth, Beauty and Riches, dancing caroles with the God of Love. Within a spring he saw the image of a rose which he longed to pluck. The spring was the fountain of Narcissus. The God of Love shot the poet with his arrow of desire so that he longed to pluck the rose, though now he saw it was surrounded by thorns. The God of Love gave him a long lecture on the Art of Love. Reason descended from her tower to warn him of Love's dangers. Fair-Welcome encouraged him to pluck the rose. Danger rushed out to prevent him. The lover, as we must now call the poet, was sleepless with the joyous pain of love and came to the castle of Jealousy. Here, at line 4058 the poem ceases rather than finishes. It has deployed the archetypal symbols and themes of love, the May morning, the enclosed garden, the spring or fountain, the beautiful lady, and the sweet-smelling rose which is love itself, in a varied lively style. The narrative is intrinsically interesting yet also allegorical and symbolic. All stories incarnate propositions, but this one in particular gives, through the allegorical persons and their actions, a creative analysis of the mind, its desires and moods, in relation to the demands of the outside world—an analysis that does not murder to dissect. By placing the story in a dream Guillaume releases the imagination; by making it apparently autobiographical he personalises and authenticates the events. The structure of the poem expresses major movements of the medieval European imagination, its progress towards internalisation, individualisation and a civilising concept of sexual love.

'Le Roman de la Rose': Jean de Meung

From Guillaume's poem sprang a long line of dream-poems about love modulating into the more wordy versions of Machaut, out of which came *The Book of the Duchess*, and with further change other poems by Chaucer. Guillaume's unfinished *Roman de la Rose* was itself finished by a very different poet, Jean de Meung, about 1270, who added 18,000 lines of a very different style. Guillaume was courtly; Jean was a university scholastic, argumentative, learned, coarse, radical in thought, more interested in sex than love, comic, satirical about women. It is impossible to summarise his vast addition, but he raised in the vernacular many of the themes that were debated in intellectual and courtly circles in the fourteenth and fifteenth centuries, from problems of destiny and free will to free love and the liberation of women. Jean's and Guillaume's poem made a wonderful combination that must have come as an explosive widening of horizons to many an ardent provincially educated boy, as Chaucer was. The immense joint poem was copied hundreds of times, often sumptuously illustrated. To read it is a liberal education. Chaucer knew the whole poem intimately and early in life translated the first 1,704 lines, now called in English *The Romaunt of the Rose*.

(An unknown poet about 1400 added several thousand lines more.) The whole poem is a main base of Chaucer's thought and feeling, far more sophisticated than the English romances and lyrics which he also knew.

'An ABC'

At about the same time, in all probability, Chaucer made another, very different, translation from the French. This was *An ABC* in which, in 23 stanzas each beginning with a successive letter of the alphabet, he rehearses with solemnity, vigour and conviction the praises of the Blessed Virgin. (The letters *i* and *j* were combined in medieval script, as were *u/v/w*.) In this poem he expresses both the religious conviction which is as much a part of his Gothic complexity as his cynicism and ribaldry, and also the verbal resourcefulness, the wealth of vocabulary and the flexibility of his verse. His style has a calm plenitude, his metre an easy power, only rivalled by Langland and the *Gawain*-poet, who write in so different a metrical tradition.

Chaucer's life and personality

The poet's projection of his own personality is already strong in *The Book of the Duchess*. He cannot restrain his own flippancy though the occasion is so solemn. He is so self-confident that he presents himself in the poem as rather simple. Only three manuscripts of the poem survive, and perhaps it was primarily meant to be spoken in a unified group, that of the court of John of Gaunt, as a consolation to the most powerful baron in the land after the king, whose second son he was. We may thus imagine for Chaucer an audience of the highest in the land, listening for the first time for three hundred years to a great poet in English. The very existence of *The Book of the Duchess* proclaims the acceptance of the English language at court, though an English rich in French vocabulary, and with a strong French background.

Chaucer is the first literary personality in English. Everything he writes has his own stamp on it, yet his origins, sources and intellectual and emotional range are more diverse than those of any other poet in English including Shakespeare.

In himself he illustrates the achieved formation of a definitively English literary culture out of heterogeneous elements, and is at the same time the most advanced of medieval poets.

His father was a rich London vintner. Chaucer was born about 1340 or a little before and probably educated at a London grammar school. Only London amongst English cities could compare with any of the great Continental cities. He was thus more imbued than any contemporary English writer with the new European urban spirit of rationalisation and regularity, with its capacity for arithmetical calculation and recognition of public, clockwork time, its sense of material reality, its cool scepticism. The urban spirit was a 'modern' spirit, that allowed for a sometimes sentimental piety, which caused philanthropy to become, through hope of heaven, a comfortable bedfellow with self-interest. But London was also closely connected with the court, which was a much more archaic, personalised institution. The king, that archaic image of loyalty and of personal, not commercial, bonds between people, needed money, and the City could supply it. Merchants' sons like Chaucer quite frequently became courtiers, and Chaucer's life from adolescence lay with royal courts, first of all as page with the Countess of Ulster in 1357. Here he could have added to the Latin and arithmetic learnt at school the French poems of exciting sophistication written by Machaut and others. In the autumn of 1359 he took part in the dismal rainy campaign in northern France, was captured, and was ransomed by the king. A gap in the records from 1360 to 1366 and an uncertain reference allows us to guess that part of that time he studied law at the Inner Temple. A safe-conduct (a sort of passport) for travel in Navarre, between France and Spain, in 1366, suggests that he served with the Black Prince for a time in Aquitaine, like many of his friends. By 1366 he was married to Philippa, one of the queen's ladies-in-waiting. In 1367 Chaucer himself became a member of the king's household, a 'yeoman'. Thereafter he had a working courtier's career of a variety of posts, some sinecures, some not, including a long spell at the customs (1374–84) and a couple of years as Clerk of the King's Works (1389–91), an administrative job looking after the maintenance of royal buildings. He must be the only great poet who was also an accountant. Most obviously significant from a literary point of view was his first journey to Italy, from December 1372 to May 1373. Chaucer's knowledge of Italian literature, which presumably derived from his Italian experience, brought another powerful resource to his writing. He knew Petrarch by name though probably did not meet him. Italy was the most advanced country in Europe at the time and must have stimulated Chaucer's genius, but even more important was his acquisition of poems by Boccaccio and Dante. Having lived, apart from journeys, for a long time in London, mostly over the gate at Aldgate, he moved to Greenwich in Kent about 1385. His wife died in 1387, and he himself in 1400.

Such a life gave a wide range of experience. He kept friendly with all the hostile factions of the court and his friends included the poet Gower, the lawyer Strode, probably some at least of those knights who were tainted with Lollardy (see below p. 255), and great London merchants like John Philipot – in a word, a cross-section of courtiers, soldiers, scholars and merchants. He had no patron, in contrast to Machaut and Froissart, for example; but he was on good terms with Gaunt and his son Henry Bolingbroke who became King Henry IV. In his poems he often addresses ladies in general, and without making him either a great lover or lecher we may surely imagine him on friendly terms with beautiful and intelligent women.

'The House of Fame'

After *The Book of the Duchess* Chaucer's next poem was also in four-stress couplets and much influenced by French dream-poems, but now the Italian influence begins to make itself felt. *The House of Fame* (2,158 lines long), of which only three manuscript copies survive, was written between 1374 and 1380 while he was at the Customs (about whose clerical work he complains in the poem). It is an enigmatic poem, rich in varied subject matter and comedy, uncertain in direction, and unfinished. Its structure resembles *The Book of the Duchess* in that, after a prologue on dreams, we have first an account of a book, Virgil's *Aeneid*, mainly focused on Dido's unhappy love and death. Then an eagle catches the poet up into the skies in a brilliantly comic episode that for all its flippancy evokes the ancient image of the poet's flight into the heavens, expressive of dissatisfaction, unrest and aspiration, reaching out to the celestial living centre of creation, away from dull earth. The fame which the goddess of that name gives out in arbitrary reward in her grand temple is treated with contempt: the true house of Fame is a wicker house sixty miles long full of personalised rumours and stories. Chaucer despises fame but is interested in ordinary human people and events, though he treats them with humorous satire. A man of great authority comes forth to make an announcement – but the poem stops just before he speaks. Chaucer could not finish it. He could not bring himself to speak for authority. The poem is a Gothic medley of mood, and often of grotesque description, a revolutionary, anti-formal poem, spontaneous in effect, which cannot even formulate the problem that lies, we feel, somewhere behind it. At times it reads like one of the rare prologues to early secular plays.

Chaucer is truly Gothic in his liking for tension, debate, problems. The times were very difficult: England was as usual in a mess. King Edward III, worn out by love and war, died in 1377. Edward, the Black Prince of Europe's chivalry, had died the year before. Richard, the Prince's son, aged eleven, succeeded to the throne and, as was often and all too truly quoted from the Bible, 'Woe to the land where a child is king!' (Ecclesiastes x. 16). Oppressive and ill-judged laws culminated in the Peasants' Revolt of 1381, and the mob who broke into London to burn and pillage swarmed through the gate over which Chaucer lived. He never comments on political events, being perhaps too dangerously near them, certainly seeing two sides to every question. Chaucer is interested in people and feelings, in religion, science and philosophy, the personal or the cosmic, rather than in political systems, theories and reforms. He combines a relish for life with a pessimistic quietism. Langland's anguish passes him by: he prefers a scientific treatise to a political sermon. Yet questioning, uncertainty, a response to the current of the times runs along with the irrepressible urge to laugh, resulting in a constant ambivalence of tone, an increasing difficulty in saying anything 'straight'. *The House of Fame* thus genuinely though indirectly reflects the nature of the times.

'The Parliament of Fowls'

Chaucer's questioning continues in the next poem, *The Parliament of Fowls*, with a bigger problem at its heart, similar in structure, but with an even wider span of interest, a better control, shown in a more splendid metre. The great five-stress, ten- or eleven-syllable line, the staple of mature English verse ever since, appears for the first time in English, knitted into a new elaborate seven-line stanza, the nobly-named 'rhyme royal'. Chaucer probably evolved it on the model of Italian verse in Dante and Boccaccio, and the poem, 699 lines long (99 stanzas and an inserted lyric), is one of the finest in the language. This time, once more through the story of an ancient Latin book, the poet imagines the flight into the heavens of an ancient Roman, Scipio Africanus, and the command to him to do well. But he has a still unformulated problem and the heavens cannot satisfy him. He dreams that he himself is brought into the garden of Nature – effectively, of this world – where under Nature as God's deputy all the birds are met to find a mate, for it is St Valentine's day, 14 February. The three noblest birds are the predatory hawks. They have the right to be first to choose, but they all love the same beautiful formel eagle ('formel' being the technical word for the female). Who should have her? She is not to be constrained. It is a classic love-dilemma in life; and a typically Gothic 'question of love' of a kind that the groups of young men and women, like those of Boccaccio's *Decameron*, in courtly society liked to debate. The lower vulgar birds join in and make it a rowdy argument, while the question is broadened. What is the sense of such love? There are plenty of other fish in the sea. The formel eagle has anyway no desire for a mate, and in the end the issue is postponed for a year with the debate left characteristically unresolved. Other echoes are aroused; the vulgar birds are amusingly characterised in their down-to-earth sense and lack of sensibility, but social unrest and challenge is recognised. Beneath all is an undercurrent of questioning about the whole nature of love and life. A beautiful description makes a transition from the garden to the Temple of Venus where beauty is allied to a hot-house anguish of love. Not all refined love is either happy or good. This passage is directly borrowed from Boccaccio's poem *Teseida* in the manner of traditional poets and has a decorativeness absent in English before Chaucer. *The Parliament* is a further rich amalgam of the resources of the European literary mind from Classical Latin to French and Italian. *Le Roman de la Rose* is the matrix, but the Italian influence has broadened and clarified the material, which includes (in the vulgar birds) what might be described as pragmatic English sentiment. The diction shows a further advance in extending the vocabulary in both courtly and abrasively popular styles. It is an astonishing poem.

There were courtly 'literary' societies, such as those of the Flower and the Leaf mentioned in *The Prologue to the Legend of Good Women*, and in France such societies met on St Valentine's Day. A reading of *The Parliament* and other St Valentine's Day poems may have been part of the process and product of literary festivities – genuinely oral. *The Parliament* is also profoundly literate. Its sparkling surface is supported by a structure derived from the impassioned reading by a subtle mind of Latin, French and Italian works, though this has not impeded sharp observation and imitation of everyday life. The poem ends by the poet turning to yet other books with which to solve his problems.

'The Consolation of Philosophy'

So he turned to a major philosophical work in Latin, to which he would have been first introduced, along with much other learned material, by Jean de Meung in his part of *Le Roman de la Rose*. Now he went to the original, in difficult Latin, the *De Consolatione Philosophiae* of Boethius, written about 523 AD. Boethius had had a brilliant career in government under the Ostrogoth Emperor of Rome, Theodoric; but the Emperor like all tyrants became suspicious, and Boethius was imprisoned and eventually killed in 524 AD. He was extremely learned in Greek and Latin, and his translations of various Greek works into Latin were part of the foundations on which medieval men laboriously re-created a structure of knowledge after the disastrous fall of Rome. He was a Christian who wrote some impressive theological works. While in prison he set himself with noble resolution to face the problems of the apparently arbitrary incidence of good and evil, happiness and unhappiness, good and bad fortune, as they occur in life, arguing by natural reason, no doubt supported by, but without recourse to Christian faith. His book represents the course of his thinking. It begins with a portrayal of himself, distraught, in prison, visited by the beautiful lady Philosophy. She reproaches him for his complaints, and the rest of the work, in five books, is composed of a dialogue between the author-inside-the-poem, and Philosophy, in sections of prose, in which she offers rational consolation, interspersed with fine lyrics expressing wonder and joy. It was an immensely influential work throughout the Middle Ages until the new world-view developed in the seventeenth century. It attempts what non-philosophers have always thought that philosophy should do, to reconcile us to the trials of existence by offering some rational overall scheme of purpose and significance. As philosophy it is derivative; it offers no method for analytical thought. When medieval scholastic philosophy started in the twelfth century it began with Boethius' translations of some of Aristotle's work on logic and rapidly outgrew even that. But scholastic philosophy based on logic and dialectic offers little support either to the distressed spirit or to the literary imagination and Chaucer shows no significant knowledge of it. A noble spirit shines through the *Consolation* that sustains the reader; the book is interested in problems, such as that of 'felicity', which do not interest real philosophers. It offers an imaginable picture of the moral universe in an apparently logical exposition; its prose has a wide range of reference; its poems express something of the glory of the universe beyond all suffering; no wonder princes (Alfred the Great and Elizabeth I) translated it, and so many others read and commented on it. The mixture of prose and verse, the device of presenting the author within his own work, the exhortation of the author by a superior lady, and the mythological picture of Fortune with her wheel, were influential on other works for many centuries. Dante, Chaucer, Langland, the *Gawain*-poet (in *Pearl*) reveal the book's direct or indirect influence, as even Milton does.

The Consolation of Philosophy represents that victory of mind over matter, that achievement of serenity over circumstances of anguish, which life demands of so many of its victims in all periods. Chaucer turned to it not out of circumstances of personal tragedy, as far as we can see, but from his fundamental sympathy with and pity for the human condition. He translated its difficult Latin prose and verse, with the help of a French translation and commentary, into elaborate English prose, about 1382–5, and henceforth few of his works are without some sign of its influence, while four or five splendid short poems are on entirely Boethian themes.

At about the same time, in the mid-1380s, Chaucer was working on two great poems whose stories called for profoundly Boethian treatment, a mixture of comedy (in both medieval and modern senses) and tragedy; of lyric idealism and stark realism. These are *Troilus and Criseyde*, five 'books' and over 8,000 lines long, in 1,177 'rhyme royal' stanzas, and *The Knight's Tale*, 2,250 lines long. This (or the closely contemporary *Legend of Good Women*) is the first English poem in that difficult, delightful metre, the five-stress, ten- or eleven-syllable line (making use of final *-e* as required) as combined in couplets. In each poem Chaucer drew on a different poem of Boccaccio's, interpreting the story in each case in the spirit of Boethius to convey his own Gothic sense of the pain and joy of life, with a profoundly Christian feeling for both the importance and the insignificance of individual destiny.

'Troilus and Criseyde': the story

In the complex sentence that fills the opening stanza of *Troilus* the poet offers to tell us of the 'double sorrow' of Troilus in loving, and invokes a conceit from Boethius, stating that his verses weep as he writes. Thus literacy is personified in a strange way, for the next stanza gives us a sense of the poet standing before us, as it were acting aloud his story, when he refers to his own sad expression, suiting his sad material. Our sense of the narrating poet, contemplating from various points of view the story about which he writes, or sings, his poem, is the source of the richness and teasing ambiguities of the work. In his eight-stanza introduction Chaucer runs the gamut from solemnity about and sympathy for young lovers to a detached flippancy. The actual narrative begins by telling how the 'great divine' who could foretell the future, the lord Calchas, deserted Troy for the besieging Greeks, abandoning his daughter, the young but already widowed Criseyde. Troilus, son of King Priam and after his brother, Hector, the greatest warrior of Troy, is very young, and contemptuous of love, but he sees the golden-haired Criseyde, in a widow's black dress, in the temple and is immediately smitten with love. How soon are the proud humbled. The bitter-sweet pain of love is so great that Troilus, the most sensitive of all medieval heroes, takes to his bed. His friend, Pandarus, discovers him and, as emotional in his way as Troilus, 'well nigh melts for woe and ruth'. In a scene of realistic dialogue presented with delicate humour he wheedles the cause of Troilus' pain out of him and promises to help, because Criseyde is none other than his own niece. Pandarus' age, like Criseyde's, is an enigma. But we should think of Troilus and Criseyde as in their late 'teens, and Pandarus little older.

Book II begins with a scene of quite remarkable realism entirely invented by Chaucer in which Pandarus comes to Criseyde's fine house (like one of the houses of the nobility in the late fourteenth century along the Strand, between Westminster and the City of London with a lovely garden). In a long fencing dialogue of great psychological realism he discloses, to Criseyde's dismay, that she has a noble lover. Why, she thinks to herself, should she, now free, love and lose her liberty? For love is the most stormy life, and hard on women, who are often slandered and betrayed. But in her garden, while walking with her nieces and other women, one of her nieces sings a beautiful song about the nobility and bliss of love – part of the recurrent lyric beauty with which the story is told. As Criseyde lies in bed 'a nightingale upon a cedar green' sings a lay of love that makes her heart fresh and gay.

By a series of intrigues and letters Pandarus at last contrives a meeting in Troilus' brother's house between Troilus, feigning sick, and Criseyde, during which Troilus is virtually speechless from passionate shyness, and Criseyde is all understanding womanly tenderness. Eventually Pandarus gives a dinner party in his house to Criseyde when he knows, by the stars, that there will that night be a storm of rain. Troilus is hidden within the house. Does Criseyde know? Who can tell? Pandarus persuades her to stay, and the poet comments,

But O Fortune, executrice of wyrdes — agent of destiny
O influences of thise hevenės hye!
Soth is, that under God ye ben oure hierdes — shepherds
Though to us bestės ben the causes wrie. — hidden

But execut was al bisyde hire leve	carried out
The goddės wil; for which she mostė bleve.	remain
The bentė moonė with hire hornės pale,	crescent
Saturne, and Jove, in Cancro joynėd were,	
That swych a reyn from heven gan avale	descend
That every maner womman that was there	
Hadde of that smoky reyn a verray feere;	real fear
At which Pandare tho lough, and seydė thenne,	
"Now were it tyme a lady to gon henne!"	hence
	[III, 617–30]

(Fortune is the personification of the ups-and-downs of worldly life, made familiar by Boethius, while 'wyrdes' is 'destiny', a similar concept, each thought to be ultimately under Providence, but remote from God. The influences are those of the stars like the planets Saturn and Jove (Jupiter), which manipulate us unless we bypass them by direct submission to God. Saturn and Jupiter were joined with the moon in the sign of the Zodiac Cancer, a conjunction which occurs only once in 600 years, but did actually happen in May 1385, about the time Chaucer was writing *Troilus*.)

Here we have the full Chaucerian Gothic range, the highest heavens connected with local human affairs. The poet comments on his story with full human sympathy and yet a touch of ironic detachment; he is both philosophical and concrete. The rest of this book tells with extraordinary richness of detail how Pandarus manipulates Troilus into bed with Criseyde, and Troilus' swooning, reverent, yet sensual delight. Criseyde has given him her pity and her mercy, and now loves him fully, though the pains and raptures are told from Troilus' point of view, and we never have represented any sensual delight of Criseyde. His love ennobles Troilus even further, and the book ends with Troilus' superb hymn to universal love, translated from the *Consolation*, in which that love which controls earth and sea is claimed to be the bond of nature that also links lovers. Thus Troilus is with Criseyde, 'his owen hertė swete', in the last line of Book III.

But al to litel, weylaway the whyle	alas, the time
Lasteth swich joie, ythonkėd be Fortune.	[IV, 1–2]

So begins Book IV, with a sharp juxtaposition. Such is the tragic Boethian view of this world, in so far as men allow themselves to be governed by Fortune. Having risen to the top of the wheel, a fall must come. Book IV tells the painful story of how Criseyde is unjustly sent to the enemy Greeks by the Trojan Parliament for reasons of political expediency. In order to preserve her reputation she refuses to elope with Troilus, but is ultimately seduced by 'the sudden Diomede' when in the Greek camp 'with wommen fewe, among the Grekės stronge. Troilus is agonised but faithful and is finally killed by the 'fierse Achilles'.

Boccaccio's Filostrato *told in the light of Boethius*

So far the story is taken from Boccaccio's youthful poem, *Il Filostrato*, which is told with a sexual relish that turns into a cynical anti-feminism. Chaucer must have had Boccaccio's text in front of him and translated much of it from stanza to stanza. But in translating he transformed it, cutting out stanzas, and slotting in comments, stanzas and whole episodes, so that in the entirely traditional manner of modifying a received story he improved it in every way, deepening the philosophical tone by Boethian commentary as he contemplated the Boethian tragedy of Fortune, and changing the characters; ennobling Troilus, making Criseyde more lovable and complex, turning Pandarus into the supreme 'fixer', and giving English henceforward the word 'pandar' for a bawd. Chaucer raised the social level, gave poetic splendour, yet enlivened the realism, added much humour, greatly increased the pathos. The characters, recognisable types, are generated *by* the action as Chaucer conceived it, rather than themselves generating the action (and in that respect fulfilling a Boethian, traditional image of the human role). They live in our minds as they enjoy themselves and as they suffer.

The actual story finishes with Criseyde's betrayal and Troilus' death; it is, as Chaucer says, 'litel myn tragedye'. A tragedy in the medieval Boethian definition (also repeated in the *Prologue* to *The Monk's Tale* in *The Canterbury Tales*) is the fall of a great man from high to low. But the poem continues beyond the end of the story, and we have an astonishing glimpse of Troilus' soul released from 'this wretched world' to ascend blissfully into the heavens, where he laughs at the woe of those who mourn for him. And the poet concludes the poem by recommending 'young fresh folks' of either sex, in whom love grows up with their age, to avoid feigned love and to love Christ as God, who betrays no one. This extended, surprising, complex ending, condemning pagan worldliness and idolatry, is the Boethian answer to Boethian tragedy; to have a spirit that rises above the world. Yet it is worldly experience that must paradoxically justify the rejection of worldliness in order to turn tragedy into what the Middle Ages called 'comedy', that is, a story with a happy, good ending, like Dante's *Divine Comedy*, ending in Heaven.

Presentation of the story

No brief account can give more than a hint of the richness of the poetic narrative of *Troilus*, lyrical, meditative, humorous and sombre, by turns. The poet contemplates the story from many different points of view, now serious, now almost flippant. Sometimes he gives the impression of an omniscient teller, and reports what goes on in the characters' most secret minds, at others he expresses ignorance of the kinds of fact that could easily have been known, invented or guessed, such as how old Criseyde is, or whether she had any children. (Boccaccio tells us she had none.) Chaucer thus deploys the possibilities of a traditional reporter of a known story who cannot change the main outline, yet he also invents and changes. His variable and dramatic presentation of the story has led modern critics to speak of Chaucer's narrative as if it were the dramatic monologue of a foolish and ignorant narrator, a dramatic character within the poem. This is to exaggerate and limit one aspect only of the Gothic variability of point-of-view. It also mistakenly attributes a modern cynicism to the variability of style, and particularly to the traditional sententiousness, hyperbole or word-play which Chaucer uses. When Chaucer writes sadly, 'Swich is this world . . .' (V, 1748–50), the sentiment is true, justified by the story, soberly expressed. It is surely mistaken to regard it, because it is not in essence original, as the comic expression of the silly old buffer telling the story. Indeed to do so is to attribute a real triviality to the narration which is quite unjustified. Similarly, when richly decorative reference is made to the stars of heaven shining as Criseyde goes to bed (V, 1014–22), or as Troilus sends for Pandarus (V, 1107–11), the effect is not to deride human actions in comparison with cosmic beauty and grandeur, but to see them in their glorious setting, with complex implications of their general significance, including the wholeness of human experience. To isolate and concentrate on a foolish narrator in this and other of Chaucer's poems is to fragment, by modernistic analysis, and to distort, the Gothic and archaic wholeness of Chaucer's vision.

Yet in asserting this we can retain the insight given by the concept of the narrator. There really is a cynicism, a dramatic detachment, frequent irony, a moral neutrality in Chaucer, which are genuinely modernistic, though they contribute to the Gothic tension of his work. Chaucer recognised these elements in himself and rejected them at the end of *The Canterbury Tales*.

'The Knight's Tale'

The Knight's Tale, composed about 1386, but now so-called because it was later included as told by the Knight in *The Canterbury Tales*, is another version of the mixed sorrow and joy of the world. In this case Chaucer much reduced his source, Boccaccio's inflated epic, *Teseida*, but he again placed the story in a Boethian light, and added colourful martial and mythological descriptions. He presents the glory and the horror, the success and the tragedy, of the hard brilliant world of chivalry, mingling passion with courtly realism, humour and touches of cynical wit. Two young nobles, Palamon and Arcite, cousins and friends, are captured in war and imprisoned for life by Theseus, Duke of Athens. This is again a story set in classical antiquity, though Chaucer envisages it in idealised and partly contemporary terms. He gives us a glimpse of chivalric splendour as Theseus returns home from war in triumph.

The redė statue of Mars, with spere and targe — shield
So shyneth in his whitė baner large
That alle the feeldės glyteren up and doun; — fields
And by his baner born is his penoun — pennant
Of gold ful riche, in which there was ybete — embroidered
The Mynotaur, which that he slough in Crete. — slew

Thus rit this duc, thus rit this conquerour, rides
And in his hoost of chivalrie the flour. flower
[*CT* I, 975–82]

Change Mars and Minotaur for the lion of England and the captured lilies of France (still on the royal banner) and you have Edward III, whom Theseus certainly calls to mind.

From their dark prison Palamon and Arcite see in the palace garden the beautiful Emily, sister of Hippolyta, the wife of Theseus, and immediately fall in love. Their love makes them hate each other. After a varied series of chances they get out of prison and each brings a following to fight in a tournament for Emily. Arcite wins, an accident injures him, and he marries Emily only on his deathbed. Eventually Palamon, who was first to see Emily, marries her. This action is 'controlled' by the gods, Mars, Venus, Jove and Saturn, historically appropriate to pagan times, and for Chaucer a mythological, poetic embodiment of what the fourteenth century considered the scientific truth of astrological influence. The temples of the gods, and the occasion of the tournament, are elaborately described. Though Chaucer is in general more interested in love, in the inner life and domestic detail, than in public themes or adventure and fighting, there is no irony in his presentation of the glamour of chivalry. Nor does he jib, either, at the pain and horror of wounds and death; the sorrow is as prominent as the glory. The poem is summed up at the end by two great speeches by Theseus and his father Egeus, full of proverbial traditional wisdom about the inevitability of suffering and death, making a virtue of necessity and accepting the wisdom of divine Providence. Once again, as at the end of *Troilus*, there is a fine insistence on a resolute and not too mournful acceptance of sorrow and death. Excessive self-indulgent mourning does neither the dead nor the living any good. This life is a 'foul prison', to leave it is no loss; meanwhile let us make the best of it – a truly Gothic vision of 'the mixed life' where joy and tragedy co-exist under God.

What may I conclude of this longė serye process
But after wo I rede us to be merye,
And thanken Juppiter of al his grace? [*CT* I, 3067–9]

'The Legend of Good Women'

Soon after writing this Chaucer returned to what had been, up to the composition of *Troilus*, his favourite topic, the loss and betrayal of love. About 1386 he wrote a series of poems in the same metre as *The Knight's Tale* in *The Legend of Good Women*, a secular parallel of saints' lives, based on Ovid, about women betrayed in love. They have pathos, some delicacy, some ill-judged flippancies. They are rather repetitious, and betray some impatience with the subject. We may assume that he had written himself out on the subject, having come to a middle-aged acceptance of the mixed nature of life. Furthermore the poem was a rare instance with him of a commissioned work, as we may deduce from the *Prologue*, which by contrast is one of his liveliest pieces. It tells how he has a passionate devotion to books and reading.

> Save, certeynly, whan that the month of May
> Is comen, and that I here the foulės synge, birds
> And that the flourės gynnen for to sprynge,
> Farewel my bok and my devocioun!
>
> [Prologue F, 36–9]

The lines in which he recounts how he gets up at dawn to adore the daisy in the meadows have a wonderful sense of early summer freshness, for all the half-humorous courtly preciosity of daisy worship, and the allusions to opposing courtly factions 'the Flower' and 'the Leaf'. At the end of the day the poet goes home to his house and has his servants make him up a bed in the garden, where he sleeps and dreams that he is visited by the God of Love and his queen Alceste. Chaucer evokes a mythological image of what could well have been a real meeting with king Richard and his beloved queen Anne. The God of Love berates the poet for writing about Criseyde, false in love; but the queen excuses him for his stupidity and lists all the works he has written so far, including 'Palamon and Arcite'. (Chaucer has taken the opportunity by this device to list his works. Though he always presents himself so deprecatingly he is more conscious than any other medieval poet of his , *œuvre*, and of his place, not an inferior one, in the European history of poetry, from Homer onwards.) The queen suggests that in recompense for his fault he shall write the lives of women 'true in loving'. It is this suggestion which is probably a gracefully indirect representation in mythological imagery of a commission by the young queen to write the poem which follows. The scene is charming and delightfully personal, even if the task was a little perfunctorily performed, and in fact never completed, stopping just short of the end of the ninth story when other references later show that nineteen or more were planned. He revised the *Prologue*, however, about 1396, improved its structure, and added to the list of his works. (The first version of the *Prologue* is now referred to as F and the second as G, after the manuscripts.)

'The Canterbury Tales'

Although the *Legend* was a partial failure it was also, as a collection of stories insufficiently varied, a dry run for the major work of English Gothic literature, *The Canterbury Tales*. By this time, about 1387, Chaucer had achieved assured command of the European literary tradition in Latin, French and Italian, of his own language and metre, and of the powers of literacy. The *Legend* showed that he was no longer compelled to write from some inner need or unhappiness. Far from drying up, he was now at the peak of his powers, able to survey and draw upon all the wide and varied styles and types of writing that he knew, to command them to his own purposes, with no need to express himself, but looking upon humanity with profound interest, sympathy and pity, with humour and ironic detachment, and above all as an unusually self-conscious entertainer, an artist with words. He proceeded to write a sort of 'anatomy' (to use Professor Northrop Frye's concept) or descriptive analysis, mostly in the form of stories, of European secular literary culture, and thus by implication of English secular culture itself. The range is truly astonishing, from shepherdess to duke, from bawdy comic popular stories to faithful married love, to tragedy, to puritanical religion; from everyday domestic realism to allusions to the whole body of scientific knowledge. *The Canterbury Tales* in its multiplicity is the most inclusive single work in English literature. It is like one of the great Gothic anthologies, the Auchinleck or Thornton manuscripts, not only copied but composed by one man; yet because of the nature of traditional literature and Chaucer's genius, through that one man a whole culture speaks.

The audience of The Canterbury Tales

The Canterbury Tales was immediately immensely popular, and over eighty fifteenth-century manuscripts survive, copies of copies, none from Chaucer's own hand. The work is a tribute to his own genius, to the multiplicity of English Gothic literary culture, and to the courtly and learned audience which he both served and dominated. In his audience were the Royal family, of formidable passions and considerable literary taste; high-born ladies; courtiers, many of them soldiers hardened in battle and practised in administration, some of them Lollards; lawyers such as 'philosophical Strode' and learned literary men such as the poet Gower (both addressed at the end of *Troilus*); country gentry who like himself were also justices of the peace and members of Parliament; rich and important city men such as Walworth, and Philpot, the merchant who fitted out a successful war-fleet at his own expense and thus shamed the nobility for their martial ineptitude. Both these men were Chaucer's colleagues at the Customs. Philpot at least was a personal friend, while both were knighted for their brave decisive actions that stemmed the Peasants' Revolt. Part also of the audience were humbler but learned men in the city such as Thomas Usk, an under-sheriff and author, eventually executed in the dangerous political changes of the day and Hoccleve, a younger poet, while Lydgate, monk of the abbey of Bury St Edmund's was Chaucer's most devoted reader and most famous literary disciple.

The basic concept

Chaucer probably began *The Canterbury Tales* about 1387. He had already written 'Palamon and Arcite', which marks his attainment of the fullest self-realisation, and some other shorter poetic narratives. In order to organise and add to them he conceived of people to tell them, developing the way that the English romances had been written in imitation of the oral style as it were for a minstrel, so as to make a consonance between tale and teller, rather as characters were invented to suit actions in traditional narratives, including his own *Troilus*. The stories are the equivalents of actions. Then going beyond the minstrel situation, he presumably asked himself, what would be a characteristic story-telling group of mixed characters? The answer was a group of pilgrims. A pilgrimage suited Chaucer's imagination well. It embodied a shifting point-of-view, from character to character. It was a mixture of people, and had become rather a holiday occupation, yet with still a religious base, so it was a mixture of the secular and the religious. Its transitoriness, the moving over margins and boundaries, suited an exploratory imagination which learnt from its failures and rarely repeated successes. In the interplay of characters between the tales Chaucer created realistic dramatic vignettes of explanation, criticism, confrontation and reconciliation that are purely secular, modern and entertaining. They seem to be completely original *rapportage*, yet are fully poetic in their richness of meaning.

The General Prologue

First, in *The General Prologue* Chaucer describes his group of pilgrims gathered in the Tabard Inn at Southwark, just south of London Bridge, a setting familiar to many of his readers and easily imaginable by us today. He places himself as a character among the rest. After the opening line, 'Whan that Aprill with his shourės soote', and the evocation of spring, when 'smalė fowelės maken melodye' and everyone longs to travel, each pilgrim is described in a list of characteristics, giving aspects of their appearance and history, which is an informal version of the old stiff formal descriptions of rhetoric. The Knight is described as a hard-bitten Christian frontiersman – 'He was a verray parfit gentil knyght'; his son the Squire 'as fressh as is the month of May'; the Prioress with her little dogs, 'And al was conscience and tendre herte'; the lusty Monk, 'A manly man, to been an abbot able'; the Friar, 'And over al, ther as profit sholde arise/Curteis he was and lowely of servyse'; the Merchant, 'Sownynge alwey th'encrees of his wynnyng' ('always boasting about how much money he made'); the Clerk of Oxenford, 'And gladly wolde he lerne and gladly teche'; the Lawyer, nowhere so busy a man, 'And yet he semed bisier than he was'; the Franklin, 'It snewed in his hous of mete and drynke'; the Cook, with a running sore on his leg, 'For blankmanger [white-meat stew], that made he with the beste'; the Shipman who when he took prisoners 'By water he sente hem hoom to every lond' (i.e. made them walk the plank); the Doctor, 'He was a verray parfit praktisour' (a parody of the praise of the Knight); The Wife of Bath, who had had five husbands, 'Withouten oother compaignye in youthe'; the poor Parson, 'But riche he was of hooly thoght and werk'; his brother the Plowman, 'That hadde ylad of dong ful many a fother' (load); the Miller, a stout carle, 'Wel koude he stelen corn and tollen [charge] thries'; the Reeve, from Baldeswell in Norfolk, 'a sclendre colerik man'; the pimply Summoner (a sort of lay ecclesiastical policeman), 'That hadde a fyr-reed cherubynnes face', accompanied by the deceitful effeminate Pardoner with long yellow hair and squeaky voice, 'I trowe he were a geldying or a mare'; a few others, and finally, the Host of the Tabard, Harry Bailly, well known personally to many of Chaucer's first audience (as probably were some of the others), a fat man with popping-out eyes, 'A fairer burgeys is ther noon in Chepe' (i.e. in Cheapside in London). All are described in this crisp, varied, pregnant, amused style, each line full of implications, with hints of praise or, more often, of satire, apparently casual, unillusioned yet tolerant, realistic yet describing each character as the best of his or her kind.

Bawdy comic tales

At the Host's suggestion the pilgrims agree to tell stories on the journey to Canterbury and back for a prize supper, and the Host accompanies them. The lot falls on the Knight to begin. He tells 'Palamon and Arcite' and would probably have won the prize. Following this noble tale the Miller, now drunk, insists on telling 'a legend', which turns out to be the wittiest, most polished, comic poem in English, like *The Knight's Tale* about two young men in love with the same girl, but inverted from courtly to vulgar; a bawdy international comic tale based on the crude expression 'kiss my arse'. The coarseness of the story is offset by the courtliness and wit of the style, which is very patronising about the villagers, their language and their way of life, if very appreciative of the heroine Alisoun's provincial allure. It is 'a churl's tale' says

Chaucer, unfairly to churls, since it is written from a courtier's point of view by a courtier for a gentry audience. The story is set near Oxford and one of the young men is a graduate student in lodgings; the Reeve ripostes with a similarly brilliant story about two Cambridge clerks and the mill at Trumpington. These tales are the nearest in English to the French thirteenth-century *fabliau*, and are similar to the bawdy tales in Boccaccio's slightly earlier prose work, the *Decameron*, though Chaucer enriches his versions with rhetorical artistry.

Other tales follow, in varied sequence. *Fabliau*-type tales are told by the Merchant, a brilliant piece about an old knight and a young wife; and the Shipman, about a merchant, his wife, and a lustful monk, in which the wife comes off best, and which was probably originally meant to be told by the Wife of Bath. Somewhat similar, in that they are international comic popular tales turned to particular account, are the tales told by Summoner and Friar as satires against each other. All are in plot structure even more fantastic than romance or saint's life, but they are placed in contemporary settings and told with domestic realism. The absurdity of comedy thrives because it transmutes the commonplace, and these remain the most amusing as well as some of the most poetic narratives in English.

Religious folk-tales

By contrast the Lawyer tells the romantic religious folk-tale of Constance, whose endurance of wicked mothers-in-law, and lonely sea voyages, sustained by her Christian faith, bears out her name. Here the refreshment comes from remoteness of time and place as well as extravagance of action, though even here Chaucer reveals his strong feeling for historical and scientific actuality, in details of settings and in astrological reference. Of a similar kind of secular saint's life is the Clerk's more personally appropriate tale of patient Griselda. This tale which enrages modern feminist sensibilities was invented out of traditional elements by Boccaccio, who placed it last in the *Decameron*. It became immensely popular throughout Europe. Chaucer knew it from a French translation, and raised the tension of the improbable events by telling them with the most vivid realism. The poem is consequently painful but also beautiful if accepted as praise of patience. Its strong chaste style with little colour is very suitable to the Clerk, though it is immediately followed by an envoi, or postscript, which mocks the whole concept – don't think to find wives as patient as that nowadays! – of which it is impossible to tell whether the speaker is the Clerk or the poet. Chaucer is quite ready here as elsewhere to break the fictional realistic 'frame' for the sake of a joke.

Confessional prologues

His interest in characterisation was as strong as it is modern. The Wife of Bath introduces another type of narration, with her long autobiographical *Prologue*, recounting in intimate detail the hard life she led her husbands. This is partly the development of the 'confessional' form, found in Jean de Meung's part of *Le Roman de la Rose*, arising out of the thirteenth-century post-Lateran interest in confession and the inner self, creating a new individualism. Jean de Meung uses the device of confession to satirise friars, putting an account of his own misdeeds in the friar's own mouth. Chaucer too uses it as satire, for he makes the Wife boast of attitudes and acts that a whole string of morbidly anti-feminist ecclesiastical writers from Jerome onwards had complained of. The Wife's *Prologue* in itself becomes something of a *fabliau*. At the same time, in picturing so vividly the Wife's gusto, and in attributing no real evil to her, we have a real sense of the circumstances of her life, and Chaucer leads us not only to laugh at but to laugh with the Wife. We feel we know her well in appearance, motive and feeling. There are two other similar 'confessional prologues', by the Pardoner and by the alchemical Canon's Yeoman, who joins the pilgrimage later. These have the same Gothic ambiguity. The Pardoner's, about dread of the Plague, and the Canon's Yeoman's, about the pains and perils of alchemical experiments, draw vivid pictures of contemporary low life, as well as expressing both traditional concepts and something of individual character.

Tales whose moral goes against the teller

The tales these pilgrims tell vary further. The Canon's Yeoman's is a uniquely poetic anecdote of technological trickery in London; the Pardoner's tale is a sermon *exemplum* or illustrative anecdote – the traditional story of three thieves who betray each other for gold. It is adorned by a glimpse of an unusually mysterious – for Chaucer – old man who himself seeks death but cannot die. The Wife's tale is another folktale of a more romantic kind, on the question of sovereignty in marriage, vaguely attached to Arthurian times but given a personal twist by Chaucer. In these tales about death, covetousness and sex, the message of the tale works against the teller, who nevertheless tries to turn it to his or her own advantage. The Pardoner in particular seems to be taken in by his own eloquence, and having previously confessed his shabby tricks in his Prologue, tries them out at the end of the tale in earnest, drawing on himself the Host's brutal contempt, and giving an enigmatic turn to the presentation of his own character which may not be consistent but is highly effective.

Romances

Secular romance is represented by a range of poems. The Squire's is least satisfactory and Chaucer failed to finish it. Its magic content hardly suited his sense of reality. It is followed by the supremely successful *Franklin's Tale* which Chaucer calls a Breton lay, though he seems to have adapted it from a story by Boccaccio. It embodies a series of characteristically Chaucerian paradoxes. A faithful if excessively tender-hearted wife foolishly promises to give herself to a would-be seducer if he ensures her husband's safe return by removing some rocks on the coast of Brittany. He does so, long after the husband's return. Thus faithful love engenders unfaithfulness. (It is another folklore theme, 'the rash promise'.) The rocks represent danger but also honour, integrity. Her husband in agony says she must keep her promise.

> Trouthe is the hyeste thyng that man may kepe. [*CT* V, 1479]

Such self-sacrificing nobility calls forth corresponding virtues and all ends with generosity and faithfulness. The moral is that we cannot avoid risks in life, and we should not manipulate the environment or we shall find disagreeable consequences.

Another aspect of romance is found in the story of *Sir Thopas* told by the pilgrim – Chaucer himself. It is a parody of the silliest and feeblest characteristics of the English rhyming-romances. At the literalistic level it is wonderfully bad, and it is a characteristic Chaucerian jest to attribute it to himself as one of the pilgrims. In fact it is brilliant, and extremely funny.

Classical and modern instances

There are yet more kinds of tale. Those attributed to the Doctor and the Manciple, brief sensational stories from classical antiquity, are not particularly appropriate to the tellers and are more reminiscent of Gower in the generally sober flatness of narrative which presents their moving or ironical events. *The Monk's Tale* is different again, a whole series of brief tragedies or 'falls', preceded by the Boethian definition of tragedy, and extending from that of Satan, through classical heroes to two modern instances. Such great men did not need to be good for their falls to attract sympathy. The story of Hugo of Pisa, from Dante, is the most pathetic because of the children's suffering, a thing which always moved Chaucer's pity.

Religious tales

The specifically religious tales are both attributed to the more naturally pious female sex. The tale attributed to the Second Nun, who is not otherwise characterised, is a version of that Life of St Cecilia which so moved Christina of Markyate (see above, p. 19). Chaucer tells it without irony but it is no more than a mechanical exercise in rhyme royal. He tells us in Prologue F to the *Legend* that he wrote it. It was probably written in the early 1380s, at the height of his powers, and its poetic weakness does not mean that it is less 'sincere' or less representative of Chaucer's real interests. The other religious poem is the superb *Prioress's Tale*, a religious folk-tale, of the little boy murdered by the Jews, told with deep pathos and especial sympathy for a 'mother's tender heart', and with a realism that modulates into a celestial idealism.

Elaborated beast-fable

Of all the poems, the one which represents the most inclusive triumph of Chaucer's art is *The Nun's Priests's Tale*, only partially appropriate to the teller. It is the traditional fable of the Cock and the Fox, frequently pictured in church imagery, and sometimes told by medieval preachers as an allegory of the Fall. Chaucer deliberately takes it literally ('My tale is of a fox', he says) but he elaborates its narration with all manner of rhetorical device and comedy, including a parody of rhetoric itself, and not omitting a passing touch of pathos for a murdered Anglo-Saxon royal child-saint, Kenelm.

Serious prose moral meditations

Not all the so-called tales are strictly narrative. Two are serious prose moral meditations, both by men. After the debacle of *Sir Thopas* Chaucer sets himself to tell the *Tale of Melibee* 'a little thing in prose', entirely serious and of some length. It is not insignificant that Chaucer allocates this non-fictional sober piece to himself, after the self-mockery of *Sir Thopas*. It is not ironical, and testifies to his serious concern with the appropriate conduct of life. The work is a translation of a French prose allegory about Meliboeus's wife Prudence and their daughter Sophie (Wisdom), itself derived from Latin, and a popular European work about the right and peaceful conduct of life, full of proverbial, entirely sensible, conventional wisdom. It gives the serious basis of Chaucer's secular thought and is a well-written piece of prose, though a close translation. The last 'tale' of all is also in prose and probably a translation from the French, though the immediate source is lost. It is a meditation by the Parson on the Seven Deadly Sins and on the need for Penitence, testifying without irony to deep religious conviction. No full understanding of Chaucer is possible without reading these two prose pieces. The *Parson's Tale* moves straight into a final prose passage called *Retracciouns*, in which Chaucer speaks in his own voice and quite seriously condemns all his secular works, from *The Book of the Duchess* to *Troilus* and those Canterbury Tales 'that sounen into [incline to] synne'. Secular literature, art for its own sake, is condemned. At the end of his life Chaucer condemns his own finest and most advanced literary works. Of all his paradoxes this is the greatest.

Archaic and modern in Chaucer

We may largely explain it by relating it to the general dichotomy already touched on between the 'archaic' and the 'modernistic' attitudes of mind, each of which was strong in Chaucer. (See D. S. Brewer, *Tradition and Innovation in Chaucer*, London: Macmillan, 1982, pp. 1–21.) By the 'archaic' is meant those attitudes of the mind, mainly received from tradition, which are unselfconscious, which conceive experience in personalised terms, which originate values, and which, though often mutually inconsistent, are so closely linked by custom and acceptance as to constitute a whole, and a whole view of life, which is felt to be sacred. It is the set of attitudes that is often, though inadequately, summed up as 'the primitive mentality'. In a sense every living person has in part a 'primitive mentality', shares in the archaic mind, because we cannot avoid having basic unprovable values, and we inevitably personalise issues and problems. Equally, no living person is fully archaic. Everyone has some scepticism, develops some critical self-awareness, analyses self and experience, and in consequence begins to fragment the wholeness of experience, to detect morally neutral aspects of life, become modernistic. In the history of Western culture the developments arising from the empirical scientific revolution of the seventeenth century, whose ultimate consequences have so drastically changed our outlook since the Middle Ages, have encouraged 'modernism'. Modern thought tends to be specialised; subjects are not connected with each other; the objective world is not personalised; quantitative methods prevail; much experience is morally neutral; utilitarian standards are invoked. No one is entirely modernistic in mind, any more than archaic, but certain personalities, and different stages of culture, have different proportions of the mixture. Amongst many important factors in the development of the modern mind are those associated with the development of towns, commerce and empirical science, already noted as an influence on Chaucer. We may here single out as a crucial aspect of modernism the development of practical, useful *arithmetic* (not the numerological, 'magical', thus archaic, patterns of number used by some medieval poets). Arithmetic is reflected in various ways in Chaucer's mercantile background and his accounting experience, but more particularly in his scientific interests, which space does not allow for more than a passing mention of here. They were however extensive and are often touched on indirectly in his work. Among his scientific interests the most outstanding is astronomy, which involved the extensive use of calculation. There are many astronomical references in Chaucer's work, often in relation to the measurement of time; the regularity of the measurement of time is a most important new development in the fourteenth century, both socially and economically and in science. Chaucer's interest in astronomy is plain in the substantial translation he made in 1391 called *A Treatise on the Astrolabe* to instruct his son Lewis. The astrolabe was a quite complicated instrument used for the measurement of the position of the stars. In it, moreover, Chaucer explicitly denies interest in *astrology*, the art of foretelling the future, which is best understood as the 'magical' 'archaic' aspect of astronomy (and whose currency in modern times illustrates our unappeasable hunger for the archaic). The church was always hostile to arithmetic, rightly seeing it as a solvent, or at least an evasion, of moral values. Chaucer's interest in calculation, quantitative, morally neutral, specialised, is the intellectual counterpart of his personal scepticism and detachment, his interest in art as entertainment divorced from moral considerations, which he refers to in his *Retraccioun*s as 'souning into synne'. It also went along with the naturalism of much of his writing, which corresponds to the Neoclassical attitudes to literature which match the empirical scientific revolution of the seventeenth century.

We thus see in Chaucer a remarkable case of a mind equally divided between the 'archaic' and the 'modern' at a period when the modern was developing fast but was still relatively weak in the culture as a whole. Moreover, the 'archaic' desire for connectedness was strong in Chaucer himself, as we may see, for example, in Troilus's song in praise of love (III, 1744 ff.) and in the structure of *The Franklin's Tale*, where honour and truth are linked to the acceptance of physical danger from the rocks in the sea. We find other examples of the divided mind among the tensions of the Gothic period, but in no poet was the modern so developed as in Chaucer, nor the tension, we may guess, so severe. It is remarkable that for so much of his life Chaucer managed to hold together such a variety of conflicting interests apparently without strain, though the accusation of rape which was made against him in 1380 may reveal one failure of control. We are conscious of hidden depths even in his comic poetry. But at the end of his life, tired with age, it is clear that Chaucer could no longer sustain the struggle for control and he let go, perhaps with relief, perhaps with regret, all those secular poems which in various aspects represent the modernistic spirit. Looking back, from our different world, we may be more conscious than he could be of how much of wholeness was in his literary achievement; how narrow, in a way, was the archaic religious totality and unity to which he eventually returned. But it was unified and sacred, as the modern can never be, and Chaucer's spiritual insight, historically conditioned as we all must be, was probably just.

But simpler minds recognised him as the greatest English poet without such subtleties, and he was honoured by burial in Westminster Abbey in October 1400. His sweetness of temper had brought him many friends; his poetic genius assured him of direct influence for the next two centuries. In the twentieth century his genius and the interest of his mind seem greater than ever.

7 Chaucer's Friends and Followers in England and Scotland

Gower, Clanvowe, Scogan

CHAUCER's friend and contemporary John Gower was too old to be significantly influenced by him: later contemporaries and followers make his eloquence and richness of style a convention whose literary value it is nowadays easy to neglect because they overdid it, but they 'naturalised', as well as distorted through one-sided emphasis, Chaucer's work.

John Gower was a gentleman who owned land in Kent and Suffolk, had had some legal training, and was on the fringes of the court. He illustrates the multilingual culture of educated English society in the fourteenth century, though he was rather old-fashioned, as learned men may be. He first wrote a poem in French, *Mirour de l'Omme* ('Mirror of Man') of which nearly 30,000 lines survive in only one manuscript. In the latter part of his life he was engaged on major Latin works, *Vox Clamantis* ('the Voice of One Crying', *cf.* Isaiah xl. 3) and the *Cronica Tripertita* ('Three-part Chronicle'), expressing apocalyptic concern and horror at the state of England in an often powerful rhetorical style. He wrote other shorter poems in French, Latin and English on the personal theme of love, and on public concerns, especially on the need for peace. Ultimately, unwearied, though troubled by illness, he wrote *Confessio Amantis* ('the Lover's Confession') in English, in octosyllabic couplets of great regularity, without monotony, comprising a Prologue and eight books of uneven length amounting to 33,444 lines, begun about 1386. Because unrelieved reading of wisdom dulls a man's wit, says Gower in his Prologue, he will write a book 'Somwhat of lust [pleasure], somewhat of lore'. Since few men write in English (he is thinking of courtiers but emulating Chaucer), he intends to write a book 'for King Richard's sake' because once, on the Thames:

As I be botė cam rowende   rowing
So as fortune hir tymė sette
My liegė lord par chaunce I mette;
And so befel, as I cam nyh,
Out of my bot, whan he me syh   saw
He bad me come in to his barge . . .
And bad me doo my besynesse
Some newė thing I scholdė boke   write in a book
That he himself it mihtė loke.
40* . . . 52*
[G. C. Macaulay (ed.), *Works* (EETS, 1900)ES 81]

However, reflecting the general disgust with Richard in the last decade of his reign, to 1399, when he was deposed and murdered, Gower later re-dedicated his poem to the usurper Henry Bolingbroke, who became Henry IV, with whom he already had some literary connection, as had Chaucer.

Gower puts himself into his own poem, as did all the great fourteenth-century poets, and represents himself as an unsuccessful but hopeful lover, confessing to Genius (a name referring to fertility), who is priest of the goddess Venus. In confessing the poet, Genius relates many stories to illustrate various virtues and vices. The stories come mostly from classical antiquity, though there are also some traditional tales, as, for example, the story of Florent (I, 1407–1861), an analogue of *The Wife of Bath's Tale*, illustrating the virtue of obedience in love, and of Constance (II, 587–1612), drawn, like Chaucer's *Lawyer's Tale*, from the Anglo-Norman chronicler Trivet. Book VII is an encyclopaedic summary of knowledge, while VIII has only the story of Apollonius of Tyre, an archetypal 'family drama' popular until Shakespeare's time, and the basis of *Pericles*. The whole work is thus another Gothic miscellany and 'anatomy' with a simpler, more rigid, less naturalistic structure than *The Canterbury Tales*. There is some inconsistency in the presentation of Genius, the priest of Venus, who sometimes condemns sexual love, and strongly recommends chastity, but to insist on this mistakes the nature of the analysis. The structure of stories is the 'action', the character of Genius the product, and the variety of Gothic inclusiveness determines his attitudes in individual cases within a general complex morality.

Gower is always concerned with moral themes and has not Chaucer's empirical interest in character, but he has a wry style, a gentle sympathy especially for women, and above all a steady narrative flow in telling 133 stories. He ranges unhurriedly, untiringly, clear-sightedly, over the gamut of sin and virtue, not baulking at such stories of incest within 'the family drama' as those of Canacee in Book III, and Apollonius in Book VIII, which Chaucer quite seriously condemns in the Prologue to *The Man of Law's Tale*. He can evoke clear pictures, as of the ladies riding in the wood – a scene reminiscent in tone and style though it is more elaborate, of *Sir Orfeo*:

On faire amblendė hors thei sete	ambling
That were al whytė, fatte and grete,	
And everichon thei ride on side.	everyone; side-saddle
The sadles were of such a pride	
With perle and gold so wel begon	
So richė syh sche nevere non;	saw she
In kertlės and in copės riche	
Thei werėn clothėd, allė liche,	
Departed evene of whyt and blew;	
With allė lustės that sche knew	delights
Thei were enbrouded overal.	
Here bodies weren long and smal;	Their; slender
The beautė faye upon her face	their faces
Non erthly thing it may desface.	

[Macaulay, *op. cit.* IV, 1309–22]

The style is precise, avoiding Chaucer's extremes of literalism and hyperbole, of pathos and outrageous comedy, in a word, his extravagance. Gower does not hold up the narrative flow for rich rhetorical description like Chaucer, nor does his style reveal any influence from the English rhyming romances apart from the general resemblance to *Sir Orfeo*.

At the end of the *Confessio Amantis* the lover-poet concludes that he is too old to love, and the poem draws gracefully to its conclusion. There is even a rare pleasing touch of extravagance as he writes a letter to Venus using his tears for ink, pleading to be released from the pains of love. He concludes by praying for the state of England (for the king in the earlier version), with that concern for the public good, for peace and unity in the land, which is another of his attractive traits, and he finally casts his eye on heaven so that:

Wher resteth love and allė pes
Oure joiė mai ben endėles.
[Macaulay, *op. cit.* VIII, 3171–2]

A closer friend, perhaps, of Chaucer's, though a lesser poet, was the Lollard knight Sir John Clanvowe, who wrote, beside a devotional tract in English, *The Two Ways*, a charmingly Chaucerian debate poem, *The Boke of Cupide* (*c.* 1390). Another was Henry Scogan, tutor to Henry IV's sons, for whom he wrote *A Moral Balade.*

Lydgate

These men shared Chaucer's courtly milieu, but Chaucer's most devoted reader and imitator was Lydgate 'the monk of Bury' (*c.* 1370–1449), who in sheer bulk of writing carried Chaucer's achievement even further. His output is simply vast, literacy uncontrolled, a late-medieval verbal flux like that of Skelton or Rabelais, without their coarse literalism, their sense of the body's grossness, which might ballast the hot-air balloon. Lydgate is the sort of writer who gives rhetoric a bad name. He wrote a *Troy-book* of over 30,000 lines (1412–20) thus going far beyond *Troilus. The Siege of Thebes* of nearly 5,000 lines, (1420–2) which was reprinted throughout the sixteenth century with Chaucer's work, has a Prologue attaching it to *The Canterbury Tales. The Fall of Princes* of over 36,000 lines (1430–40), hugely expands the brief tragedies of *The Monk's Tale. The Complaint of the Black Knight* springs from *The Book of the Duchess*, and so forth. He also translated the moral allegory *The Pilgrimage of The Life of Man* from a French poem by Guillaume de Deguileville, though allegory is not a Chaucerian mode, and wrote several 'Mummings' or masques, and many other religious and secular pieces. All were produced for patrons. Lydgate's monastic base, the great monastery at Bury St Edmunds, was close to the centre of national life, and he knew how to please both great nobles and the citizens of London. For a couple of centuries he was grouped as equal with Chaucer and Gower. There is indeed a generosity, a fullness and an attractive modesty in Lydgate whiich can be glimpsed in his frequent praise of Chaucer:

That madė firstė to distille and rayne
The golde dewe dropes of speche and eloquence
Into our tungė, thurgh his excellence

And fonde the flourės first of Retoryke
Our rude speche, only to enlumyne
That in our tungė was never noon hym like.
[J. Lauritis, R. Klinefelter and V. Gallagher (eds), *The Life of Our Lady*, (Pittsburgh: Dusquesne Studies, 1961, 1632–7)]

In his 'Chapitle of the governance of Poetis' (*Fall of Princes* III, 3837 ff), he gives an excellent description of the Gothic poet, a noble Rhetor, one who flourishes in wisdom and science (i.e. learning), not socially or morally superior, but deserving of the support of princes. He can touch deep notes of conventional wisdom in the *Troy-book*, which Professor Pearsall sees as the cornerstone of his achievement, and pours out the riches of his vocabulary most effectively in the commonplaces of 'A Balade in Commendation of Our Lady':

Paradys of pleasance, gladsom to all good
Benygne braunchelet of the pigment-tre
Vinarye envermeilyd, refrescher of oure food, wine-cellar; vermilioned
Lycour ayens langour that pallid may not be,
Blisful bawm-blossum, bydying in bounte
Thi mantel of mercy on our myschef spred,
Or woo awake us, wrappe us undyr thi weed. Before woe; cloak
[J. Norton-Smith (ed.), *Poems*, (Oxford: Clarendon Press, 1966), p. 26, ll. 43–9]

Amplification by repetition was Lydgate's chief literary device, though he deploys many rhetorical patterns and a little wordplay. He gives us an extreme example of rich late-Gothic surface decoration, of which the inner structure would normally be abstract, intellectual, non-mimetic, but which in Lydgate's case often fails because it is too weak to sustain the surface. In other words, he is short on meaning. The metre similarly lacks an inner structure, a norm, and in consequence continually stumbles. His vocabulary is often rich and 'aureate', but without compensatory literal force.

Hoccleve and others

Thomas Hoccleve (*c.* 1370 – *c.* 1430), another contemporary, is in some ways the opposite of Lydgate. His chief merit lies in the flavour of authentic realism he gives, especially in the autobiographical passages. These occur in *La Male Regle de T. Hoccleve* ('the bad conduct of T. Hoccleve') written about 1405, the *Regement of Princes* ('Rule of Princes') (1412), *Thomas Hoccleve's Complaint* (1422) and the *Dialogue with a Friend* (1422). How true the account is cannot be told, but an interesting picture of a clerk's life emerges, with the drudgery of writing in the office, the self-pitying youthful self-indulgence in food and drink, chasing girls without the nerve to sleep with them, taking a boat on the Thames, his poverty, a nervous breakdown, a bullying wife and chafing marriage. He portrays himself modestly and sympathetically as a weak, foolish, nervous man, but it is paradoxically a strong portrait. His other poems – addresses to the Virgin, balades to King Henry V and great men at court, *A Letter to Cupid*, translated from the French, etc. – are less ornate and repetitious than Lydgate's, often with a conversational flavour and a well-managed metre. In *The Regement of Princes* he praises Chaucer's eloquence as eloquently as he can, contributing to the traditional view of Chaucer, and accompanies his praise with a portrait, posthumous but convincing, in British Library Harley MS 4866, f. 34:

> O maister deere and fadir reverent
> Mi maister Chaucer, flour of eloquence,
> Mirour of fructuous entendement,   fruitful meaning
> O universal fadir in science,
> Allas that thou thyn excellent prudence
> In thi bed mortel mightist naght byqwethe.
> [*Cf. Works*, Part III, F. J. Furnivall (ed.), (EETS, 1897) ES 72]

A minor poet, but a man of feeling, Hoccleve's significance lies mostly in his modern self-awareness, and the consequent lively evocation of the sense of a real 'man talking to men', a fresh aspect of early fifteenth-century literary life.

The Chaucerian line slowly diffuses itself throughout the fifteenth century until it merges with the other native streams of lyric, rhyming romances and the drama. It can be summed up in the miscellany of pieces that were attached, though not attributed, to Chaucer's name in the first sixteenth-century printed edition of Chaucer's work edited by Francis Thynne in 1532. This included Clanvowe's *Boke of Cupide*, Scogan's *Balade*, Gower's *The Praise of Peace*. Among them are two of the best fifteenth-century English Chaucerian poems, *The Flower and the Leaf* and *The Assembly of Ladies*, each purporting to be written by a lady – an unconscious tribute to Chaucer's feminism. They have charming conventional descriptions of spring and gardens. *The Flower and the Leaf* is the better of these two courtly allegories. Until it was shown, in the late nineteenth century, not to be by Chaucer, it was a favourite with poets and had been translated by Wordsworth.

Scottish Chaucerians

Far and away the best of these attached poems is *The Testament of Cresseid*, which is printed immediately following *Troilus*, and was indeed designed as a pendant. It is by the Scottish poet, Robert Henryson, to be mentioned later. English, spelt and pronounced Inglis, was the natural language of those Scots who lived south of the Highland Line and were not Gaelic-speaking Celts. This part of Scotland was part of the broader 'English' tradition, though more immediately centred on Edinburgh and having its own characteristic variations. It was not in any way Celtic, and the Highlanders were a feared and hated set of primitive tribes speaking a foreign tongue.

The Scottish tradition of English begins with John Barbour's racy romance-chronicle, *The Bruce* (1375), written in octosyllabic couplets to celebrate the acts of Scotland's hero, and keep them in memory by writing:

> To put in writ a soothfast story
> That it last aye furth in memorye [I, 14–15]

Its merit is its plain patriotic and human vigour:

> A! Fredome is a noble thing! [I, 225]

Probably the first Scottish poet to write in a more rhetorically ornate and self-conscious tradition was the author of *The Kingis Quair* (The King's Book), probably the Scottish James I (1394–1437), though since he spent many years as a prisoner in England he became so anglicised that the poem could be taken as English rather than Scottish. It only survives in two manuscripts written in Scottish dialect. The poem is a dream-vision about love, with medievalised classical mythology and a Boethian base. Thoughtful, tender and resolute, it is Chaucerian in the poet's self-presentation and the range of style from astrological adornment to plain directness.

Henryson

The best of any poets writing in English in the fifteenth century are two Scots, Robert Henryson (*c.* 1425 – *c.* 1500) and William Dunbar (*c.* 1460 – *c.* 1530), conventionally described as 'Scottish Chaucerians'. Certainly they both praised Chaucer, and regarded him as the father of English poetry. He had improved the language, and they had the advantage of his (and Lydgate's) additions to available styles and types of writing, but they have their own characteristics different from Chaucer and each other. Their poetry survives in a number of scattered manuscripts and prints, mostly of the sixteenth century, and no internal chronology of the poems of either has been established.

Henryson was a schoolmaster in Dunfermline, about whom little else is known. *The Testament of Cresseid* obviously derives from Troilus and is a brief (615 lines) insertion into the action of *Troilus V*, in which the poet, meditative and engaged, describes the character and subsequent life and death of Cresseid. He first presents himself as an elderly man on a cold winter's night reading by the fire in his oratory.

> I mend the fyre and beikit me about — made up; warmed
> Than tuik ane drink, my spreitis to comfort, — spirits
> And armit me weill fra the cauld thairout.
> To cut the winter nicht and mak it schort
> I tuik ane quair, and left all uther sport, — book
> Writtin be worthie Chaucer glorious
> Of fair Creisseid and worthie Troylus
> [*The Testament of Cresseid*, (D. Fox (ed.), *Poems of Robert Henryson* (Oxford: Clarendon Press,1981), *Cf.* p. 112, ll. 36–42]

Cresseid he sees as a lascivious but loving woman ('Sa gigotlike [wanton] takand [taking] thy foull plesance,/I have pietie thow suld fall sic mischance' 83–4), whom he cannot but pity – a characteristically Chaucerian and humane attitude, though Henryson's moral conviction is stern. She returns to her loving father, who continues to cherish her after Diomede has rapidly tired of her, and in a prayer she reproaches Venus and Cupid:

> Ye causit me alwayis understand and trow — believe
> The seid of lufe was sawin in my face. — seed; sown
> [136–7]

They strike her with leprosy (which was sometimes then associated with sexual depravity). Henryson takes this, under the veil of mythology, as both a divine punishment and an example of the fickleness of Fortune. Cresseid joins the leprous beggars, and on one occasion Troilus passes by. She is so disfigured outwardly that he does not recognise her, but a memory of 'fair Cresseid', 'his own darling', arises, 'a spark of love' is kindled and out of 'knightly pity' he gives a purse of gold. Cresseid does not even recognise him. It is a piercing little scene, characteristic of a moving, morally austere poem.

Henryson's major work is *The Morall Fabillis of Esope the Phrygian*, a poetic version of one of the commonest of schoolbooks, with a very un-Chaucerian Prolog. In this Henryson makes an interesting statement of the medieval theory of allegory of a kind in which Chaucer has no interest at all:

> Thocht feinyeit fabils of ald poetre — Though; feigned
> Be not al grunded upon truth, yit than
> Thair polite termes of sweit rhetore — polished
> Richt plesand ar unto the eir of man,
> And als the cause quhy that thay first began — why
> Wes to repreif thee of thi misleving*
> O man, be figure of ane uther thing
>
> **either* false belief *or* evil conduct *or both*
> [*Cf.* D. Fox, *op. cit.* p. 3, ll. 1–7]

Henryson activates the ancient paradoxical commonplaces about the goodness of poetry: as by labour the earth produces flowers and corn wholesome and good for man's sustenance,

> Sa springis thair ane morall sweit sentence — meaning
> Oute of the subtell dyte of poetry, — style
> [12–13]

so the sweet kernel comes from the hard nut. But the hard nut is also sport, and too much study dulls the spirit. Thus does the poet reconcile, with traditional inconsistency, the pleasure and utility of poetry, what Chaucer calls mirth and doctrine. Henryson says he is translating into the mother tongue from Latin by request of a lord, into 'homely language', for he never understood rhetoric – the modest, slightly self-mocking stance of the Gothic poet, subjecting himself to the requirements and the judgement of the audience.

The fables are beautifully told, not over-ornate with rhetoric, but with a full steady pressure of economic and beautiful language, comprising thirteen stories, each with a moral, in 2,975 lines. They articulate the great commonplaces of human experience:

> Yit efter joy oftymės cummis cair
> And troubill efter grit prosperitie, [290–1]

But this sententiousness is enlivened because it arises from contemplation of humanised animals, as here of the town mouse and the country mouse. Chaucer's favourite astrological references to time are invoked on the playful supposition that they are understood naturally by the fox who says 'My destenie and eik my weird I watt [know]' (l. 649). There is a continual play of light humour. Yet the serious underlying morality is not jibbed at, trivialised, undercut, or treated with irony, and though warmly felt, it is not shrilly expressed. The high prudence of omnipotent God (ll. 1622–3) lies behind all, and as in this story of the preaching of the swallow, animates the firmament, all creatures, 'The somer with his jolie mantill grene' (l. 1678), frosty winter, and the ploughmen and seed-sowers at work:

> It wes grit joy to him that luifit corne
> To se thame laubour baith at evin and morne. [1725–6]

There is a satisfying well-grounded wholeness and beauty in both vision and style; full of art, without artfulness. The poem *Orpheus and Eurydice* is to be compared with *Sir Orfeo*, indicating what a difference Chaucer had made to the tradition, in showing how to elaborate diction, incorporate learning, comment sententiously, explore inner feeling and describe outer landscape. Henryson again concludes with a *moralitas*, referring to Boethius, which analyses the story in allegorical terms. The *moralitas* reveals the intellectual abstract force which underlies Henryson's apparently simple narratives, and gives further glimpses of his power. Recent research by Professor J. McQueen suggests a numerological structure in some of his poems (see also below, p. 169). Henryson also wrote some fine religious lyrics; the delightful short pastoral *Robene and Makyne*; the mixture of ballad and romance, *The Bludy Serk* (shirt), which also moralised; and, true Gothic poet that he was, *Sum Practyses of Medecyne*, of great verbal ingenuity, with some rough humour at the expense of doctors, and a touch of coarseness appropriate to the subject.

Dunbar

The coarseness and the astonishing verbal dexterity are even more evident in William Dunbar, whose artistic versatility mirrors the brief brilliance of courtly culture in the Scotland of James IV, which perished with him at Flodden Field (1513). Dunbar may have had noble connections and taken his master's degree at St Andrew's University in 1489. He had some courtly position and had a court pension till 1513, but he took priest's orders in 1504 and after Flodden he may have acquired the benefice sought in some of his poems, for records of him then cease.

Dunbar wrote in every conceivable short form and is the very apotheosis of the Gothic poet with his wide range in style as in subject matter, from enamel to excrement. The artistry of his poems is complete, so that the reader always feels comfortably certain that no stylistic, metrical or structural lapse will drop into bathos; and yet, even because of the superb control, the reader is conscious either of a lack of heart, or a heart effectively concealed. Dunbar is never slow to push himself forward, developing the traditional style with typical verve:

> Sanct Salvatour! send silver sorrow,
> [J. Kinsley (ed.), *The Poems of William Dunbar* (Oxford: Clarendon Press, 1979), p. 69]

In this address modelled on Chaucer's only begging poem,

the witty 'Purse', he boldly adjures the king. Another poem presumably to the king is about his headache and general dullness – one feels he must have had many a hangover. Yet there is no pathos or self-pity. 'How Dumbar wes desyrd to be ane Freir' begins with a dream dialogue with St Francis, then merges into a claim that the poet has travelled in England and France as a friar and always 'tricked people'. St Francis then turns into a fiend who vanishes with stink and fiery smoke, but the poem is comic satire, hovering on the verge of dream-vision and confession, the poet's own self much more of a self-conscious mask than the equivalent appearances in Dante, Chaucer, Langland, Gower, *Pearl*, Lydgate, etc., where half the charm is the ambiguous relation to the real person of the poet. Dunbar is perhaps most himself in the uproarious and coarse 'Flyting [abuse] of Dunbar and Kennedie'. Kennedy was a contemporary poet and they jointly contributed strings of abuse of each other which reveal a remarkable and practised facility. Vulgar abuse was probably part of a medieval jester's and minstrel's courtly repertoire, here brought to an elaborate if not fine art. More sympathetic is the famous poem of twenty-five stanzas, usually known as 'Lament of the Makaris' ('poets'), beginning:

> I that in heill wes and gladnes — *health*
> Am trublit now with gret seikness,
> And feblit with infermite: — *enfeebled*
> *Timor mortis conturbat me.*

The refrain ('the fear of death disturbs me') comes from the service for the dead and had been similarly used by Lydgate. The roll of poets is in itself moving, including 'the noble Chaucer', Henryson and many Scottish poets now unknown.

Dunbar knows something of love, though nothing of tenderness. 'In secreit place this hyndir nicht' has a lovely first line but goes on to give a comically gross rendering of a dirty townsman's love-plea to his girl, a witty extension and extract from *The Miller's Tale*. The most famous poem of this kind is his 'Tretis of the tua mariit Wemen and the Wedo', a dazzling virtuoso display of mingled coarseness and courtliness in alliterative verse. The poet in a 'goodly green garth' hides in a ditch to overhear three gay ladies with long golden hair, delicate soft faces and beautiful clothes, talk of love. But they speak in blunter terms than the Wife of Bath, whose influence here is strong, in an exhilaratingly rich Scottish vocabulary, and the poet finishes with a kind of *demande d'amour* – you most honourable auditors, which of these three wanton wives would you like to have as your own? Although Chaucer's sympathetic warmth is lacking and we do not respond as to living people, there is no tragic satire. It is shrewd, entertaining, popular, derisive comedy, and the vigour and variety of the vocabulary itself is an entertainment. Were he not so fully in control one might say that Dunbar is drunk with words.

The same skill and delight is shown at the opposite end of the scale, as if subject matter were immaterial to Dunbar. He writes the most elaborate forms of those 'fresch anamalit termes celical' ('fresh enamelled heavenly terms') for which he praises the 'reverend Chaucere, rois of rethoris all', in 'The Goldyn Targe'. In this poem he describes how at dawn, when 'Up sprang the goldyn candill matutyne' and pearly drops shook in silver showers and birds sang on the tender crops, he dreamt how he saw a ship arrive on a river in a bright landscape from which came a hundred ladies, as fresh as flowers, in kirtills green, 'With papis quhite [white] and mydlis small as wandis'. He sees Nature and Venus and many another mythological figure and personification. The poet himself is wounded by Beauty, but the action is slight. He awakes, and praises Chaucer. The poem is the decorative aspect of *The Parliament of Fowls* raised to the nth degree, reminiscent of some bright late-fifteenth-century tapestry of the Garden of Love. A somewhat similar beautiful piece is 'The Thrissill and the Rois' ('The Thrush and the Rose').

Almost every separate poem of Dunbar's, short as they mostly are, from burlesques to moralisings, from meditations to Marian lyrics, is another deft variant on a recognisably traditional topic, which with untiring zest and artistry Dunbar extends without breaking the received form. What he writes, whether scatological abuse or aureate devotion, is in a sense the purest poetry, its perfection unmarred by verbal weakness, the culmination not only of the verbal traditions represented by Chaucer, but also of others, such as the alliterative tradition, yet to be discussed. He is the nearest the English tradition comes to the contemporary French poet

Villon, though he does not strike the Frenchman's uniquely personal plaintive note.

The tradition, however, was not concluded. Gavin Douglas in the early sixteenth century, Sir David Lindsay a little later, and many others in succeeding centuries show the vitality of 'Inglis' in Scotland. That, like the equally continuous tradition in England, with Skelton and Hawes in the early sixteenth century, is matter for another volume. We now return to the fourteenth century in England, to pick up the thread of the central English tradition, the alliterative, with its roots in Old English.

8

Alliterative Poetry

'Wynnere and Wastoure'

CHAUCER makes his Parson repudiate all 'fables and swich wrecchednesse'. He would be glad, says the Parson, to give lawful pleasure to the company:

> But trusteth wel, I am a Southren man,
> I kan nat geeste 'rum, ram, ruf' by lettre,
> Ne, God woot, rym holde I but litel bettre. [*CT* X, 42–4]

So he will tell a pleasant tale in prose. Thus he notes the three techniques of writing in the fourteenth century – rhyme, alliterative verse and prose. The Parson allows the possibility of some virtuous matter in alliterative verse, but he singles out the remarkable characteristic of its distinctness as a regional form. South seems commonly to be opposed to both north and west. In the second half of the fourteenth century appear nearly thirty substantial poems whose origin lies mainly in the north and the West Midlands. They are written in the alliterative long line, which consists of four main stresses, the first three of which usually begin with the same letter, and is sometimes called head-rhyme. As in Old English and with Layamon, there is no regular number of unstressed syllables between the stresses. Chaucer's, 'rum, ram, ruf' is an unkind distortion but picks out the main element.

The West Midlands include Worcestershire and Herefordshire, home of Layamon and of the alliterative prose of the Katherine Group of homilies, of other fragments of alliterative verse and of Harley 2253, which has much alliteration. In this area seems to have been preserved some continuity of knowledge of written traditional alliterative verse from Old English times, while the four-stress line is quite natural to English, and its music persists through even Shakespeare's and Milton's five-stress blank verse into the nineteenth and twentieth centuries. The rather self-conscious Englishness of the alliterative poems, together with their use of French and Latin sources, suggests a reaching out to new material by an established community expanding its interests, yet re-evoking, while developing, traditional modes, creating for itself anew the old ideal of a community hearing its traditional stories in native verse. Probably the earliest poem that survives of the new movement is *Wynnere and Wastoure*, so good that it must have had predecessors now lost. It was composed about 1350 but is only recorded in one of the fifteenth-century manuscripts compiled by the Yorkshire gentleman Robert Thornton, now British Library Additional 31042. The poet immediately sounds several notes that will be characteristic:

> Sythen that Bretayne was biggede and Bruyttus it aughte,
> Thurgh the takynge of Troye with tresone with-inn,
> There hathe selcouthes bene sene in seere kynges tymes,
> Bot never so many as nowe by the ninthe dele.
> [*Cf.* I. Gollancz (ed.), *Winner and Waster* (Oxford: Clarendon Press, 1930; repr. Cambridge: D. S. Brewer, 1974) ll. 1–4]

(Since Britain was made (*literally*, built) and Brutus owned it, through the capture of Troy by treason inside, there have been wonders seen in many kings' times, but never as many as now by the ninth part.)

Britain, whose rulers are descended from those of Troy, is a remarkable land, though the poet goes on to complain that the modern wonders are all of cleverness and deceit, cunning words, unfriendliness, cowardice and regional prejudice:

> Dare never no westren wy, while this werlde lasteth
> Send his sone southewarde to see ne to here
> That he ne schall holden byhinde when he hore for eld es. [8–10]

(No western man, while this world lasts, dare send his son southward to see nor to hear, that he should not rather [?] keep back when he is white-haired for age. [Obscure: perhaps meaning that the man being old, would regret sending his son, who would be corrupted in the south – a familiar English notion.])

Everything is bad, he continues, nature is disturbed, young men of low birth marry ladies and Doomsday must be near. (This is stock material and appears in another Thornton poem, *Tomas of Ersseldoune*, containing various prophecies.) Moreover, in the past there were lords in the land who loved to hear those 'makers of mirths' who could find solid material with wise words, of a kind that was never made or read in any romance that ever was heard.

Bot now a childe appon chere, withowtten chynwedys,
That never wroghte thurgh witt three wordes togedire,
Fro he can jangle als a jaye and japes telle
He schall be levede and lovede and lett of a while
Wel more than the man that made hymselven. [24–8]

(But now a child in appearance, with a bare chin [*literally*, without chin-clothing] who never put three words together by his own intelligence, from the time that he can chatter like a jay and tell jokes shall be believed and loved and made much of far more than the man who himself has composed.)

This is a complaint *against* minstrels, mere frivolous entertainers, repeaters of other men's words, of a kind Langland was to make, on behalf of poets. It is a complaint also against modern audiences. By implication is evoked the figure of the poet, old and sage, with serious things to say that are nevertheless heartening. The author says that all literature should be didactic, but is not; he is reacting in theory against the Gothic poem which, as often with Chaucer, mixes the serious and the frivolous, though he himself in practice makes a bid (as 'maker of mirth') for entertainment value. Indeed in the course of his poem he blends the serious with the comic in satire, and mixes dream-vision, allegory and unresolved debate, in a typical Gothic mixture, to express his vigorous concern for the contemporary English economic and social situation, which as usual, is bad.

The poet tells how he went in the west through a spring landscape, which is not, however, completely restful:

Bi a bonke of a bourne, bryghte was the sone
Undir a worthiliche wodde, by a wale medewe;
Fele floures gan folde ther my fote steppede.
I layde myn hede one ane hill, ane hawthorne besyde.
The throstills full throly they threped togedire. [33–7]

(Along the bank of a stream – the sun was bright – beside a fine wood and a choice meadow. Many flowers were entwined where my foot trod. I laid my head on a mound, by a hawthorn. The thrushes argued sharply against each other.)

Wild geese gnaw the bark of trees, the jay chatters and the noise of water in the rough streams is so great that it is almost night before the poet can fall asleep. There may be a touch of humour in the exasperation, but this western landscape is harsher than the soft charms of the French and Latin originals of the conventional sunny May-morning opening of a dream-vision poem. When the poet at last sleeps he has a vision of a lovely green country shut in by a long hill, and sees in two woods two opposing armies. On a cliff is a beautiful red-striped 'cabin', presumably one of the elaborate tents known as 'pavilions', with the Garter motto in English on it. A formidably attired knight appears by the pavilion, and we realise he must be Edward, Prince of Wales, the Black Prince. A king then appears, in his magnificence, and berry-brown his beard (as we learn later, he is about forty years old). In one army are warriors from all over Europe, and also the Pope, the orders of friars, and lawyers and merchants, mostly described through satirical descriptions of the invented heraldry of their banners. The other side are briefly described as serious soldiers, 'bold squires of blood'. Each side sends a representative to argue their case to the king, Winner to represent the mixed army, Waster to represent the soldiers.

The kynge waytted one wyde, and the wyne askes,
Beryns broghte it anone in bolles of silvere.
Me thoghte I sowpped so sadly it sowede bothe myn eghne.
And he that wilnes of this werke to wete any forthire
Full freschely and faste, for here a fitt endes. [213–17]

(The king looked widely around, and called for wine. Men brought it immediately in silver bowls. It seemed to me that I drank so much it bleared both my eyes. Let him who wishes to know further about this business fill up briskly and quick, for a section ends here.)

The poet breaks the frame here, destroying all perspective, putting himself completely *in* the poem at the fictional level (drinking the same drink as the characters) and in the next line putting himself right outside with his advice to the audience to fill up their cups, in parody of a minstrel's call for a drink to help him along. The poet here for a moment distances himself from the material of the poem, but he does not create an 'ironic' narrator, even though he allows us our own judgement of what he tells us. Winner and Waster put forth arguments to justify their respective prudence and extravagance in terms of the national economy. The problems of circulation of money and goods, of saving and spending, are familiar, if in different terms, in our own day. The concern for the poor, for social justice, for the problems of inequality, are the same, though different ages, like Winner aand Waster, come to different conclusions. Although the poem is incomplete probably not much is lost, and though the arguments are put forcefully it is highly unlikely that the poem presented a firm conclusion in favour of one side or the other. To some extent both Winner and Waster are necessary, and the arguments are artificially distinguished and heightened to create a Gothic tension which is, in itself, a sort of answer to the problems. Each side attempts to see itself in terms of ultimate values, of what is right in the final, therefore religious, analysis, but there is every reason to suppose that the poet, though feeling the problems strongly, saw both right and wrong on each side. The debate form allows the poet to present several points of view within a multiple whole, and he does not try to resolve them or produce a consistent answer. It is refreshing to have poetry on matters of public concern, but the poet is not writing a treatise on practical economics. For all his protestations he has a certain licence for Gothic poetic non-responsibility.

'The Parlement of the Thre Ages'

The British Library Thornton manuscript, Additional 31042, contains another alliterative poem, *The Parlement of the Thre Ages*. These two poems have more in common with each other than with later alliterative poems. Their dialect is much the same, and a considerable number of words and phrases are shared. They could be by the same author. But more likely these similarities, especially of language, are part of the common stock of poetic words and phrases shared to some extent by many alliterative poems, which constitute a regional school. Whether the school reflects an oral tradition, or a new literary creation, is not clear. There are other similarities between these two poems: a spring setting at the beginning, a dream-vision sequence, rich descriptions of nature and clothing, knowledge of books, a religious concern for right behaviour, pleasure in the brilliant if transitory world. All this establishes, not unity of authorship, but a sense of similar audiences and concerns. The Thornton manuscript is one of two compiled by Robert Thornton, about 1440 (see below, p. 176), and though the relative lateness of date has allowed both the spread of the alliterative poems and their mingling with other forms of romance, the type of manuscript is similar to those of other alliterative poems and suggests the same social level. We may assume an audience of small gentry, clerics, the auxiliary gentry of great houses, mostly in the West and North Midlands extending eventually to Lincolnshire and Yorkshire. They were provincial, with some hostility to the south, but they were well-read, and concerned with national as well as with general ethical problems. In *The Parlement of the Thre Ages* we have an excellent sample of good provincial culture, with its interest in hunting, and the presentation of the Three Ages of Man, doing full justice to the courtliness of youth, the anxieties about property of middle age, and the pains and piety of old age. There is a well-informed account of the traditional Nine Worthies (three classical: Hector, Alexander, Julius Cæsar; three Jewish; Joshua, David, Judas Maccabeus; three Christian: Arthur, Godfrey of Boulogne, Charlemagne), and the longest list extant of titles of romance stories in medieval English literature.

Alliterative romances

The interest in romance is always significant because the purely fictional images of romance by their freedom from practical compulsions reveal some of the deeper inner needs of any community. Although there is a pronounced religiously utilitarian bent in the alliterative school in general, as in so much fourteenth-century literary culture, the pride of life shown in rich descriptions also emerges in romance. About the same time that *Wynnere and Wastoure* was written two other alliterative poems based on French poems were written in Gloucestershire, the county which adjoins Worcestershire to the south, by unknown authors. *Joseph of Arimathie* (709 lines long) has been tentatively dated to the mid-fourteenth century. It is based on that part of the French *Queste del Saint Graal* which tells how Joseph of Arimathea preserved the dish now called the Grail, containing the blood shed by Christ on the Cross, and eventually came to Britain. The Grail story eventually became fully incorporated in the Arthurian legend, which is the nearest the English have come to a national mythology. Although this is a religious romance the author particularly excels in portraying battles. *Joseph of Arimathie* is found only in the vast religious miscellany, the Vernon manuscript, probably written about 1400, which includes the alliterative version of the Biblical story of Susannah, called *The Pistill of Susan.* The presence of these poems in this miscellany shows that the alliterative poems had spread through the country and mingled with other types of writing. *Joseph of Arimathie* has little of the characteristic alliterative vocabulary, either because it was composed so early that the vocabulary had not developed or, equally possible, because it was composed, like Langland's *Piers Plowman*, on the fringe of the main area in which the poems originated. The same may be said of the romance *William of Palerne*, surviving in one manuscript on its own, which was commissioned, as the author tells us, by Humphrey de Bohun, Earl of Hereford, for those of his people who did not know French (ll. 5529–33). It was probably written a little before 1361 at one of Humphrey's Gloucestershire manors, Whitminster or Haresfield, a little before 1361, the year Humphrey died. The author apologises for his clumsy handling of the metre (ll. 5521–6); it seems likely that he felt that the alliterative metre was particularly English. The French poem on which the English version is based is an enjoyable romance of the twelfth century telling how William, son of a king in Sicily, is victim of a plot by a wicked uncle, but is saved by a kindly werewolf. This beginning in the English manuscript is lost. The English text begins where the boy is brought up by a cowherd. Eventually he comes to serve the emperor of Rome. He falls in love with the emperor's daughter and she with him. They become lovers in secret. They eventually have to escape, sewn up in bearskins as a disguise, and helped by the werewolf. There is a delightful account of their journey. William wins glory, identities are re-established, and all ends happily. The fundamental matter is thus the folkloric one of the family drama, incorporating the typical romance themes of withdrawal from society, love, testing and re-integration within society. The education of the hero, both specific and general, is another telling element. No one objects, at any rate at the end, to the lovers' pre-marital sex, it being justified by its faithfulness. The English version is rather more clumsy in style, but often with additional vivid touches and in one instance an extra episode of a rather knock-about kind. With this poem may be included *Chevalere Assigne* (370 lines long) of uncertain date, a version of the folk-tale of the Swan Knight, perhaps an early example of the alliterative style, based on French and making very little use of the characteristic alliterative vocabulary. It deals with the 'family drama', parental malice, the separation of children, and the education of the hero. The treatment is rather more vigorous and humorous than in *William of Palerne*. *Chevalere Assigne* is found only in the important collection of romances, British Library MS Cotton Caligula A ii, which also has one of several versions of *The Pistill of Susan*, and was copied out late in the fifteenth century.

The translation of these early works from French, and of others, *Alisaunder of Macedoine* and *Alexander and Dindimus*, from Latin, suggests a building up of work in English to meet a growing demand in the west and north for literature whose material was of European interest and which ought to be represented in a properly English style. There is a touch of regional self-consciousness in the north and west absent from the metrical rhyming and tail-rhyme romances, and less noticeable in the south-western part of the country. Langland appears to draw from this more south-westerly area since he sets the opening of his poem on Malvern Hills, some twenty miles south and west of Worcester, and this may be why he uses little of the characteristic vocabulary of the alliterative 'school'. Nor does Langland assert his Englishness or show any interest in English or British history, though he writes with a profound concern for the state of the nation similar to that found in other alliterative writers but notably absent from the rhyming romances and the work of the civil servant and courtier, Chaucer.

Historical poems

The alliterative school includes a number of historical and battle poems consonant with a national concern. There are several long poems on Alexander and a very long one on *The Gest Hystoriale of the Destruction of Troy* (c. 1375) particularly notable for its scenes of storm and battle. The Troy story was about 'the adventures of our noble ancestors' (*Destruction*, l.5) and references to it appear especially in the prologues of alliterative poems. These old stories, as the Prologue to the *Destruction* says, are liable to be pushed out of mind by new ones, but old stories in the accounts of men who actually saw the actions described may be a solace to some. The main thing is to find out the truth. In this pre-scientific thought-world such an aim does not prevent a writer from manipulating his sources by adding, omitting or amplifying; he seeks an essential truth to life, not an imitation of things as they actually happened, for all his protestations. From our point of view he mingles fiction and history, but even modern history is a matter of interpretation, and it is as imaginative re-interpretation that many medieval narratives should be judged. Nevertheless medieval authors necessarily recognise some kind of difference between 'fable' and 'truth', though their criteria are different from ours. The Prologue of *The Destruction of Troy* gives a useful summary of the usual medieval view, found by implication as late as Shakespeare's *Troilus and Cressida*, that Homer (whose Greek could not be read) was a liar and a propagandist biased in favour of the Greeks, and that the true story of the Trojan war is to be found in the Latin histories, supposedly eyewitness accounts in Latin by Dares Phrygius, a Greek, and Dictys Cretensis, a Trojan, which actually date from the sixth and fourth centuries A.D. respectively.

The Morte Arthure

The most notable of these historical alliterative poems takes up English/British history at its most exciting point, the national myth of Arthur. The *Morte Arthure* (4,346 lines) is impossible to date precisely (say *c.* 1360). It gives an extraordinarily vivid sense of the feel of a real military campaign, and displays strong partisanship on the side of 'our' men, who are undoubtedly English. After a pious invocation to 'great glorious God' the poet addresses the audience:

> Ye that liste has to lyth, or luffes for to here
> Off elders of alde tyme and of theire auke dedys,
> How they were lele in theire lawe and lovede God Almyghty,
> Herkynes me heyndly and holdys yow styll,
> And I sall tell yow a tale that trewe es and nobyll
> Off the ryealle renkys of the Rownnde Table.
>
> [Thornton MS f. 53, 12–17]

(You that wish to listen, or love to hear of elders of ancient times and their strange deeds, how they were loyal in their law and loved God Almighty, listen courteously to me and remain quiet and I shall tell you a tale that is true and noble about the royal warriors of the Round Table.)

After a rehearsal of Arthur's conquests a banquet is described at which ambassadors arrive from the Emperor of Rome to summon Arthur to do homage. The episode, ultimately derived from the French poet Wace, may be compared with Layamon's treatment (see above, p. 13). After a splendid banquet the ambassadors are sent back with insults. When Arthur has prepared for war in France he has a dream of himself as a dragon, defeating a bear signifying the emperor Lucyus. A particularly full and at times grotesque account tells how Arthur himself, who dominates this poem, kills the giant of Mont St Michel. Before the battle there is a touch of realistic detail, as Arthur takes the cold air (l. 944), which later caught the attention of Malory who was normally uninterested in such superficial realism. The fight is preceded by an effective formal description of Arthur's arming, of a highly traditional kind (ll. 900–19, *cf.* p. 162 below). In a later battle there is some resemblance to the victory of Crècy, though other episodes of the fighting of single knights recall rather the fantasies of normal romance. Arthur fights his way through Tuscany and at Viterbo the Romans acknowledge defeat. That night Arthur has a second significant dream, this time of Fortune's Wheel, that frequent medieval image of the life of kings and of every man, reminding us that all who live must die. Arthur sees the eight Worthies around Fortune's Wheel. He himself, being the ninth, is lifted up on it, then crushed. Philosophers interpreting the dream warn him to prepare his soul for death and reproach him for his cruelty and bloodshed. The poet juxtaposes such legitimate blame with enthusiastic endorsement of much bloodthirsty warfare, oscillating between admiration and implicit criticism of the reckless bravery that in both fact and fiction characterised fourteenth-century warfare – as it sometimes does that of the twentieth century. Human nature does not always change. The poet probably knew the discussions and condemnations by churchmen of military brutality, but he was also a patriot. A somewhat similar ambivalence arises in the attitude to Gawain. Arthur at the peak of his triumph, at the top of Fortune's Wheel, hears of his nephew Mordred's treason and his queen Gaynor's marriage to Mordred. He rushes back and at the assault made in landing on the coast, Gawain, who has in the past been wildly reckless, and is now described by the poet as beyond all reason, falls into a frenzy as if he wished to destroy himself. He gets into disastrous difficulties and makes a speech recognising that he has thrown himself and his men away (l. 3802). Yet when he is killed he is the subject of moving laments, first by Mordred, the foe who has killed him, and then, in a rightly famous passage, by Arthur himself. This too was taken up by Malory though it was transferred with modifications to Hector's lament for Lancelot, abandoning the grisly realism of the poem.

> Than gliftis the gud kynge, and glopyns in herte
> Gronys full grisely, wyth gretande teris
> Knelis downe to the cors and kaught it in armes,
> Kastys upe his umbrere, and kyssis hym sone,
> Lokes one his eyeliddis that lowkkide ware faire,
> His lippis like to the lede and his lire falowede.
> Than the corownde kyng cryes full lowde,
> 'Dere kosyne o kynde, in kare am I levede,
> For nowe my wirchipe es wente and my were endide.
> Here es the hope of my hele, my happynge of armes,
> My herte and my hardynes. Hale one hym lengede
> My concell, my comforthe, that kepide myne herte.
> Of all knyghtes the kynge that undir Criste lifede
> Thou was worthy to be kyng, thofe I the corowne bare.
>
> [f. 94v, ll. 3949–62]

(Then the good king looks and grieves at heart, groans terribly, with pouring tears, kneels down to the corpse and held it in his arms, raises his visor, and immediately kisses him, looks at his eyelids that were well closed, his lips like lead and his pale face. Then the crowned king loudly cries, 'Dear kinsman by blood, I am left in sorrow, for now my honour has gone and my war ended. Here is my hope of well-being, my good fortune in battle, my heart and my bravery. Wholly to him, who guarded my heart, belonged my counsel, my comfort. You were worthy to be the king of all knights who lived under Christ, though I wore the crown.')

The poem then with no flagging of interest follows the story to its familiar end, in the death of Arthur from wounds received at the hands of Mordred, who in this poem is his nephew. But there is no mysterious boat, no queens, to fetch him away. This poem is more down to earth.

Not a word is wasted. Stylised in a Gothic manner, with abrupt changes of tense and syntax, and with touches of realism, it admirably renders complexity of feeling. Some other parts of the poem have equally sharp juxtapositions, such as the constant invocations of the mildness of Mary side by side with approval of ferocious behaviour towards the enemy. Even if there is a touch of criticism of Arthur, he and his men are referred to as English, and the poet, as English as they, constantly refers to 'our' side. As modernist outsiders we may be puzzled, but for those 'inside', who have experienced, or can by imagination experience, a national war, the inconsistencies, and the zest with which the slaughter of the enemy can be portrayed, are natural enough. The whole poem is more archaic than modern in tone. There is no narrator distanced from the poet, speaking dramatically in a voice different from his, by which ironic effects may be produced.

The unflagging style, though not much varied, is rich, luxuriant and hyperbolic, and the poem's vitality has generated controversy among critics. It used to be called a romance, but since there is no love interest, no withdrawal from society, no testing of the hero (except in the episode of Arthur's fight with the giant), no reintegration in society in a happy ending, it cannot be that. Its chief modern student, Professor Göller, calls it an anti-romance. It is certainly a tragedy: some have called it an epic. It is something of a history, both in telling Arthur's story and in the associations that are consciously or unconsciously felt with contemporary warfare. There may be a political message to Edward III, who was a keen Arthurian, to take warning from Arthur's fate. To debate the terms 'romance', 'epic' and 'history', is necessary, because if any is accepted it conditions our approach, understanding, emphasis and critical judgement; but it is not surprising that our Neoclassical genres and their names, with their assumptions and accompanying value judgements, fit awkwardly to that Gothic miscellaneity which the eighteenth century called, with disapproval, 'mixed modes'. The medieval poet, having received the main outline of his story, which he cannot change, exploits each aspect of it as seems most fitting at that particular point, borrowing from elsewhere, inventing, omitting, with less concern to reconcile minor inconsistencies and to produce a worked-out overall coherent view based on naturalistic premises than modern critics expect. In this respect Shakespeare himself is fully medieval. There may well be more unity, deriving from a 'pattern of culture', in such work than is at first realised, but to convey a single overall point of view within the work is not the main object of the poet.

These poems must serve as preliminary examples of the central tradition of medieval English poetry. The fourteenth-century alliterative line was derived from Old English poetry, or was re-created from misty memories of it in relation to the natural rhythms of English, in ways not yet fully understood. It was first used to naturalise European culture in those parts of the country more remote from the international Gothic culture of the courts of Edward III and Richard II. In that period, the second half of the fourteenth century, when the very different Chaucer was less provincially fulfilling the same purpose, the English alliterative line was the natural vehicle for two poets, the *Gawain*-poet and Langland, as good as any English poets since, except Shakespeare, so great that they each need a chapter of their own. Other poems, inevitably, fail to reach the same standard and some fall far below it, without losing value as witnesses to various stages and interests of literary culture.

The later stages of the tradition will be best mentioned following the *Gawain*-poet and Langland (below, p. 177 and p. 209).

9
The *Gawain*-poet

'Sir Gawain and the Green Knight': the story

GAWAIN, not Lancelot, was the original principal knight of King Arthur. Gawain was the son of Arthur's sister Morgause, and the relationship of uncle to sister's son was of great antiquity and power. The chronicles of the history of Britain (not only England) which, after Geoffrey of Monmouth's *History of the Kings of Britain* (1135), incorporated Arthur into the long story from Troy to the Anglo-Saxons, maintained Gawain's pre-eminence. Lancelot was the product mainly of the romantic inventiveness of Chrétien de Troyes in the late twelfth century, and of the continuation and expansions by thirteenth-century French romancers of Chrétien's unfinished poem about Lancelot and Guinevere, *Le Chevalier de la Charrette*. The English alliterative poems disregard Lancelot and follow the chronicle tradition. Gawain is represented as the idealistic young hero of the greatest of all English romances, the alliterative poem *Sir Gawain and the Green Knight*, 2530 lines long and divided into four sections called *fyttes*. It was composed about 1370 and survives in a modest little manuscript, British Library Cotton Nero A x, with three other poems, *Pearl*, *Patience* and *Cleanness* (or *Purity*; all are modern titles). This manuscript was written and illustrated with four rather poor pictures about 1400. The four poems are all probably by the same unknown poet who lived among the hills and moors of Derbyshire in the North Midlands. Here he will be called the *Gawain*-poet, as has been the custom, though a few scholars refer to him as the *Pearl*-poet and the manuscript as the *Pearl*-manuscript.

Sir Gawain and the Green Knight begins with a prologue going back to the fall of Troy, noting the foundation of Rome by Aeneas, and how his grandson,

fer over the French flod, Felix Brutus
On mony bonkkes ful brode Bretayn he settez — hills; founds
wyth wynne — joy
Where werre & wrake & wonder
Bi sythes hatz* wont therinne — times; dwelt
& oft bothe blysse and blunder
Ful skete hatz skyfted synne. — quickly; shifted since
[f. 91, 13–19]

*-*tz* is pronounced unvoiced like the *ss* in *lass*

More wonders have happened in this land, says the patriotic poet, than in any other, and of all the kings Arthur was the *hendest* ('most courtly'). Therefore, says the poet, he will tell of a wonder that happened in Arthur's time, 'if you will listen to this lay a little while'. He thus evokes the idea of the traditional communal audience. The poet, however, intrudes no more, until in the last few lines of the poem he refers to the witness of 'Brutus bokes', repeats the first line at l. 2525, and concludes with a prayer of a traditional kind.

The story opens with the description of a glorious Christmas and New Year feast in Arthur's hall. All those present are young and are the most famous of knights and the loveliest of ladies. The glamour is enchanting; the poet combines action with description in a way to baffle summary. The setting is realistically suggested yet ideal, a secular heaven of successful youthfulness which we can easily imagine though we have never known such splendours in ordinary life. On New Year's day Arthur, as tradition often averred, will not begin the feast till a wonder has occurred. As they wait a huge man enters the hall on horseback as a challenger. He is frightening but handsome, and green all over, dressed with a Gothic richness of decoration which the poet lovingly describes, though he cunningly leaves the information about the greenness to the end of his description of the entry. He continues:

And al graythed in grene this gome & his wedes,
A strayt cote ful streght, that stek on his sides,
A meré mantile abof, mensked withinne
With pelure pured apert, the pane fule clene
With blythe blaunner ful bryght, & his hod bothe,
That watz laght fro his lokkez & layde on his schulderes;
Heme wel-haled hose of that same grene,
That spenet on his sparlyr, & clene spures under

Of bryght golde, upon silk bordes barred ful ryche,
& scholes under schankes there the schalk rydes.
& alle his vesture verayly watz clene verdure,
Bothe the barres of his belt & other blythe stones
That were richely rayled in his aray clene
Aboutte hymself & his sadel, upon silk werkez,
That were to tor for to telle of tryfles the halve.

[f. 93v, 151–65]

(And this man and his clothes were all arrayed in green – a tight-fitting very narrow coat, that clung to his sides, a delightful cloak on top of that, adorned [*literally*, honoured] within with fine fur easy to see, the edging very clean with very bright joyous fur, and his hood also, that was raised from his hair and laid on his shoulders. Neat hose well drawn up of that same green colour, that fitted close to the calf of the leg, and clean spurs below of bright gold upon silken bands richly ribbed, and there the man rides without shoes on his feet [*literally*, under legs: *or*, with light shoes – *scholetz* – on his feet]. And all his clothing truly was clean greenness, both the bars on his belt and other joyous gems which were richly placed on his clean clothing about him and his saddle, on silk embroideries, that it would be too hard to tell of half the details.]

The very style is also the meaning. Even in this short passage there is copious and repeated use of generalised adjectives of unabashed praise, as *clene* (one of his favourite words implying pure and fresh as well as 'not dirty'), and also *blythe* and *bryght*. These are often emphasised by the emphatic adverb *ful* whose only function is reinforcement. Another notable characteristic is the use, as descriptive adjectives applied to objects, of words which, to our modern way of thinking, more naturally describe the appreciative response of the beholder to the objects than the objects themselves, like *blythe* of fur and jewels. This characteristic, for which no rhetorical term seems quite appropriate, extends in this passage to the past participle of a verb, as for example where the cloak is not only *meré*, 'pleasant', and also 'merry', but is *mensked*, 'honoured', by the fur lining, itself *pured*, 'made pure', 'refined'. Some editors translate *pured* as 'trimmed to one colour'; this may give the physical basis of what is meant, but loses the appreciative moral approbation which is also conveyed. In such usages the poet re-creates, or creates anew, an 'archaic' wholeness of observer and object, combining without confusion the material aspect of what is seen with the moral and spiritual appreciation of the observer. There is no irony in such a passage, no division between the narrator and the poet standing behind him, no two 'voices' saying the same words but with different implications, one of them misleading, between which the reader must discriminate. Though most modern critics think there is irony in the similar description of Arthur's court, I do not think this likely. This poet is writing in a traditional style which (like ordinary popular language) is hyperbolical, general and repetitious, if considered from the point of view of literalistic meaning. The theory of modern literature, and some modern literature itself, repudiates such a popular style, with its relationship to oral and manuscript conditions, in which poet, object and reader (or hearer) are united in accepted standards. Perhaps such a style is impossible in modern English. This style's generality and imprecision is the opposite of literalism. Though often general it is not abstract, and the poet can also give a specific concrete basis of description when necessary, to which he can anchor the general meaning, as when he tells us of the Green Knight's stockings, well-fitting and unwrinkled. The physical detail of properly managed dress implies the wearer's admirable qualities, as a smartly-dressed soldier implies one who is brave and efficient. The poet takes particuar delight in rich and beautiful objects which he praises even though they reflect the quality of one who appears to be an enemy. The thing that is good in itself pleases him. Thus the praise of the Green Knight's appearance does not mean that we should also approve of his rudeness or side with him against the court. Equally, though we identify our interests with those of the court, which is 'our' side, we note that, though the court is ideally good, even Arthur's knights may be struck dumb, though not all for fear.

The Green Knight proposes a 'Beheading Game' which Gawain takes on himself from Arthur with conspicuous courtesy, and he decapitates the Green Knight, unfortunately causing him no inconvenience. The story centres on how Gawain keeps his promise to accept the return blow in a year's time. On the next All Saints' Day, November 1st, Gawain sets out on his 'anious vyage' ('anxious journey') to keep his dreaded tryst, having been formally armed. His shield has a portrait of the Blessed Virgin Mary, to whom he is devoted, on the inside, and on the outside, as a blason, the pentangle device, the geometrical 'endless knot' of five interconnected points, each of which symbolises five of Gawain's virtuous qualities. He is faultless in his five 'wits' (i.e. senses); has never failed in his five fingers; puts all his trust in Christ's five wounds; takes courage from Mary's five joys; and as his fifth five has always practised generosity, fellowship, cleanness (i.e. chastity), courtesy and pity. These five are a part of medieval religious number-mnemonics (ten commandments, seven deadly sins, five joys, etc.). They have no arithmetical utility and little æsthetic appeal to modern minds. They may seem unduly schematic, but as the poet uses them they symbolise in the interconnectedness of the pentangle the Christian chivalry of Gawain, and the archaic ideal of a united whole of being and acting, physical, moral and spiritual. They express the essence of Gawain, though they are not a device for 'characterisation' in any novelistic way. The pentangle is not mentioned again. It is not part of the sequence of events; it expresses basic assumptions.

Gawain travels indomitably through harsh weather to arrive, apparently by accident, on Christmas Eve, at a fine castle in the wilds of Derbyshire. There, most courteously treated during the Christmas feast, he is sexually tempted on three successive days at the end of the year by the lord's wife while the lord is away hunting. The temptation scenes, where Gawain is in bed, are most wittily described, with fencing conversation between the lady and the knight as in a decent Restoration comedy, if such can be imagined. They are interspersed with vigorous descriptions of the lord's hunting and slaughter of, successively, deer, a boar and a fox. The juxtaposition of the hunting with the bedroom scenes, made without comment, and with no allegorical intent (as in later poems, see below p. 211), creates a larger recognition than either could give separately to the ambivalent charms, excitements and dangers of the carnal world of sex and death.

Gawain has promised an 'exchange of winnings' with his host (another archaic practice) and on the first two days duly 'hands over' the kisses he has been forced to accept from the lady, and notionally receives the proceeds of the hunting. On the third day he 'hands over' three kisses but secretly retains a girdle she has persuaded him to accept on the grounds that it can magically preserve life. Early on New Year's Day he must leave for the tryst of the Green Chapel, which fortunately, as the lord has assured him, is 'not two miles away'. The story is conducted with admirable suspense as Gawain travels through the snowy hills. There, at the Green Chapel, which is probably a barrow, a prehistoric burial-mound of the kind to which superstition attached stories of death-dealing demons, he meets his foe, undergoes two feints with the beheading axe, and finally escapes with only a nick in the neck. It is a wonderful climax. The Green Knight reveals himself as the lord of the castle, who has plotted to destroy Gawain by getting his own wife to seduce him. If he had actually been seduced Gawain would have had his head chopped off. Gawain would have been totally faultless, and thus unharmed, had he not by accepting the girdle marginally given in to the lady. His chastity has proved as powerful a life-saver as the Green Knight's own more dubious magic, and the 'magic' girdle, far from being a preserver, is his only source of weakness. The lord explains that it has all been a plot by Gawain's aunt, Arthur's sister, Morgan le Fay, who is an ugly old lady Gawain has been introduced to in the castle but has not recognised. The lord, whose name is Bertilak, is under her control. She hates Guinivere, and had sent Bertilak as Green Knight to frighten Guinivere to death by seeing his decapitation in Arthur's court. The Green Knight is remarkably genial considering that his plot has failed, and he asks Gawain back to the castle; but the idealistic Gawain is deeply mortified at even so slight a shortcoming as he has shown, and he returns to Arthur's court. There all the knights take the view, as the Green Knight does, and as I do, that Gawain, though not inhumanly perfect, has triumphantly succeeded, not failed. Gawain, however, decides to wear the lady's green girdle as a badge of shame. Arthur's knights choose to wear a similar device as a baldric to acquire honour by showing their association with Gawain. What for the best of men is a sign of weakness represents for the rest of us an ideal we should find it hard to reach. But many modern critics disagree, and consider Gawain to be a failure.

The nature of the style

The warm idealising tone of the style, so important to the whole, is conveyed by the constant use of unambiguous

1. God and Devils from the Royal manuscript.

2. The Nativity from the Additional manuscript.

3. The Crucifixion from the Evesham Psalter.

4. Resurrection and Jonah and the Whale from the York Psalter.

5. A Tournament from Froissart.

6. Lovers in a Garden from the Harley manuscript.

7. Hunting scene from the Hardwick Hall Tapestry.

8. A Feast from the Royal manuscript.

9. Lydgate presenting the Bible from the Harley manuscript.

Hou he þi seruaunt was mayden marie
And lat his loue floure and fructifie

Al þogh his lyfe be queynt þe resemblaunce
Of him hath in me so fressh lyflynesse
Þat to putte othir men in remembraunce
Of his persone I haue heere his liknesse
Do make to þis ende in sothfastnesse
Þat þei þat haue of him lest þought & mynde
By þis peynture may ageyn him fynde

The ymages þat in þe chirche been
Maken folk þenke on god & on his seyntes
Whan þe ymages þei beholden & seen
Were oft vnsyte of hem causith restreyntes
Of þoughtes gode whan a þing depeynt is
Or entailed if men take of it heede
Thoght of þe liknesse it wil in hym brede

Yit some holden oppinioun and sey

10. Chaucer and his text from the Harley manuscript.

11. Conway Castle from the Harley manuscript.

12. A Ploughman from the Luttrell Psalter.

13. Christ Entering Jerusalem from the Additional manuscript.

14. Christ in Majesty from the Royal manuscript.

15. The Battle of Agincourt, 1415.

16. The Black Death from the Additional manuscript.

17. Baruch reading before the King from the Royal manuscript.

18. Fortune's Wheel from a 15th-Century manuscript.

19. Salisbury Cathedral.

adjectives of praise like *gode* (used many times of Gawain), *hende* ('courteous', not used mockingly as in Chaucer), *faire, ryche, bryght*. Other adjectives attribute the observer's approbation to the object – *blythe, gay* – or attribute a moral quality to objects – *noble, wlonk* ('noble'), etc. Others simply reinforce a noun, as *glyterande golde*. Such adjectives are evaluative, not descriptive. Although they are frequent they do not clog the style, which is powerful, having a high proportion of verbs and nouns. The vocabulary is large, and many nouns, in particular, are rare, of northern origin, ultimately from Old Norse. They help to pile up the synonyms that the poet's concept of the alliterative line needs but, more significantly, they are intrinsic to his picture of a complex and splendid world of nature and civilisation, tense with potential conflict, whose vital forces, ancient and new, have to be mastered with effort and brought into a related unity. The vocabulary includes the general and the idealising with the concrete and even the technical (as in the description of the 'breaking' of the deer (ll. 1319–64)), and ranges from the lady's colloquial speech to stylised but fresh description, as of the passing seasons (ll. 500–35). It has few abstract words. Even within the individual word aspects of meaning are included which are now normally divided. To traditional hyperbole and repetition is added witty word-play, as when the lady says 'ye are welcum to my cors' (l. 1237) where *my cors* could mean as elsewhere in Middle English, and as Gawain insists on taking it, simply 'me', but could be taken, as the next lines suggest, more literalistically as sexual invitation, 'my body'. The poet wittingly recognises, uses and rejects literalism in this pun.

The syntax is often loose and far from the prose order of words, in part because of the needs of alliteration. Its looseness allows the poet to use many co-ordinate sentences which move forward in juxtaposition, without much subordination. This emphasises description and action, but the convoluted order also helps to create the poet's characteristic interlinkings, and magnificently enacts in its windings a subtle complex situation, as in Gawain's request to Arthur to take over the apparently deadly game, which expresses and orders so many factors in an elaborate courtesy (ll. 343–60).

The metre works in the same way. The four stresses of the long alliterative line, three with the alliterating letter, are rightly described by the poet as of ancient tradition in England. They are linked in 'loyal' words – a characteristic adjective – and as he says of his story,

> I shal telle hit astit, as I in toun herde — quickly
> with tonge
> As hit is stad and stoken — placed and set
> In stori stif and stronge — brave; powerful
> With lel letteres loken — loyal; locked together
> In londe so hatz ben long. [30–6]

Most of this passage is in different metre. The alliterative long lines are in stanzas of from about 13 to 24 lines long which are concluded by a one-stress phrase which catches them up, called the 'bob', and four two-stress lines rhyming twice, which go with a delightful swing and gaiety, varying the pace and lightening the tone, called the 'wheel'. The one-stress phrase is the nearest the poet comes to a meaningless tag and its use is mainly as a 'musical' pause before he changes speed and rhythm in the lively 'wheel'.

The sources

The sources of the poem are numerous. The poet insists on the traditional nature of the story. His Gawain is the traditional English Gawain. The poet's descriptions of rough weather recall the established skills of the alliterative poets. The story is set in a recognisable English landscape. The arming topic is extremely ancient and appears in *Beowulf*. But this topic is also frequently found in medieval French romance and the poet knows these very well, though he shows no knowledge of the modern courtly fourteenth-century French poets used by Chaucer, such as Machaut. It seems likely that Gawain's reputation for courtesy comes from the great thirteenth-century Arthurian romances, but the poet had more specific sources. Although the beheading-game motif and various episodes of sexual temptation are very ancient and were widespread in French romances, the beheading scene that is closest is a version of the story of Carados that appears in the thirteenth-century French continuation in verse, by an anonymous poet, of Chrétien's unfinished story of Perceval. Here, the unknown challenger turns out to be the hero's father. There are two short thirteenth-century French Gawain-romances, *Le Chevalier à l'Epée* and *La Mule Sans Frein*, which the *Gawain*-poet knew and used, and another beheading of a churl by Gawain in *Hunbaut*. This latter poem, like the story of Carados and another poem about Yder, also has a temptation scene. The *Gawain*-poet alone creates a unified story out of the two main elements of sexual temptation and beheading. From ancient elements he creates a new structure, mythic, yet realistic in its verbal realisation.

The values and symbolic meaning of Sir Gawain and the Green Knight

At the level of the verbal realisation the poem is rich and varied. Many significant medieval ideas and concepts are evoked. Courtesy ranges from good table-manners and the ability to make pleasant conversation to a daily beauty of personality that shines in dealing with others. Gawain is not thought of as particularly courteous in the English chronicle tradition, but in the thirteenth-century French romances this aspect of his character became particularly notable. With it went a marked amorousness verging on sexual promiscuity. The poet rejects this, but he obviously knew about it, and it is as if the lady of the castle tries to fix upon the English Gawain the loose reputation of the French version. There is thus a certain ambiguity about courtesy. It is a virtue, yet it implies the 'love-talking' for which Gawain is celebrated in the poem. Courtesy and chastity, both good in themselves, may come into conflict. If a lady asks you to go to bed with her, courtesy may make it seem impolite to refuse. That does not mean that courtesy is always the same as sexual promiscuity. It means that you have to be clever to be good. Hence the wit. The emotional and verbal tension, in which potential incompatibilities are yoked together, have little to do with romantic love, and much to do with the excitement of sex. The obligation of chastity is superior to that of courtesy. Values good in themselves may come into conflict. When that happens we have to establish a hierarchy of values, and not destroy one or other.

Other values also come into the same situation. 'Truth', that complex amalgam of loyalty, courage, faithfulness and honesty, is thought by some to be Gawain's chief virtue, but all the virtues are interlinked. Gawain's truth to his word brings him to the tryst; his truth in his loyalty to his host, though he is not represented as thinking of it at the time, obviously reinforces, or is part of, his chastity; and his chastity, his faithfulness to God and the Virgin, is an element of his truth. But chastity is seen as the master-value here and elsewhere in medieval literature, for example in the great thirteenth-century French prose religious romance *Le Queste del Saint Graal*, later translated by Malory (see below p. 273). Courage is obviously a fundamental aspect of any virtue, since without it none can be maintained when tested. Generosity is also important in that it is the opposite of greed, even greed for life, which is an aspect of cowardice. The poem encourages such reflections about values without being in the least moralistic.

Though Gawain is an ideal figure the sense we are given of his fears and relief and joy, and his minor failure at the end, ensure that he is not so idealised that we cannot believe in him as a human being. Moreover towards the end, in touches of description, and through Bertilak's and the court's amused response to his natural but excessive self-condemnation for his slip, we attain a certain detachment from our hero. Yet he remains the protagonist. His character is typical, broadly-sketched and does not develop; he is not presented as an autonomous developing *personality* as a novel might show him. The whole action and the nature of the other characters can only be understood as they refer to him. They are not novelistic, plausible, independently-motivated personalities; if taken as such, they become incomprehensible. Why, for example, should Sir Bertilak wish to cuckold himself in order to decapitate Gawain? Why need he decapitate Gawain at all, since the ostensible object of the whole action had been to frighten Guinivere to death, and that had failed a year before? As in myth, romance and fairy-tale, all is referred to the protagonist. In romance we see the hero establish his identity and independence by withdrawing from society, being tested, and returning to be integrated in society. In this best of romances there are continual variations from the ordinary pattern. Gawain does not, like most heroes, marry. He has a higher and in worldly terms a lonelier destiny. He is isolated in feeling from the court, his chosen society, though the court associates itself with him. Ultimate personal integrity, full status as an individual, involves the capacity to stand in spirit *really* alone. In this poem the *pattern* of the story, as in myth and fairy-tale, is more significant than personalised characterisation. The juxtapositions in the story of 'nature' and 'nurture' (Gawain is called 'fine fader of nurture' l. 919); of the exchange of gifts, itself a subtle contest; of the three temptations and the three blows; all tell their own complex story. Like so many stories, it is a story of sex and death, though with its own medieval message of triumph over the material world of cause-and-effect by the exercise of spiritual strength and self-control. At the deepest level of structure the story is a most original version of the family drama, in which the Green Knight is a father figure, and his lady the seductive aspect, and Morgan the malevolent aspect, of the mother figure. This is the only way in which we can explain the otherwise absurd account of the action given by the Green Knight himself. The hero's quest, instead of being a departure from home, as is usual in fairy-tales, is a return to home, where he must solve the problems of emotional bonds, and from which he emerges, not unscarred, as a mature, though young, adult. The poem sets 'archaic' against 'modern', as Professors Burrow and Benson have shown; older 'romantic', 'symbolic' and 'psychological' modes are thus combined with newer, more realistic, representational modes. The poet's triumph is to reconcile 'archaic' and 'modern', though critics differ in their judgement of the outcome, and many think of Gawain as a failure and of the poem therefore as a criticism of romance. Variety of response is itself a witness to the poem's richness and complexity of meaning.

'Pearl': the story

The same richness and similar underlying themes occur in the *Gawain*-poet's other poems, but they are very different in subject matter. No one has yet solved the problem of the order in which they were written, and it is still just possible, though unlikely, that they may be shown to be by different poets. The establishment of the chronology of Shakespeare's plays in the nineteenth century revolutionised criticism of his work, but there does not seem to be quite the same sense of development in the *Gawain*-poet's works, perhaps because we have lost the earlier ones. *Pearl* may show a development from *Sir Gawain and the Green Knight* in that the protagonist, now the poet himself, is a father, not a 'child'. Its basis is the poet's lament for his dead two-year-old daughter. He relates how his grief caused him to argue with himself, as it were, about the Christian meaning of death. The logic of acceptance of the beloved's security in heaven forces the bereaved father on earth to give up selfish grief while accepting the misery of loss. Once again a lonely integrity of life is the conclusion. The poignancy of the basic situation, delicately and indirectly suggested as the basis of the intellectual and emotional progress, can only be fully appreciated by parents, whereas for the appreciation of romance we all have the experience of being children. The loss of children and the experience of death generally pressed far more painfully, because so frequently, on the fourteenth century than it does on twentieth-century advanced industrial societies. Even the hard-boiled Boccaccio has a poem in Latin lamenting the death of his illegitimate daughter Octavia, and even Chaucer, little interested in family relationships, relates in his *Prioress's Tale* the mother's agony over the death of a child. Chaucer's tale is traditional and provides consolation through a miracle. The *Gawain*-poet is less sentimental and consoles himself, if consolation it can be called, by elaborately brilliant art and sober religious conviction.

The poem begins with a statement about his 'precious pearl'. 'So smal, so smothe her sydes were' (l. 5), 'Allas I leste hyr in on erbere' (l. 9) ('Alas, I lost her in an arbour'), which clearly signifies that no simple object was lost, but a person, evoked in the language of romance. It is agony to think of her colour clad in mud. The poet mourns her in the flowery spot where she is lost, presumably her grave, in August, in a high season, when corn is cut with sharp sickles, which probably indicates the time of the great festival of the Assumption of the Blessed Virgin on August 15th and thus a time of nature's harvest and supernatural ascension. Though the nature of Christ teaches him comfort, his 'wretched will' continues in woe. He falls asleep on the mound and is transported in spirit to a land shining with the splendour of imperishable jewels, where he sees a maiden clad in gleaming white and adorned with a great pearl standing on the other side of a stream, at the foot of a crystal cliff gleaming with 'royal' rays. He knows her, yet cannot believe his eyes, which eagerly 'question her fair face'. A 'gladdening glory' glides into him, the vision 'stings his heart', he is abashed and stands 'as hende as hawk in hall'. The process of hesitant recognition in that strange bright landscape is most moving. He asks with humility, is she his pearl whom he has so mourned? She replies with a calm detachment contrasting with his tremulous joy.

A long complex dialogue ensues in which she responds sometimes rather tartly to his confusion, and his reluctance to accept her heavenly status. She reproaches her 'jeweller' for thinking that our Lord would lie who promised to 'raise our life' (*cf.* l. 305) and for wanting to cross the water before his time. He must suffer and not kick against the pricks. He touchingly asks her not to be annoyed – she was his joy, and he misses her so much. What sort of life does she lead? It is a blissful life she says, for she is taken in marriage with the Lamb of God, though so young. How can this be, he says, since Mary herself is the Queen of Courtesy? The answer is that everyone in heaven is king or queen. His earthly literalism finds it hard to understand the equality combined with hierarchy in heaven which is brought about by the workings of courtesy, which is God's grace. And how can she, who was not two years old and knew neither *Pater Noster* nor *Creed*, be made a queen? (There is here as elsewhere perhaps a touch of sardonic humour in the poet's presentation of himself, arising out of the situation of a child instructing her rather stupid father.) She tells the parable of the workers in the vineyard to explain that salvation does not rest on mere deserving. God's *'fraunchyse'* ('generosity'), His grace, makes up the lack of merit when it is incurred by innocence. She is spotless and now, saved by the suffering of Christ, is one of the virgins who in *Apocalypse* (the *Revelation of Saint John*), are seen with God. The poet sees the apocalyptic vision, the glorious sight of the jewelled Jerusalem, the heavenly city, and his beloved with the blessed. He is so transported with love-longing that he plunges into the sundering stream, but it is not God's will, and he awakes to reconcile himself in 'this doel-doungoun' (l. 1187), in the grievous prison of this life, to the will of God. Nature and supernature are connected but different, and must not be sentimentally confused.

Symbolisation and values

Such visions of a dead child are not unknown to grieving parents, it is said, even today: the experience is one of common humanity. It is worked out with extraordinary beauty in terms of fourteenth-century anxieties and problems which can still be related to modern needs. Modern Christians might not be so worried about the fate after death of a child, but it is salutary to be reminded of the selfish aspect of mourning, and of the claim to significance as human beings even of the weak, the innocent, the unintellectual, the defenceless. Though our own symbolisations would be different our griefs are much the same.

Again the poet takes traditional themes, accepts them and makes them new. The topos of 'a lady instructing the author' goes back to *The Consolation of Philosophy* of Boethius in the fifth century. Dante is instructed and guided by Beatrice; Langland by the Lady, Holy Church. No doubt each is a variant of a psychologically symbolic mother-figure or Jungian Anima, the creative and sustaining female element in a man's mind and life, the part played so often in the fourteenth century by the image of the Virgin Mary. In *Pearl* there is a special freshness because the lady is the poet's daughter and the normal authoritative parent–child relationship is reversed. The dialogue is dramatic. The introduction of the poet's own self into the poem, used by many fourteenth-century European poets from Dante onwards, is given further interest by the relationship. It still seems not useful to speak of a Narrator, though most critics now do. The poet dramatises his former self, it is true, but if we cut that self off from the now speaking poet, as modern dissection encourages us to do in the creation of a Narrator, we greatly limit the emotional effect of the poem. The poet's loss becomes a mere hypothesis, to be entertained as an interesting artistic *tour-de-force*.

The dream-vision allows a poet a great range of free subjective exploration which has the validation of personal experience, or of what is claimed to be so, without materialistic limitation. It is peculiarly apt to express illumination through memory, through actual experience as revelation and through a kind of prophecy. It is both in and out of the world. The poet of *Pearl* does not abuse the freedom and wander into uncontrolled fantasy. The whole point of the poem is by his vision to assert the reality principle of the painful here-and-now.

The form

The power of the poem is strengthened by its feeling being channelled into an extraordinarily complex form. It is written in stanzas of twelve lines each rhyming on only three rhymes, with internal alliteration usually on two out of four stressed syllables in variable position in each line. There are 1212 lines, in 101 stanzas. The poet likes symbolic numbers. He used fives in *Sir Gawain and the Green Knight*; in *Pearl* he makes even greater use of twelve. Twelve is a significant biblical and folkloric number, especially in *Apocalypse*, and in Gothic design (the first Gothic church, St Denis in Paris, was founded on twelve pillars because of the symbolic biblical significance, not structural utility, and King's College Chapel in Cambridge has twelve bays). So the poet builds his poem on an analagous perfect structure of twelves. By the number 101, the 'perfect' number 100 plus one, the unity of God is probably meant. The stanzas are in groups of five, linked to each other by a device known to the rhetoricians as *concatenatio* (concatenation), which echoes the last line of one stanza in the first line of the next. The last line of the whole poem comes back to the first, 'Perle plesaunte to prynces paye' ('Pearl pleasing to the delight of princes', l. 1) turning to 'And precious perles unto his pay' ('And precious pearls for his delight', l. 1212), in which both spiritual progress and interrelationships are created in another 'endless knot'. Within these structures are others. The whole form of the poem enacts its meaning.

The diction

The diction like that of *Sir Gawain and the Green Knight* is elaborate and rich, and the word-play, sound-echoes and puns, are particularly remarkable; an example is the pun on *makeles/maskellez*. The meanings of words are strained with a wittiness that is occasionally baffling. The concatenation itself is built on multiple meanings of the same word. 'Pearl' has several meanings: as a precious stone and signifying beauty, desirability, freedom from corruption. In Latin it is *margaritas*, giving the English name 'Margery', which may be hinted at as the maiden's name. It is the biblical 'pearl of great price' of Matthew xiii, 45–6, for which a man would sell all that he has, and the poet as father is its 'jeweller', though he wrongly thinks, at first, that he owns it. The pearl is without spot, rounded as an image of eternity, an image of heaven and salvation, 'blythe of mode' ('mood'), and common to all that were righteous in life (736–9). Another word and concept of great power is that of 'courtesy', used as a link-word in the section ll. 421–80 in reference to Mary, Queen of Courtesy, empress of heaven, earth and hell, and 'courtesy' comes to mean the grace of God. Courtesy is the cause that we are all members of one body, in the Pauline similitude of I Corinthians xii, 14 ff., which we would expect to appeal to this poet.

Another notable point about the diction is that though firmly religious it is touched especially at the beginning with the warmth of the language of love in romances, just as the maiden is clad in a white dress scattered with pearls. She is as fresh as 'flor-de-lys', at the height of fashion, 'that precious sweet'. Nevertheless there is a certain rigour of style. Adjectives are not so exuberant, syntax not so widely flexible as in *Sir Gawain and the Green Knight*. The sources are mainly biblical, but the poet refers to Aristotle and some have seen reminiscences of the *Roman de la Rose*. Everything is subordinated to the grand scheme, as the individual is to his cosmic destiny.

'Cleanness': the story

The poem *Cleanness* (sometimes called *Purity*), 1,812 lines long, explores biblical imagery further in pursuit of the topic that lies at the heart of *Sir Gawain and the Green Knight*: chastity. Modern developments have so altered views and behaviour that for many people now chastity has become as meaningless as faithfulness in marriage or faith in God.

Modern people must use different symbol systems to express their sense of the meaning of life, into which ancient systems must be translated. A symbol-system is more than just that for those who believe it: it is 'reality'. God is only a symbol for those who do not believe in him. Similarly chastity is not only a symbol for integrity but also integrity itself in traditional literature. Traditionally, before the advent of scientific analysis, the world was seen in anthropomorphic terms and this meant that sexuality moulded many perceptions. In ancient societies the land's fertility was seen in terms of the king's virility. In biblical and Christian tradition idolatry is expressed as sexual sin, and idolatry is also conceived of as all the ways in which man loves objects rather than God. It became natural to associate heresy with all kinds of sexual crimes. Adultery was associated with murder. Sodomy was felt to be particularly unnatural and horrible. On the other hand marriage was used as an image of spiritual unity with God, and the highest praise of spiritual love in such writers as St Bernard and some English mystics is expressed in terms of marriage. Sexuality was also associated, as in many traditional societies, with very powerful concepts of cleanness and dirt. Chastity implied physical cleanliness, order, wholeness and holiness, and spiritual integrity, as Professor Charlotte Morse has shown. These also can be attained through ritual purification. 'Cleanness' thus becomes a highly complex concept and the *Gawain*-poet exploits this to the full. The violation of cleanness unleashes violent powers in the universe and touches on the sacred, as Professor Mary Douglas has shown. *Fylthe* is not just dirt alone, it is sacrilege. Illicit sexuality is a potent example of *fylthe* for those who, like the *Gawain*-poet, feel so ardently the interconnected passionate nature of the whole of life. Medieval society was full of the sins and crimes against chastity that the official culture abhorred. Even the religious orders whose prime commitment was to chastity were constantly and probably rightly accused of sexual incontinence, including sodomy, as well as greed and idleness. In secular life war encouraged an appalling incidence of rape, murder and theft and even in ordinary times, even in England, less violent and better controlled than most other countries, the ordinary level of disorder was distressingly high. There was thus plenty of reason for anguish, complaint, idealistic instruction and prayer, and v must see medieval literature in this setting.

'Cleanness' is the first word of the poem, and God is sa to be angry with those who, like some priests, are defile Though the poet says that there are many beautiful arg ments in favour of cleanness the poem proceeds by exampl of its opposite, for as we now realise, and the poet sensed, is by filth that divine power is seen at its most dangerou Sacrilege and sin may be imaginatively more exciting th their opposites because they break boundaries and whi destroying the old create new potentials, but the poet rejec any such consolation. He tells the parable, from Matthe xxii. 1–14 and Luke xiv. 16–24, of the Wedding Feast ar the guest who came in dirty clothes, seen in contempora terms, with the usual symbolic significance. There is r rescue or consolation for the rejected sinner. The rest of tl poem consists in powerful re-tellings of God's vengeance biblical story on the unclean, with the three major exampl of the Flood (ll. 249–544), the destruction of the cities Sodom (ll. 890–1048), and Belshazzar's feast and destructi (ll. 1333–1804). They are traditionally associated with ea other. The first two are connected already in the second lett of Peter (II Peter ii. 4–7, 19–22), and all three are connect in medieval biblical commentary. Belshazzar's sin was defile the holy vessels robbed from the Temple of Jerusale and 'vessel' was a widely accepted symbol for the hum being, into whom may be poured either filth or cleannes The poet's horrified relish for these narratives of destructio the many striking phrases, illustrate by contrast a furth aspect of the poet's interests, his passionate desire for natur order. Medieval society conceived of 'nature', the world general, as being 'naturally' good, and the 'normal' ar natural as therefore part of the moral law. In consequen how sickening (*wlatsom*) to God it was before the Flood wh men, whose only obligation was to follow nature, indulged filthy sexual practices against nature, and devils engender with the daughters of men to bring forth giants, and he w accounted best who fought the most and did the most har or as in Sodom and Gomorrah, where hospitality was violat and sodomy practised; or as with Belshazzar, whose glorio court and rich vessels were a mockery, where *lemma* ('wenches') must be called 'ladies' (ll. 1365–72), where the feast is prepared 'to serve gluttons' (l. 1505) and the place is full of boasters on benches who booze till they are drunk as the devil (ll. 1499–1501). Such perversions break the integrated order of nature. Those who cause them and refuse to repent are punished by incurring even greater disorder, the disasters of flood, fire and savage battle. There is no consolation here. Filth does not purify, and the confusion of categories that it causes cleaves in two the dear heart of that joyous (*wynnelych*) Lord who dwells in heaven and makes him angry (ll. 1806–8). Let us go clean and cheerful that he may send us grace! (l. 1811). There is a fundamental sternness here with none of the reconciliations implied in our modern literary ideas of tragedy: to put it in the modern terms that one is reminded of by the picture of devastated Sodom, no one is better off for a nuclear explosion.

The style

The chilling lesson is conveyed by the usual warmth of expression. The pathos of the Flood, the terror of the animals, the nobility of Lot, the glorious Gothic decoration of the holy vessels, and the sardonic humour of the description of Belshazzar's court, are instances of the liveliness and interest of the narration. The positive themes of courtesy and cleanness thread through the poem. The diction is as witty as ever, though the syntax less elaborate. The poem is neither nihilistic nor depressing but invigorating, though less positive and conclusive in structure than others by the same poet. It is also artistically less elaborate. The alliterative long lines are undiversified by rhyme, and though the associated episodes are significantly juxtaposed the implied propositions are not so rich as in *Pearl* or *Gawain*. *Cleanness* is the most diversified of the poet's four poems in subject matter, drawing on the Bible, Mandeville's travels (see below p. 263), and contemporary life; it is the most powerful in expression of the poet's feelings (no Narrator should be invented to deflect its impact); but it is the simplest in general effect – which is perhaps what the poet wanted in view of the point he was making.

'Patience': the story

Finally, in *Patience* we return to a more personal theme. The poem is the shortest of the four, with 531 alliterative long lines. It begins most characteristically with the wry observation that 'patience is a virtue, though it is often unpleasant'. But it often soothes when hearts are heavy from scorn. The mind, in other words, is its own kingdom. The poet rehearses the Beatitudes from the Sermon on the Mount (Matthew v. 1–11, which had also been touched on at the beginning of *Cleanness*), and then proceeds to tell the story of Jonah from the Bible with a good deal of realism, sardonic zest and humour. The point is that God was patient with both Jonah and the city of Nineveh which he had promised to destroy, and the poet takes the lesson to himself, to encourage himself to be patient in suffering poverty and in doing the will of God. It is a variant of the lesson of *Pearl*. Jonah is most reluctant to do God's will, but after a voyage and the terrible storm, described with technical precision, and a stay in the noisome belly of the whale, he is sicked up on to the shore of Nineveh and obliged to preach God's wrath. He is so successful that God forgives the people of Nineveh. Jonah is therefore furious with God and actually reproaches him for his courtesy, that key word for the poet, and for his toleration of the sins of the people.

> Wel knew I thi cortaysye, thy quoynt soffraunce,
> Thy bounté of debonerté, & thy bene grace,
> Thy longe abydyng wyth lur, thy late vengaunce.
> & ay thy mercy is mete, be mysse never so huge.
>
> [f. 88v, 417–20]

(Well did I know your courtesy, your wise toleration, your liberality of kindness, and your gentle grace, your long putting-up with injury and your delayed vengeance. And your mercy is always enough, let the offence be never so huge.)

Here God is represented very differently from the vengeful deity of *Cleanness*, because what counts is repentance from sin.

Patience and *Cleanness*, like much medieval and other traditional literature, have a moral, though are not exactly didactic. The morality does not arise from the poet himself being regarded as 'a better teacher than Scotus or Aquinas' (as

Milton says of Spenser) because a poet has the superior moral status and insight attributed to him by Neoclassical theory from Sir Philip Sidney to (in terms of the novel) D. H. Lawrence. Rather, the poet aligns himself with the wisdom and teaching of the received tradition, which he articulates and extends, but does not claim to have originated, or to be specially responsible for.

'St Erkenwald'

Another excellent alliterative poem, *St Erkenwald*, (352 lines long) has sometimes been attributed to the same poet, though the characteristic style and 'feel' are different. It appears in a separate manuscript (Harley 2250) and was written out in 1477 (as a contemporary note says), probably in Cheshire. The poem was composed about a hundred years earlier, in a north-west Midland dialect, but celebrates the London saint Erkenwald. The style is plainer than that of the *Gawain*-poet, but with some similarities of diction. The metre is well handled. The lively dialogue between bishop and judge, the vigorous presentation of civic and professional life in London, the pride in London's history, the veneration for the saint, give the poem variety, interest and weight. Why this north-west Midland poem should celebrate a London saint is a puzzle, but the fact reminds us not to over-emphasise the provinciality of alliterative poems, their poets and audiences. *St Erkenwald* is a poem that may well have been commissioned by the Bishop of London in 1382–1404, Robert de Braybroke, who established two festivals of St Erkenwald at St Paul's. The first audience might have been the Bishop, Dean and Chapter and a pious congregation at such a festival. When all is said, the London emphasis seems to exclude the *Gawain*-poet.

The 'Gawain'-poet and his milieu

Our only knowledge of the poet comes from what we can deduce from the poems. He seems well-read rather than learned, secular not religious, and a serious-minded man for all his humour. He shows no sign of a university education, nor any association either with London (unless *St Erkenwald* is his) and the new sensibility of the European great towns, or with the king's court. He is probably best imagined as a provincial *miles litteratus*, an educated knight or squire, one of the minor gentry, of which there were many scattered about the country. He might have resembled the slightly earlier Sir Thomas Gray, a border knight who when imprisoned by the Scots at Edinburgh wrote in French the immense chronicle *Scalachronica*, finished in 1362. Among such men we might think of, at a much higher social level, Henry of Lancaster, father of Chaucer's duchess Blanche. He wrote in 1352 a long French prose treatise *Les Seyntz Medicines*. He was a purely secular great lord, but the book is a series of allegories on the seven deadly sins and their cure, vividly realised in contemporary terms, rhetorically elaborate and devoutly religious, though the author refers convincingly to his own sins without undue distress. More at the presumed social level of the *Gawain*-poet was the country gentleman Robert Thornton already referred to who a little later compiled his two manuscripts in Yorkshire, in the 1440s. One is now British Library Additional 31042. It contains the only copy of *Wynnere and Wastoure* and the only complete copy of *The Parlement of the Thre Ages*, besides much else, including religious works. The other is now Lincoln Cathedral A.9 which contains the only copy of the *Morte Arthure*, as well as one of four copies of *The Awntyrs off Arthure*, a prose Alexander romance, many religious pieces in prose and verse especially by Richard Rolle, and other material. Had Thornton been an author of genius he might well have produced original works similar in type to the *Gawain*-poet, for his interests and culture were very similar. The *Gawain*-poet, a generation or more earlier, knew French well, but the native tradition in his part of the country made it natural for him to write in English alliterative verse. The milieu of such works was the network of small gentry, mingled with a few greater lords, across the Midlands and the north, from west to east. They exchanged manuscripts, often, no doubt, like Thornton, copying them themselves. Such manuscripts may be imagined as read privately, or in household groups, perhaps at such a centre as Haddon Hall in Derbyshire. The dialect of the present text of the *Gawain*-poet's works is that of Derbyshire, which was probably the poet's own dialect. At Haddon Hall the fourteenth-century dining hall is still to be seen, and is easily imagined, with its high table on the dais and other tables along the length of the hall, as the setting of Arthur's court in the poem. Behind it are the withdrawing rooms with fireplaces where the author himself, or a squire or a chaplain, might have read the poems to lord and lady, squires, attendant gentry, steward, the lady's attendants.

The fading of the alliterative chivalric tradition

There are several poems which reveal the continuing influence of *Sir Gawain and the Green Knight*, but they demonstrate a decline, and are not in alliterative verse. There seems to have been no institutional or social base to continue the tradition. The tradition of chivalric alliterative poetry lasted better in the far north and Scotland, particularly in an Arthurian vein. *The Awntyrs off Arthure*, 715 lines long, composed in the north around 1400 is perhaps the most original and best. It is in two parts. The first portrays a grim encounter by Gawain with the ghost of Guinevere's mother at the mysterious Tarn Wadling in Cumberland. The second part tells of Gawain's encounter at Arthur's court with a Scottish knight who claims that Gawain has dispossessed him. The supernatural vision and moral instruction of the first part may seem to sort oddly with the legalistic wrangle of the second. The familiar problem of unity in medieval literature arises. It is not to be solved by inventing forced connections of an organic or causal kind, but by allowing the juxtapositions and apparent inconsistencies within the poem to react upon each other in the reader's mind, out of which reaction significance arises. In this poem Gawain is the link. His attitude to life and particularly to possessions, is the theme. Meanings are created under the poet's guidance by the active co-operation of the reader's mind, working on comparisons and contrasts. The poem is more than the message on which it is based, and the message is not difficult. It is traditional and humane. Pity the poor; do not be seduced by worldly goods; but the world has much good in it to be enjoyed. The device of juxtaposition as implicit comment is here similar to the juxtaposition of bedroom and hunting scenes in *Sir Gawain and the Green Knight*, and the episodes in *Cleanness*, though the poem is not in the same class.

The later Scottish poem *Golagros and Gawain*, 1,365 lines long, has a similar divided episodic structure. The multiplicity of points of view incorporated in such poems makes their interpretation variable yet creative.

The last poem fully in the alliterative chivalric tradition is so only in a self-conscious, even antiquarian spirit. *Scotish Ffeilde* was composed to celebrate, and thus was certainly written soon after, the English victory over the Scots at Flodden in 1515, when James IV and the flower of the Scottish nobility were destroyed. The particular subject matter of the poem is praise of the noble family of Legh in Cheshire, by a gentleman who was presumably one of them. Panegyric for brave deeds is an extremely archaic theme for poetry. Such praise, coexisting with rough derisive satire, seems to be the earliest of all poetic themes. But in this case the poet was consciously imitating the battle poetry of the alliterative tradition. He was not a good poet. It is possible to praise the work as competent imitation, and we can imagine a gentleman of the house of Legh, or related to it, with literary and antiquarian interests, turning his hand to pleasing the family in a traditonal way with a traditional, but undoubtedly old-fashioned poem. It was no longer a living tradition.

The poet relies extensively on *Morte Arthure*, but has an extensive acquaintance with other alliterative poems. Such knowledge is worth remembering. Very few manuscripts of alliterative poetry have survived. There must once have been very many more. They would have been like that of the *Gawain*-poet's works, modest in size and appearance, with little or with poor illustration. In the seventeenth century they looked hopelessly old-fashioned and trivial, and unless rescued by antiquarians were used to wrap food or light the fire. This last was literally the fate of part of the famous Percy manuscript, which contains one of the two versions of *Scotish Ffeilde*.

The Percy manuscript, now British Library Additional MS 27879, is itself a rescue operation, for it was written in the mid-seventeenth century on paper. It still has over 500 pages. Some enthusiast must have copied texts from a number of manuscripts now irrecoverably lost. Besides the fuller text of *Scotish Ffeilde*, it contains the only text, almost hopelessly corrupt, of *Death and Liffe*, related to Piers Plowman (see below p. 209). Most of its 192 separate items are seventeenth-century popular ballads on medieval subjects, of variable and mostly poor quality. There is, for instance, a ballad, *Fflodden Ffielde*, also written to the glory of the Stanleys. There are Robin Hood ballads, *Chevy Chase*, ballads of Gawain, Lancelot, the death of Arthur, a poem on Merlin, part of a late romance called *The Squier of Lowe Degree*, and other 'loose and humorous songs'.

One of the new modes of feeling developing in the seventeenth-century spirit was a genuine sense of the 'pastness of the past', of its difference, consequently its interest and value. This was partly a product of, and partly a reaction against, the modernistic spirit and Neoclassical concepts. A genuinely archaic attitude feels so much at one with the past that it does not differentiate itself from the past. All exists in a timeless present to which preservation and conservation for their own sake have little relevance. Conservation is a modern concept. A spirit of conservation, nowadays sometimes condemned as 'mere' antiquarianism, begins to be found in the seventeenth-century revival of Old English, in collectors of manuscripts like Sir Robert Cotton, to whom we owe so many manuscripts in the British Library; Richard Holdsworth, Master of Emmanuel College, Cambridge, whose choice collection of medieval romances went to Cambridge University Library; and, in the eighteenth century, in Bishop Percy amongst others. Percy 'improved' the ballads he found in the manuscript to produce the famous anthology *The Reliques of Ancient English Poetry* (1765) which is at the root of so much of the revival of interest in medieval English literature, and consequently of much great Romantic poetry of the late eighteenth and early nineteenth century. Percy discovered the manuscript in the house of his friend Mr Humphrey Pitt, where the maids had begun to tear leaves from it to light the fire.

The copying out, the rescue and the editing of the poems in the Percy manuscript illustrate the development of aspects of the modern spirit which are alien to much that is medieval, but which also allow us to appreciate medieval life and literature partly for their very differences. While we can never entirely lose our archaic sense of timeless values, the critical modernistic spirit as it notices differences becomes self-conscious and relativistic. Chivalric honour, by no means entirely dead today, yet often questioned, is a case in point.

Recognition of the fading tradition of chivalric alliterative poetry has necessarily led us far into the seventeenth century and the more rapid development of the modernistic spirit. A final consideration of the absorption of alliterative poetry into other traditions of English literature must be postponed until we have turned back to the fourteenth century and have taken into account in the next chapter the work of the other great poet who uses the alliterative line, William Langland, and his followers. Langland offers a quite special mingling of the archaic and modern attitudes of mind.

10

Piers Plowman

Medieval provincial culture and the desire for salvation

THE greatest of the alliterative poems, *Piers Plowman,* which is also one of the half-dozen greatest poems in the English language, takes its origin from the West Midlands, but allies itself with all levels of English society, shows a notable interest in the poor, and rapidly moves to London and Westminster. It asks the great question that stirred men's minds everywhere in Europe in the fourteenth century; what shall I do to be saved? A valuable side light on *Piers Plowman* comes from the long contest in a small Pyrenean village on the margin of France, in the earlier part of the century – Montaillou. It was a conflict between the Inquisition and a small group of heretics centred in the village where peasants, mostly illiterate but not uncultured nor untravelled, spent the long dark evenings by the light of the fire, in rooms thinly partitioned from the beasts, eagerly discussing how their souls might be saved. There was a deep concern for pardon. The story is told by E. Le Roy Ladurie, *Montaillou* (Paris: Gallimard, 1975; English translation, London: Scolar, 1979).

Thanks to unusual documentation we get a remarkable glimpse into the daily life in Montaillou of that peasant culture which was the basis of all medieval European civilisation. The lack of social distance between the classes in small communities of peasant farmers and shepherds, with a priestly family and a few gentry, gives the village of Montaillou some representative quality, though the usually dominant influences of city and court were faint. Montaillou's culture was verbally fluent and interested in abstract thought. There was no contempt for manual labour; poverty was both abhorred and admired. The power of books was felt to be great, and there was some family and solitary reading, but there was also profound distrust of books and all authority. Within a deeply religious view of the world which we may call 'archaic' was a pragmatic human scepticism and materialism which we may call 'modern'. There was considerable questioning, for example, of the doctrine of the Resurrection (though also an eager credulity in the fantasies of astrology and the heresy of Catharism). There were blasphemous jokes, a disbelief in images. Catharism itself had a strongly literalistic bias, which took absolutely literally Jesus's injunction, 'Be ye perfect' (Matthew v. 48), to absurd and sometimes cunning and vicious extremes.

We have to make some allowances before comparing this with England. This was southern France, with a stifling social system based on house and family. England had a more flexible social structure. The village priest of Montaillou, who tyrannised the village was at the same time a clandestine heretic of vigorous sexuality – a French rather than English mixture. England had little heresy and never suffered the Inquisition, whose persecution and documentation made both the situation at Montaillou, and our knowledge of it, possible. But though nothing quite like it could have happened in England, Montaillou represents some of the general characteristic stirrings of the age in Europe in general and England in particular.

In England's looser but comparable frame, it was also at the margin, the West Midland border country, where in the latter part of the fourteenth century the literalistic Lollards found refuge; where, in the nineteenth century, Revivalism flourished, and were, even today, belief in the Devil has not disappeared. In these border regions, from where in earlier times Layamon and the *Ancrene Riwle* had come, arose an even greater and stranger writer, Langland, the poet of *Piers Plowman.* he takes up the English alliterative line and begins his poem in the Malvern Hills in west Worcestershire. One tradition places his birth at Cleobury Mortimer under the high wild heather-covered hills of Shropshire, just west of Worcestershire and the Malverns. Another gives his father as Stacy de Rokayle, one of the small gentry who lived in Oxfordshire, just to the east of Worcestershire. A group of manuscripts of the third version of his poem seems to have been written in the Malvern district. We may imagine how the current questions of the time stirred a young man of genius, in a lively, fluent, but provincial and restricted society, to question anxiously and to seek further knowledge. It is the tremendous search for salvation in the varied world, amongst its puzzles and frustrations, that the poet pursues with passion, anguish, satire, comedy, a touch of despair and an irreducible hope. His poem is a moving record and re-creation of a life-time's debates within a divided self, generated by anxiety to 'do well', to be saved, in a world full of attractions, distractions and distresses, where the poor are oppressed and corruption flourishes. His long pilgrimage, an 'anxious journey' more arduous than Gawain's, comes back to its beginning, where nothing is changed but the experience of the pilgrim, and resolution continues. Langland is enmeshed in his contemporary situation, but he reminds the reader of T. S. Eliot's intersection of the timeless moment with time, England and nowhere, reduced to a condition of absolute simplicity, in which the voyager must 'fare forward' and never cease from exploration.

The A-text of 'Piers Plowman': the story

England is, as usual, in a mess. What is the solution? What shall I, what must everyman do, to be saved? Langland wrote only one poem, but it was the poem of his whole life, growing with it. The poem must have been, in a sense, his real life. The first version is called the A-text, written probably in the early 1360s. He begins with a Prologue, both conventional and original, with a haunting first line,

> In a somer sesoun whanne softe was the sunne,
> [W. W. Skeat (ed.), (Oxford: Clarendon Press, 1886)]

but description immediately moves to action. He clad himself, he says, as if he were a *schep*. The word can mean both 'sheep' and 'shepherd', and the characteristic pun, not exactly comic but touched with self-deprecating humour, might be said to sum up the quality of the whole poem, for sheep and shepherd are a unity of opposites, are concrete realities yet potent symbols. He went in 'habit like a hermit', he says, habit indicating both dress and manner, but 'unholy of works', another paradox. He travelled wide through the world to hear of marvels, but a wonderful thing happened to him one May morning on the Malvern Hills. When tired out he fell asleep to the music of a brook on the high eastern slopes (and there are those who think today that they know the very spot). In a marvellous dream he sees a 'wilderness', the great view eastward from the Malverns, an undulating plain on which he sees men in vigorous activity about the world, ploughmen and minstrels, and winners and wasters of all kinds. It is like a Brueghel picture of small animated figures, vibrantly and often scathingly described in direct colloquial language whose poetry owes nothing to poetic diction of the kind used by the *Gawain*-poet and some other alliterative poets. On one side is a tower on a hill (perhaps Bredon Hill with its former castle) and on the other a deep dale and a dungeon – a forbidding Norman keep. As for the people in between, a few are good and ill-rewarded, most are selfish and corrupt. The descriptions become more detailed, lively and satiricial and at the end of the Prologue there is no doubt that here is England.

After the Prologue of 109 lines, the poem continues in a series of sections, varying in length from under 200 to over 600 lines, which are called in Latin *passus* (so spelt in both singular and plural) which means 'step(s)'. The more usual word for such sections is *fyttes* but this normally applies only to romances. The English equivalent to *passus*, 'pas', is used in *William of Palerne* and may have been more associated with south-western alliterative poety. *Passus*, 'steps', seems a peculiarly fitting word for the somewhat wandering but continuous advance of *Piers Plowman*, whose chief protagonist, the poet himself, is so continuously on foot in his search. The equivalent word *canto*, what is sung, as in Dante's *Divine Comedy*, is less suitable.

The poet begins Passus I by saying he will now explain what it is all about. A lovely lady in linen comes down from the castle and comments that most people, provided that they receive honour on earth, desire no more and want to hear of no other heaven. What does this signify, asks the poet, presenting in the poem a *persona* of himself as a stupid ignoramus, which belies his confidence as a poet half-a-dozen lines before. (This continual changing of point of view on the part of the poet reflects a real dividedness in him from which much of the power of the poem derives, but it requires an equal flexibility from the reader who, if he or she expects clear Neoclassical divisions and a frame between fiction and reality, may easily be baffled.) The tower contains Truth, says the lady, who created you all; the dungeon is the Castle of Care, and there dwells Wrong, the Father of Falsehood, who betrayed Adam and Eve. She herself is called Holy Church, and the poet kneels to her, asking for instruction, for, he says he has no *kynde knowynge* ('natural knowledge'). You're a 'doted daff' she says, you learnt too little Latin in your youth: but you know in your heart that you should love God better than yourself, and Truth tells that love is the 'triacle of Heaven'. The world, she implies, is always seeking for treasure, but Truth is the best treasure. How does one know Truth? By falsehood: then we slide into an account of Falsehood as exemplified in the king's court where Meed, another beautiful lady, who is partly fair reward and partly bribery and corruption, is dominant. A complicated satirical action ensues to illustrate these matters. The dream-vision finishes and another begins. In Passus V Repentance preaches 'and made William to weep', and the Seven Deadly Sins personified in various ways come to confess. The Sins are seen as people. They have abstract names but are concretely described, the most remarkable instance being the famous 'description' of Glutton, which is no confession but a visit to a disreputable London pub, whose hilarity, and Glutton's fearful hangover afterwards, are described with zest. The actuality of people here makes a striking contrast with the archaic demonic imaginations of the Seven Deadly Sins by the author of *The Ancrene Riwle,* and with the elaborate intellectual and modernistic analysis of the sins in Chaucer's *Parson's Tale*. Langland is somewhere between.

After the 'confessions' a thousand people weep and wail for their sins and enthusiastically set out on pilgrimage to discover St Truth; but there is a check – where is he? Then, without warning,

> 'Peter' quod a plough-man, and putte forth his hed,
>
> [Passus VI, 1.28, *cf.* W. W. Skeat (ed.) (Oxford; Clarendon Press, 1886)]

and he says that the best pilgrimage is honest work. This is

Piers Plowman. He may already have been a popular personification of 'the honest working man.' The peasants in 1381 invoked Piers Plowman, along with John Schep, the priest, John the Miller, John Carter, etc., and it is unlikely that such a use came from reading *Piers Plowman*. It rather shows, on the contrary, Langland's own basis in ordinary life. After asserting that the best pilgrimage is honest work, Piers in Passus VII sets everyone to work appropriate to their stations in life, for he is no revolutionary, except in so far as the insistence on good behaviour is always so. Those who will not work must be beaten by Hunger. Women must sew to make clothes, knights maintain internal order, external defence and justice, and hunt to keep down destructive animals, while Piers and the rest will get food for all. Hunger quotes the Bible to the effect that all must work either by tillage or teaching, by active life or contemplative.

The pardon

Truth hears about Piers's diligence and (Passus VIII) sends a pardon to him and all who help him, from the Pope. Even merchants receive special treatment from Truth if they spend money on good works, at which they weep for joy,

> And yeven Wille for his writinge wollene clothes; gave
> For he copiede thus heore cause, thei couden him gret thonk.
> [A viii, 43–4]

This touch of sardonic self-deprecating humour suggests that Langland had himself once been a clerk for merchants or lawyers. He cut out this reference later. A priest then comes along to read the pardon and translate it into English for Piers, since it is in Latin. Piers unfolds it, 'and I', says the poet, 'behind them both, looked at the document', putting himself into the dream. It is two lines in Latin from the Athanasian Creed, which is the long Creed sometimes known as the *Quicunque Vult* ('Whosoever wishes [to be saved]'), as it is given in the Anglican Book of Common Prayer. The Athanasian Creed was to be said daily at the service called Prime in the representative medieval service book called the Sarum Rite. The words actually quoted come at the end of the long Creed after it has related the mutually contradictory yet unified qualities of the Trinity and God's action in Christ, who suffered for our salvation, descended into hell, and will come to judgement.

> And they that have done good shall go into life everlasting: and they that have done evil into everlasting fire.

The Athanasian Creed concludes, again to quote the Prayer Book translation:

> This is the Catholick Faith: which except a man believe faithfully, he cannot be saved.

This is the context of the pardon.

Here is the crux of the poem. As the priest renders it, Do well, and God shall have thy soul; do evil and the Devil will. What sort of a pardon is this? It forgives us nothing, releases us from nothing. Piers for pure *tene*, 'vexation', tears the pardon apart, and quotes then *in Latin,* this ploughman who a few lines back knew none, from Psalm XXIII (in the medieval Latin version, called the Vulgate, Psalm XXII), verse 4: 'Though I walk through the valley of the shadow of death I will fear no evil, for thou art with me'. Such a switch in the ability of Piers to read Latin shows that here, as so often in medieval imagery, we must accept surface inconsistencies and use them as guides to the inner meaning, following the literal sense, but not literalistically. The priest has denied, quite rightly, that the pardon sent by Truth, i.e. God, is a pardon, and Piers is vexed, but immediately expresses his faith in God. Then surprisingly he says he will worry no more about his sowing, and not labour so hard, but turn to penance and prayer. The priest jeers at Piers and the noise of their interesting argument wakes the poet who in some lovely lines

waitide aboute, looked around
And sauh the sonne sitte south, evene that tyme.
Meteles and moneyeles on Malverne hulles
without food and money
Musyng on this meeteles, a myle-wei ich yeode.
thinking about this dream I went a mile
Mony tyme this metels han made me to studie dream; think
For Pers love, the plouh-mon, ful pensyf in myn herte.
[A viii, 128–33]

It is plain that the poet wants us to be puzzled, too. He

meditates on biblical dreams, as of Nebuchadnezzar and Joseph. Many a time at midnight, when men should sleep, says the poet, he has thought about the pardon and how the priest impugned it, and that Do-well is more significant than 'indulgences'.

It should be remembered here that the theory of pardons was that a man could show his proper contrition by giving money to the Church, and this would modify his pains for ill-doing in Purgatory. This was called an 'indulgence'. Granted the basic belief in Purgatory, whereby sinners after death would suffer but eventually reach Heaven, it was quite reasonable. But the system was abused. Pardons could be bought for money without the sinner really feeling contrition. They were sold by licensed Pardoners who were heavily satirised by both Chaucer and Langland, to mention only two, and the Church itself abused the system in order to raise money for good causes. The poet here reasserts his belief in pardon, and penance, real inner contrition, but denies the value of merely buying indulgences by the rich. There is no easy substitute for 'doing well'. The pardon sent by Truth is metaphorically a pardon because after all it follows the saving work of Christ, without whose sacrifice, because of original sin, any amount of 'doing well' would not save us; or to put it the other way round, we have to earn pardon, and may thus win heaven, by doing well. The question then is, what is it to do well? It is not enough, it seems, simply to carry on honestly with one's daily work, because there are so many people who will cheat and exploit. Piers responds to the intellectual challenge offered by the pardon.

Piers is not a 'character' to be read literalistically. He is an image, the leading one of many images of persons in the poem who loom up and fade away. They are as it were aspects of the poet's own mind, but they are not completely subjective, for they correspond to perceptions of external reality. They are like the characters of one's dreams, which though seemingly created in one's own mind can be surprising beyond what one could think of or expect for oneself in waking life; they can instruct, reproach, baffle, and affect the tone and thought of subsequent waking life. (Langland would have read Freud and perhaps especially Jung with deep understanding.) Piers is an archetype of general fourteenth century English thought amongst both serious-minded educated people and the ordinary peasant, yet he is also the product of Langland's creative mind. The political and religious views which Piers expresses or which are associated with him, too complex to summarise here, are new versions of old Christian truisms. They worked through the nation like a slow yeast for a couple of centuries or more.

The life of study

At the end of Passus VIII the first major movement of the poem, sometimes called the 'Visio', concludes, and with Passus IX a new movement begins, sometimes called, following some manuscripts, the 'Vita', though there is no change in quality. The poet seeks throughout a summer, asking people if any know where Do-well lives. He has a typical clash with two Franciscan friars. Then, while walking in a wood on his own, in a refreshing glimpse of nature, he pauses under a tree in a glade to 'learn the lays' the birds sing – ever an enquiring spirit! He falls asleep and dreams he meets a big man, like himself. It is Thought – his own thought – who briskly and unsatisfactorily defines Do-well, Do-better and Do-best, so that he and the dreamer argue. Then they go to Wit, a man who discourses much on good and bad actions, especially on marriage – an interesting sequel to the debate in *The Owl and the Nightingale*.

Wit has a wife, called Dame Study, who is annoyed by Wit's teaching, and delivers a tirade against men who are selfish and care for nothing but minstrels' tales while they feast. If they speak of Christ they tell blasphemous jokes about the Trinity. She is sarcastic about the folly of the dreamer. The henpecked Wit says that the dreamer had better ask Dame Study pardon, and she then graciously refers him to Clergy, arrived at by the high way of good behaviour, leaving aside, for example, riches, and the long meadow of lechery a good mile to the left. Clergy is also married to a wife, Scripture, to whom Dame Study has taught logic and music. Dame Study taught Plato to write, has taught young people grammar, and has also taught carpenters and carvers and masons. Dame Study discusses her reading. The subject of theology has vexed her; the more she works on it, the darker it seems. But, she goes on, astronomy is a hard thing, and geometry and geomancy are tricky, and if you want to do well have nothing to do with them. This is a characteristic example of Langland's associative method of progress – crabwise. The underlying development is clear enough: he is discussing the problems of learning, and expressing suspicion of useless intellectuality, all measured in relation to what it is to do well, better, and best. Clergy and his wife Scripture, like Wit and his wife Dame Study, are simple personifications – allegories. The poet puts into their mouths various comments on different aspects of the problems and themes that interest him. Provided we concentrate on what is said, and not on the 'characters', we find no difficulty. They all discuss the subjects in the same way, with the same concerns for good behaviour, or rather, satire on various kinds of bad behaviour, and with reiterated care for the neglected poor. In the end there is a kind of despair about knowing how to do well, or knowing even if it matters. 'Kingship and knighthood do not get you to heaven', says Scripture. The dreamer contradicts – belief and baptism save anyone. Scripture agrees. Also we must love everyone. Yet, says the dreamer, I am no nearer, for predestination marks the saved. (This was a great question in the fourteenth century.) We are told in all sermons to do well, but evil-doers have been saved. Also great clerks are easily led from true belief, and none is saved sooner than poor people like ploughmen, shepherds, cobblers, and such ignorant dolts.

Passus XII begins with Dame Scripture putting down her husband Clergy so vigorously that he creeps quite crushed into a 'cabin' and shuts the door and tells the dreamer to go Do-Well or Do-Wicked if he wants – whatever pleases him! The dreamer pleads with Scripture to tell him the town where Kind Wit the Confessor, her cousin, lives. Here the poet lives and suffers some years, and eats broken bread like a beggar. Then fever comes and tells him to work and pray. So he has made what is here written and other works about Piers Plowman and many other people, and Death deals him a dint and drives him to the earth.

This curious and unsatisfactory third dream reveals the poet struggling with his basic theme; what shall I do to be saved? The thread is probably autobiographical. The most likely place you could 'meet' Dame Study and Clergy and

Dame Scripture in the fourteenth century was at one of the two universities, Oxford or Cambridge. There were some advanced schools for friars, one for example in Norwich, one in Oxford itself, but Langland's obsessive satire of the friars makes his attendance at a friar's school unlikely. It would have been natural for a West Midlands man to go to Oxford, one of the most influential European universities, with several thousand somewhat unruly students, some but not all very young. Sometimes parish priests went for a year or two. Langland tells us later (C vi l. 37) that his father and relatives sent him 'to school', the usual name, as often now in the United States, for the university. There he tells us he studied the Bible, knowledge of which permeates the whole of *Piers Plowman*. The determination of Piers, after the tearing of the Pardon, to study and pray, in a sense represents indirectly the poet's recourse to the world of learning.

The university and Langland's habit of mind

At the university one began with the Arts course, comprising the *trivium* (grammar, rhetoric, logic) followed by the *quadrivium* (arithmetic, geometry, astronomy, music), all taught theoretically, not practically. After these, which took seven years, the student proceeded to theology, the analytical study of 'the sacred page'. Langland treats these subjects impressionistically, not in sequence, and it is unlikely that he waited until he had finished Passus VIII before he actually went to the university, if he did. We may suppose him to be considering, in the A-text, the *general* development of his own thought, amongst other things. It is easy to imagine what sort of student Langland would have been: eager, disputatious, discontented. The university was the highway to knowledge, but what have these intellectual abstractions, which are so complex, and make men so conceited and so flippant about serious matters, to do with practical urgent questions such as the state of the poor and the need to save one's own soul? Dame Study's progressively sceptical attitude to those sciences, astronomy, geometry and geomancy (A xi, 152 ff.) which she taught, and her absolute disillusionment with theology, illogical as they are in the mouth of such a personification, might well represent the poet's own progressively disillusioned attitude to the course. He has a strong practical bent. His mind is not abstract enough for him to be an intellectual. He hates the free play of mind. A 'modern' critical analytical attitude, as implied by the 'questions' of friars (A xi, 58) repels him; 'We murder to dissect.' He is happier with Clergy and his wife Scripture. In this respect he seems to recommend the older monastic *lectio divina,* reading the Bible uncritically but not unresponsively to feed upon it spiritually, as monks were supposed to do, though Langland typically complains that monastic life is nowadays as degenerate as that of kings and clerks. In fact Clergy reiterates the practical aspects of Do-well in the grades of the clergy, Do-best being bishops, and Scripture says nothing to the point. We may suspect that Langland dropped out of the university, if he went, in disgust.

Passus XII must have left Langland, as it leaves us, feeling dissatisfied. But he never gave up. It is likely, as we can gather from hints in later versions, that he went to London where he lived with his wife Katherine (Kit) and daughter Charlotte (Calotte). It was perhaps after being a merchant's clerk that he turned to earning a poor living as a professional beadsman, praying for souls in Purgatory, to some extent living on charity – though he scorned beggary – and kept on worrying about the problems he had already raised. Passus XII had closed up the poem because he did not at first know how to continue. But he resumed, probably encouraged by some success and interest. He abandoned Passus XII but expanded the subject-matter. He started again after Passus XI with another dream, which probably by oversight is now a dream within a dream, having forgotten to wake himself up before the new beginning. At some stage of this effort to continue he then had to go back to the very beginning of the poem and write out what was now only the first part of the new poem before the addition. He wanted to make some modifications and inevitably, being Langland, with his powerful associative faculty, one thing reminded him of another, so that as he re-wrote and modified he also expanded the original A-text, enriching an already elaborate structure. The linear development now has a series of pendants, digressions, that is, amplifications. But this image is not fully satisfactory because the pendants also relate to each other, and the result is a complicated pattern of repetitions and relationships, constantly touching on the same themes.

The B-text

With a writer so continuously re-writing his poem dates are even more approximate than usual, but probably the major re-writing was done in the second half of the 1370s, as we know from some allusions. For example, when re-writing Langland inserted into the Prologue the powerful and ambivalent political satire of 'belling the cat', which alludes to the Good Parliament of 1376. We may assume that he finished, in so far as he ever finished the new version, now called the B-text, by 1379–80, when he was around forty-five years old.

The B-text grew out of A, and is the most representative version of the whole poem. Besides his additions the poet made adjustments involving redistribution of material and renumbering of *passus*, which makes the poem more elaborate and better written but does not change it fundamentally. The same passion, the same interest in ideas which always run off into, or express themselves as, concrete particulars, the same sardonic humour, and continuously lively style, carry us on as if in a copious rough stream, with our heads not always quite above water. To take an example of Langland's method at its richest and toughest, the A-text refers scornfully to pardoners and then to priests who abandon their parishes to live in London. (Simony is bribery to get a lucrative job in the Church.)

> To singe ther for simonye, for selver is swete. [A. *Prol.*, 83]

The B-text then adds the comment that bishops and bachelors (i.e. graduates) also do the same (B. *Prol.*, 87), and serve the king as civil servants. Some serve lords, and all carry out their devotions undevoutly; one may fear

> Lest Crist in consistorie acorse ful manye. court; condemn
> I parceyved of the power that Peter had to kepe, St Peter
> To bynde and to unbynde, as the Boke telleth, Bible
> How he it left with love as owre Lorde hight commanded
> Amonges foure vertues, the best of alle vertues,
> That cardinales ben called and closynng yatis gates
> There Crist is in kyngdome, to close and to shutte shut

And to opne it to hem and hevene blisse shewe.
– Ac of the cardinales atte court that caughte of that name
And power presumed in hem, a Pope to make,
To han that power that Peter hadde – inpugnen I nelle,
will not
For in love and letterure the eleccioun bilongeth
learning; election of popes
Forthi I can and can naught of courte speke more.
Thanne come there a Kyng . . . [B. *Prol.*, 99–112]

Christ's judgement at Doomsday is seen in contemporary terms as a consistory court, i.e. a bishop's court for judging ecclesiastics, from which there was no appeal. Consistory was also the name for a council of cardinals, the highest ecclesiastics under the Pope. The Pope is the representative of St Peter, who was said to have been given the power of the keys to heaven and hell by Christ (Matthew xvi. 15). He left it with the four 'cardinal' or principal virtues, Fortitude, Prudence, Temperance and Justice (*cf.* Luke xxii. 32), the four basic virtues of classical philosophy, taken into Christianity at an early stage and seen as examples of love. There is word-play on *virtue,* for the word means both 'virtue', or moral excellence, and 'power'. Cardinals are called 'closing gates' because latin *cardo* means a 'hinge', and Langland sees the virtues as the hinges on which the gates of heaven open or shut, under St Peter's power. (Thus abstract thought moves to general and concrete.) The word *cardinal* then associates with the cardinals, in whose power was now the election of the Pope. This was a sensitive issue. In September 1378 a group of French cardinals, annoyed by Pope Urban VI's denunciation of their avarice, elected an 'antipope', a Frenchman who took the name of Clement VII. Thus began the scandal of the Great Schism when two rival Popes each claimed unique authority. The English supported Urban. Of course, says Langland, 'election' is carried out with love and learning (his two great themes), thereby ironically implying that it has not been so done in this case. He leaves the topic deliberately ambiguous here, but describes Peter's authority and the giving of the cardinal virtues later, in Passus XIX, 183–90, 274–309. Such is a sketch of the complex riches of this passage, where association of words and ideas, not logic or metaphor, provides the connections but is not merely arbitrary: it follows characteristic patterns and themes, and is based on various biblical passages. All this talk of courts is then dropped abruptly, but it is not unnatural that by associative dream-logic with courts a king should then appear, while the underlying theme of good government is pursued. This is excellent satirical, moral, political poetry. Over the density of meaning and allusion plays the light of verbal wit; the poet's deep concern is lightened but not trivialised by his sarcastic implications and by the deliberate disruption of the syntax, imitating the speaking voice. The diction relies on Latin puns translated somewhat obliquely into plain English ('closing gates'). It is learned but there is nothing aureate for its own sake.

Langland cannot resist polishing and reinforcing as he re-writes, for example in the coarse instance of popular hyperbolic speech, during Dame Study's tirade against the clever and cynical flippancies of learned men's conversation. She remarks that for all those who wish to blame the ways of God Almighty:

> I wolde his eye weore in his ers, and his heele aftwr, [A xi, 80]

which becomes:

> I wolde his eye were in his ers and his fynger after. [B x, 123]

Langland's learned ladies do not mince words.

The world and the poet

When Langland begins his great continuation of the A-text in Passus B XI, the fourth vision within the third, Fortune with two seductive damsels, one called Concupiscencia Carnis (desire of the flesh), shows him the mirror of Middle-earth. An argument over him ensues between various figures, including Elde and Holyness, which represents the way the poet, like everyone else, is torn between conflicting desires and fears about life in the world. Poverty, patience, faith and love are set against riches and learning. The figure of Nature shows the poet the glory of the world, where Reason rules all except man. The poet awakes into his previous dream, so to speak, and is met by Ymaginatif, his own faculty for thought about what is not present, the mental image-making capacity

– not Imagination in the dominant modern sense of fantasy. In Passus XII Ymaginatif in a significant passage reproaches the poet, now forty-five years old, for wasting his time in 'makings', that is, in poetry, when he would be more usefully employed praying, 'for there are books enough' (B xii, 17). Like other figures in the poem Ymaginatif reproves the poet for being too satiricial, and defends learning. This is a key passage and well represents Langland's own version of the poet-in-the-poem, to be compared with *Pearl* and *The Book of the Duchess,* not to mention Dante, Machaut and many others. The Gothic poet presents himself as of inferior status to his guide or instructor, and therefore to the reader or audience. But he also controls the audience by this device, leading them to accept instruction and guidance through their partial identification also with the poet-in-the-poem. The poet-outside-the-poem is more than himself as a figure within it, for he is represented by the other figures in the poem and the total narration as well. The naturalistic 'frame' is thus broken by the presence of the poet both inside and outside the poem, creating possibilities of irony, distance and juxtaposition of different levels of fiction. The poet in-and-out of the poem is a device rich in effect. Langland enriches it further by presenting himself both within and outside his dream-visions, which are a further level of fiction within the poem.

After encountering Ymaginatif, he awakes and (Passus XIII) goes about like a madman and a 'mendicant' (the friars too were mendicants) for many years. Then he tells us he sleeps again, and in his fifth dream goes with Conscience and Patience to dine in hall with a doctor, i.e. a learned man, a friar. This is like a little scene in a college. The 'students', the poet, Conscience and Patience, have a poor meal at the sidetables, while the doctor does himself very well at High Table and talks flippantly about serious matters, as dons will. This is sharp social comedy with a sombre base. Then Conscience and Patience meet Haukyn, who is Activa Vita, a minstrel and waferer (i.e. a maker of wafers, a kind of cook, an occupation often combined with minstrelsy in ordinary life), who represents the ordinary sinful man in the world. He may purify himself by penance and poverty. Poverty is 'a hateful good', a commonplace idea quoted in Latin (B xiv, 275 ff.) which Patience expounds.

Charity and the Harrowing of Hell

In the next dream, the sixth, the dreamer meets Anima who goes under many names; a good example of the variety with which the poet represents a single, complex, many-sided concept (B xv, 23 ff.). There is a long discussion of charity. 'I have lived in the land,' says the poet, 'my name is Long Will' (B xv, 148) 'and I have never found charity.' 'Piers the Plowman knows it,' says Anima: 'he sees into men's minds, *Petrus, id est Christus*' (B xv, 206).

The identification is not absolute; we remember Anima's variety of names. Piers is an aspect of Christ. Christ, though he is God, is fully human, the carpenter's son. It is he who exemplifies love – not the rich, the learned, the proud who to poor people 'have pepper in the nose' (B xv, 197). In the following Passus XVI comes the complicated image of the Tree of Charity, cultivated and defended by Piers, while the Devil steals the fruits. Successive aspects of the image are inconsistent with each other: the significance of the tree and of Piers changes, but the underlying themes emerge of sin, defence and redemption, and of the correspondences between the Trinity and various grades of purity of life, centred in the incarnation of God in Christ. From here on develops another theme of the progress of the liturgical year, which after the privations of Lent culminates in Easter. The poet awakes, then forgets to mention that he fell asleep again, and in his seventh vision meets a man in mid-Lent, hoary-headed as a hawthorn in blossom – it is Abraham, who also represents Faith (B xvi, 172 ff.). Another comes, called Spes, Latin for 'hope'. Faith, Hope and Charity are the three specifically Christian virtues. Faith and Hope are blended into the narrative of the Good Samaritan (*cf.* Luke x. 25), which was told in answer to the question of how to inherit eternal life, that is, how to be saved. Without the Good Samaritan, that is, active love, who is Christ, they can do nothing. After this the poet again awakes, and then we begin the great Passus XVIII. He goes forth once more, unselfpityingly, in Lent, 'wolleward and wetshoed', that is, like a tramp with no shirt between woollen coat and skin, with leaky shoes, and weary of the world. Asleep in his eighth vision he sees Christ as the Samaritan and also as a medieval knight coming to joust with the Devil, conflated with the biblical narratives of the triumphal entry into Jerusalem and the Crucifixion. It is all in time and out of time, in fourteenth-century England, in Jerusalem, in the mind, an amazing creation of unity of experience. The centre of Langland's imaginative exploration here is not the Crucifixion. He is less moved by the Gothic pathos of the dead Christ and his sorrowing mother than by the triumph of the Harrowing of Hell, of Christ the hero of an older devotional tradition. (The Harrowing of Hell was known to the Middle Ages from the apocryphal Gospel of Nicodemus of about 4000 AD which was very popular, with a number of versions in Old and Middle English.) The poet goes down into the darkness. The four maidens Mercy, Truth, Righteousness and Peace meet and talk in characteristically downright terms:

> 'That thow tellest', quod Treuth 'is but a tale of waltrot!' nonsense
> [B xviii, 142]

A great light comes:

> A voice loude in that lighte to Lucifer cryeth,
> 'Prynces of this place, unpynneth and unlouketh,
> For here cometh with croune that kynge is of glorie!'
> [B xviii, 260–2]
>
> 'What lord artow?' quod Lucifer. *'Quis est iste'* *Who is this*
> *'Rex glorie,* the lighte sone seide, *The king of glory*
> And lorde of myghte and of mayne and al manere vertues,
> *Dominus virtutum.* *lord of virtues*
> Dukes of this dym place, anon undo this yates
> That Cryst may come in, the Kynges sone of Hevene.'
> [B xviii, 314–18]

Christ says to Satan:

> The bitternesse that thow hast browe, brouke it thiselven
> brewed; enjoy
> That art doctour of deth, drynke that thow madest! (you) who
> For I that am lord of lyf, love is my drynke,
> And for that drynke today I deyde upon erthe.
> (B xviii, 361–4)

Of Langland it might well be said, 'his body thought'. The powerful ancient imagery of drinking, pervasive throughout the poem, marking the absorption and control of the sweet or bitter of life, is given new force in a plain, but exciting and noble amplitude of diction, whose concrete simplicity expresses the profoundest ideas.

The fierce exaltation of justice and righteousness is superseded by mercy and calm:

> 'After sharpe shoures' quod Pees, 'most shene is the sonne;
> Is no weder warmer than after watery cloudes,
> Ne no love levere, ne lever frendes   dearer
> Than after werre and wo, whan love and pees ben maistres.
> [B xviii, 409–12]

Bells ring on Easter morning to awake the poet, who calls wife and daughter to church with him to revere God's resurrection.

Defeat and refusal to despair

He wrote what he had dreamed, he tells us at the beginning of Passus XIX, strongly reinforcing the sense of truth discovered by meditation on experience, by 'illuminated memory'. Then the poet falls asleep in the middle of mass, and dreams, in his ninth vision, of Piers Plowman all bloody, as Christ. Conscience explains the various names of Christ, and it is essential to grasp that for Langland one name may signify a multiplicity of aspects, just as many names may signify various aspects of one thing. The literalism of 'one name for one thing' sought in the seventeenth century and later can only, in this poem, confuse in attempting to simplify. Yet another illustration of Do-well, Do-better, Do-best is found in the life of Christ. His spirit descends on Piers, who also becomes St Peter. The Church is set up as the Barn, Unity, made from the wood of the Cross. But Pope and king and commons are all selfish, will not co-operate and be just. In Passus XX the poet awakes sad and miserable, and meets Need, who attempts to console him. But he sleeps, and in his tenth vision sees Anti-Christ come, and the friars, and plague sent by Nature as a punishment. Life laughs and makes himself fashionable clothes, speaks lasciviously, thinks holiness a joke and *hendenesse* ('courtesy') a waster, begets on his mistress Fortune a bastard, Sloth. Life goes to the palace of

Revel, with Elde after him, and walks over the poet's head and makes him bald – an effectively grotesque mixture of perspectives. At the poet's protest Elde makes him deaf, and knocks out his teeth. Then the poet's wife is so sorry for him that she wishes him in heaven, because that limb of his which she loved him for when they were naked in bed is also beaten down with age (B xx, 193 ff.). Self-depreciating humour comes in together with tragedy in a truly Gothic and Shakespearean mixture. There is still no remedy but 'Lerne to love' as Nature advises (B xx, 207).

Now the assault on the barn of Unity increases. It is attacked by sins and drunken priests; friars betray it; Conscience is attacked by Sloth and Pride, and not even Contrition will help; all are bewitched by the friars. In the time of complete disaster, all have deserted. But Conscience, who represents consciousness as well as moral will, is indomitable. Unvisualised, just a name and an inner force, he is the last of the poet's many images and represents his unshaken moral determination. His speech of lonely integrity movingly concludes the whole poem with courage never to give up the search for human and divine goodness, which are comprised in the figure of Piers Plowman himself:

> 'By Cryste' quod Conscience tho, 'I wil bicome a pilgryme,
> And walken as wyde as al the worlde lasteth
> To seke Piers the Plowman, that Pryde may destruye,
> And that freres hadde a fyndyng, that for nede flateren,
> And contrepleteth me, Conscience. Now Kynde me avenge
> And sende me hap and hele, til I have Piers the Plowman.'
> And siththe he gradde after grace, til I gan awake.
>
> (B xx, 378–84)

(380 ff: . . . who might destroy Pride, and [see] that friars, who flatter because of poverty and argue against me, Conscience, may have provision [made for them]. Now may Nature avenge me, and send me good luck and health, till I find Piers Plowman. And after he cried out for grace, until I woke up.)

In just such a spirit did Blake write his lyric 'Jerusalem':

> I shall not cease from mental fight . . .
> Till I have built Jerusalem
> In England's green and pleasant land.

The C-text

Conscience did indeed keep on pilgrimage, for the poet continued to work on his poem and developed it further, using as his working copy, apparently, a manuscript of the B-text whose mistakes he often did not notice, or at least bother with. In just the same way Wordsworth kept on tinkering with *The Prelude,* the poem central to his imaginative life, for fifty years. In a similar way Tennyson began simply to copy out the poem equally important to him, *In Memoriam,* and introduced considerable revisions and deletions. Langland's further re-writing was perhaps done in the mid-1380s, and is called the C-text. The Peasants' Revolt had taken place in 1381, and maybe Langland wished to dissociate himself from inflammatory revolution. He wished also to clarify, perhaps to simplify. The C-text is less fiery. The episode of Piers's tearing of the Pardon, for example, is much toned down. This profound image of frustration will always retain an irreducibly enigmatic quality: perhaps Langland too, when he re-wrote the poem in the C-text, felt that he no longer quite understood it. But in other parts the poetic fires still flame up on familiar topics. For example, before the preaching of Conscience to the people in the A-text Passus V (which he had changed to Reason preaching in the B-text), Langland inserts into the C-text a delightful autobiographical passage (Passus VI, 1–108) about his own life in Cornhill, London, and an argument he has with Reason about his apparently idle way of life – reflecting his usual anxiety about the right kind of life to lead. Here he justifies himself as a beadsman and as a clerk who ought not to do manual labour. He makes no mention of poetry but makes the assertion, that

> in my conscience ich knowe what Crist wolde that ich wrouhte.
> (C vi, 83)

There is also a superb passage inserted after B vii, 86 (which line itself concludes a twenty-line amplification from A viii, 63), on poor labourers, which begins:

The most needy aren oure neighebores, and we nyme good hede
if we tak
As prisones in puttes, and poure folke in cote prisoners in pits cottages
Charged with children and chef lordes rente. [C x, 71 ff.

It continues for ninety-four lines. The bounds of Langland's compassion are never limited, though here as usual it over flows into satire on frauds and minstrels and workshy health beggars. The Harrowing of Hell is even more vigorous conducted in the C-text, with extra touches of deliberatel grotesque realism. Hell is prepared like a castle under siege Lucifer calls to Ragamuffin to bar up the doors, and stop al chinks against the light. Astrot (Ashtaroth) is to get th herdsman Colting and his men to drive the cattle in. Boilin brimstone (sulphur), a hellish variant on earthly boiling oil is to be prepared to throw on the heads of any who com near the walls. Strong crossbows and brazen guns are to b set ready. Mahoun is to work the mangonel (a large machin for hurling stones) (C xxi, 283–96). This is sheer exuberanc of creative associative invention. Such elaboration, known t medieval rhetorical theory as 'amplification', shows tha Langland's own temper of mind was in part the reverse o allegorical. As soon as he thought of an idea or an action, th fertility of his invention and the richness of his response t life led to the addition of concrete detail which emphasise the sense of everyday existence, and gives personality even t abstractions, or to the Devil, who was in any case in part a 'historical' figure. In this respect Langland's thought i 'incarnational'; he puts flesh on non-material realities, an he does it mainly by association. This passage was perhap the last fling of Langland's concretising associative imagina tion, indulged in out of sheer creative high spirits.

Poetry Based on association

(i) Of ideas

The process of association is particularly important in Lang land's poety, but also in all medieval poetry, though it ha been very little studied. There are two general aspects to b considered here. One is the association of ideas, arising fron mental training and personal habit of mind. The obviou example in relation to Langland and much religious poetry is the structure of associations of biblical texts with each other and with more general ideas, some of them to do with biblical exegesis. Thus the associations of Abraham with Faith, and of the three angels whom he entertained (Genesis xviii) with the doctrine of the Trinity are built up in this way, by a long tradition of biblical commmentary. Episodes concerning Abraham may be said to 'mean' these further significances while also remaining themselves. Association of ideas of a kind rather more special to Langland are the important group concerned with work, idleness, honest poverty, dishonest poverty. An example of this cluster is the amplification in the C-text of the passage concerning the pardon sent to Piers, already elaborated in B from the A-text. Thus A viii, 70, has attached to it B vii, 73–88. This was mostly cut in the C-text (B 74–7 together with a Latin quotation and 79–88), but the C-text adds the long amplification, already referred to, beginning 'The most needy are our neighbours', C x, 71–165, and another passage, C x, 186–281, including much on 'lolleres' ('idlers'). These associative 'clusters' deserve study. Only when we ourselves are used to the associations can we easily follow the line of thought, but we have to learn them because our culture no longer provides them in ordinary education.

(ii) Of things – realism

The passage just mentioned is also an example of the second general aspect of the process of association, which is association not so much of ideas as of 'things', the physical circumstances of everyday life. Langland follows in a description or a comment a sequence suggested by what would have been or could have been found side by side in actual experience; as when he says of 'lollers' that they are not found on Sundays at church, but 'I' meet them at midday, dressed in a cape, then (inevitably for Langland) as a friar, sitting in the best place at table, (C x, 242–50). Another example of association of things found together in ordinary experience is the story of Glutton's visit to the pub when he meant to go to confession, again amplified in B from A. This is the type of amplification that we later see in the C-text's addition of 'brazen guns', etc., in the scene in Hell. It is an effective device for creating 'realistic' description.

Association as metonymy

The technical literary name for association in either aspect is *metonymy*. It depends on *juxtaposition*, just as *metaphor*, from which it is at the opposite pole, depends on *similarity, likeness*. Metonymy tends to break away from intellectual pattern and often has the apparent arbitrariness and uniqueness which we find in ordinary experience. This is why it promotes 'realism'. If we do not naturally share a poet's experience – and obviously there is much that we cannot share, or know naturally, about life lived six hundred years ago – we do not easily follow what were quite natural juxtapositions for him. Hence arises much of Langland's difficulty for a modern reader, especially in the absence of a narrative. But also much of the delight of *Piers Plowman* lies in the wealth of realistic particulars connected with the general frame of reference by metonymy. Practice in reading him makes the train of association easier to follow, and uncovers an even richer texture.

Allegory

(i) Representation of intangible entities as people

Metonymy affects Langland's use of allegory, which may also be divided into two types. The first is the 'archaic' use of allegory whereby the movements of the mind, such as thoughts, perceptions and desires, are 'projected' on to the outside world so as to appear as independent people or as other entities. This is common in human thought, though it is particularly noticeable in pre-scientific cultures, hence not unreasonably called 'archaic'. Even a modern psychoanalyst writes of the virtues in as it were proto-Langlandian terms, in a rather 'allegorical', 'archaic' way, in a work that throws light on *Piers Plowman*:

> I will, therefore, speak of *Hope, Will, Purpose* and *Competence* as the rudiments of virtue developed in childhood; of *Fidelity* as the adolescent virtue; and of *Love, Care* and *Wisdom* as the central virtues of adulthood. In all their seeming discontinuity these qualities depend on each other.

Will cannot be trained till hope is secure, nor can love become reciprocal until fidelity has proven reliable.

[Erik Erikson, *Insight and Responsibility* [(London: Faber, 1966), p. 115]

Langland represents these abstractions, and others like Thought and Ymaginatif, as persons who spoke to him. Thus what is intangible, though real, takes on physical form. When this is a sin, such as Gluttony, the metonymic habit extends the description, and many details are not allegorical at all, but realistic, often satiric. The plane of abstraction is confused in theory, though perfectly comprehensible in practice, and the abstraction is vividly realised.

(ii) Representation of complex entities as people

The other general aspect of allegory reflects a move in the other direction, from concrete particulars to abstract or general names, which are then represented as persons, or from concrete to a representative action, which is then carried out by 'persons' of various kinds. This aspect of allegory works on the outside world, not on the inner mind, and one of its effects is thus to unite inner and outer. Langland knows an elaborate institution, the Church, which has many social, physical and spiritual structures, a long history, and is composed of many men and some women. He generalises from all this detail in terms of one of the Church's main functions, to guide and instruct. Of course he was not alone in this – the concept of 'Mother Church', for example, was ancient and widespread. So Langland represents the Church as a beautiful lady who gives instruction. Or he represents the general desire for money, both as legitimate reward and as bribery, as another lady; or the general conduct of ordinary men as *l'homme moyen sensuel*, a generalised person, Haukyn, Active Life. He can use such characters on the same plane of fiction as the generalised character 'king', or 'sheriff', or more generalised, 'knighthood'. The relation of characters to what they represent is both varied and shifting. Piers Plowman is thus a generalised character, 'the honest working man,' when he first appears. Once such a character appears, however, and Langland's imagination works on him, he acquires further characteristics. The honest working man becomes a figure in the poem who expresses something in Langland's own mind, his aspiration. But he also represents human nature at its best. History tells us that human nature at its best was to be found in Christ. This significance can therefore be associated with Piers. Christ's deputy on earth was first, according to medieval thought, St Peter, the first Pope, and thus Piers may represent the Pope. Eventually he represents the human goodness which Langland believes in but is hard to find. So long as we do not look for the same relationship always between a character and what he or she represents, or always for the same meaning for a character, but accept the guidance of the poem at a given point, we are usually not puzzled. Some passages, like that of the Tree of Life, will always, because of Langland's rapid switches of thought, arouse controversy in interpretation. Others, though a mixture of types of character, as when Meed rides on a sheriff, False on a juror, etc., offer no problem, and allow Langland to bring together various aspects of life, without worrying about a naturalistic imitation of life as it normally appears.

'Piers Plowman' as spiritual autobiography

The poem gives a most powerful sense of the 'ordinary' workaday world, yet it is also the only medieval poem to record the poet's own mental experiences, as it does through allegory. The poem is in one aspect a spiritual autobiography. It is perhaps curious that in the great age of English mysticism Langland is not in the least mystical, nor does he reflect anything of the richness of 'feminine' interior life. His ladies are not tender mother-figures but rather sharp-tongued English housewives who stand no nonsense from their husbands or from stupid enquirers. He has none of the Gothic sentimentality of so many poems to the Virgin or to Christ on the cross. He seems to have no sense of personal sin, even if the Seven Deadly Sins represent a kind of confession by the poet. He has what used to be thought of as a characteristically 'masculine' temperament, rationalistic, objective, realistic, extremely aggressive; yet he is forced into the inner world of the mind by the compulsions of his own convictions and by a fundamental insecurity about his own role in life. It can be argued that the richness of the interior life of women in the Middle Ages was a product of their restricted public roles. Langland, in his long robes, clothed like a 'loller', not quite a clerk, certainly not a labourer, nor a knight, in this respect on the margin of society, divided against himself, was also a product of his own choice to restrict his own public role, and to be a poet. This least feminist of poets chose to take on what was in a sense a feminine, creative, but not highly regarded role. Though it was his own choice and he continued to want it, he hated it as well. Is not the torn pardon a partly unconscious image of frustration, of disappointment with the message God sends? Surely poverty was hard to bear, when many bad men seemed to live such comfortable lives. His form of the inner life lacked tenderness to himself, and to others. The love which is his constant theme was genuine but fierce. Hence the apocalyptic tone and perhaps thought. His individuality, his need to test things for himself, his satire of and emotional independence from the church, his individualism and elevation of a purely secular image, Piers Plowman, look to the future, to the Protestant reform. His work is full of protest; but there is much that is archaic in his worship and feeling for life.

The materials of the poem

It is significant of its individualistic quality that this endlessly interesting poem has no specific source or major sources apart from the Bible and the liturgy, which themselves might be described as a major part of Langland's thought-world rather than sources. Bible and liturgy are not criticised: they are the subject of *lectio divina*, a deep well of thought, instruction, imaginative experience. Almost every sentence in the Bible has for Langland its further relationships and meanings, some of them derived from the standard medieval three- or four-fold allegorical exegesis, and generating vivid images and far-reaching implications in his meditative mind. With the Bible must be associated the sermons to which Langland often refers, and from which much of his method, material, attitudes and satire derive. Exposition of the Bible, castigation of the vices of all classes, compassion for the poor, are the recurrent themes of sermons. Langland knew the materials of the seven liberal arts and the methods of disputation as practised in the university. As a poet he knew the poems of the Western alliterative tradition, *Wynnere and Wastoure*, probably *The Parlement of the Thre Ages*, and others. Through these he knew the general tradition of the dream-vision. He must have known something of poems on the general topic of the pilgrimage of the life of man, the subject of a famous poem by the French poet Deguilleville, later translated by Lydgate. He knew the story of the Harrowing of Hell from the *Gospel of Nicodemus* in either Latin or English, and may have seen miracle plays on the subject. All this material he brought to the passionate examination of life in the world and to his own response to it in his restless wandering. He is extraordinarily original. His first greatest source is himself: 'Look in thy heart and write.' In this we note again how he reflects the new individualism of the fourteenth century. Yet his representation of the inner life is markedly externalised still in an 'archaic', concrete way that does not cut off the subjective from the objective world. He always tries valiantly to unite them: Conscience seeks Piers Plowman.

Piers Plowman is usually found in sober professionally written manuscripts on its own, or in collections, such as the huge book, Cambridge Dd. 1. 17, where a version of the B-text is accompanied by a chronicle in Latin, Mandeville's *Travels, The Seven Sages of Rome* (a religious romance) and similar pieces. It was presumably meant for use in a religious house. Altogether there are fifty-one extant manuscript copies (excluding fragments) of all three versions of the poem, some of them conflating all or two of the versions. There can be no doubt that the poem was widely read in the fifteenth and sixteenth centuries, although it was not printed till 1550 by Robert Crowley, whose motive was religious, though it was rapidly reprinted by him. The poem had come to be seen as part of the reforming movement of the Church. Caxton did not print it possibly because of its controversial and non-courtly nature (see below, p. 279). It would have been read, no doubt, by serious middle-aged responsible clerical men, religious, but not often monastic, and rarely friars. Its point of view is that of a secular clerk, with its popular elements, its sympathy for the poor and social indignation against the rich. It is no more a matter for popular tavern-minstrelsy than it is for courtier's dalliance.

Piers Plowman influenced a number of other alliterative poems. *Mum and the Sothsegger* is an incomplete satirical dream-poem, of which 1751 lines survive, concerned with good government. The author knows Mandeville (see below, p. 263) as well as Langland and was probably one of the minor gentry around Bristol about 1403–6. There is plenty of contemporary interest, and a notably charming description of a rich landscape, ll. 876–931. But there is nothing of the individualism, inner life, fire or wit of Langland.

Pierce the Plowman's Crede (850 lines) shows some natural implications of Langland's attitudes which Langland himself would paradoxically have repudiated, for it is a Wycliffite, that is, Lollard poem, (see below, p. 255), hostile to the friars. The luxury of the Dominican friars and the fat friar as big as a barrel (ll. 203–30) are satirically described. Alexander Pope once owned a copy. Even more striking is the pathos of the description of the poor ragged ploughman struggling in the mud, helped by his wife whose bare feet bleed on the icy ground, while their two small children cry at the field's end. The poem was probably composed about 1395, and two manuscripts survive.

The absorption of the alliterative tradition

Two poems show the spread of the tradition which Langland's own poem suggests. *Death and Liffe* survives only in very corrupt form in the Percy manuscript (see above, p. 178), and its 458 lines were composed some time, probably late, in the fifteenth century, perhaps in the North-West Midlands. The poem is a debate, in the line of *Winner and Waster* and *The Parlement of the Thre Ages*, between Dame Life and Dame Death. Life represents both nature and eternal life, and triumphs, through Christ, over Death. The poem is vigorous and enjoyable without any subtlety. Finally, there is a curious little poem of the early sixteenth century whose first line obviously takes off from Langland. Its nature and setting illustrate the absorption of the alliterative tradition as will be shown.

The Percy manuscript, itself an antiquarian product saved by another antiquarian, is a witness not to the survival of the alliterative tradition but of a rescue operation. Why did the alliterative line, and the style of mind it represents, decay as a dominant factor in the work of any single poet or group of poets almost as mysteriously as it appears, or reappears, in the mid-fourteenth century? The work of Dunbar (see above,

p. 138), the last significant poet to use it, offers one clue. Although Dunbar's handling is as lively and vigorous as that of any other metre or mode that he uses, the alliterative line is only one of the options open to that extraordinarily versatile poet. He uses it predominantly for coarse abuse and courtly satire, and he does not deploy to any considerable extent the characteristic themes and juxtapositions of the fully realised alliterative tradition. The heart of that tradition is a certain earnestness of purpose (with whatever incidental humour or wit) in confronting serious matters of the well-being of the soul or of society. Juxtaposition of episode, blunt argumentation, descriptions of nature, battles and courtly splendour, satire and rough humour are carried on a tide of powerful feeling and deep concern for a whole related set of values, though the public and general interest, rather than the purely personal, predominates. This bias, which accounts for so much that is good and great in the alliterative tradition, may also account for its decay. Alliterative verse, preferring inclusive juxtapositions of subject matter rather than a line of argument, may have come to be felt to be in a sense too 'poetic', or too cumbersome, too inclusive and 'archaic' a medium for the messages serious men now wished to deliver. Prose, more logical, more specialised, less musical, less difficult to compose and understand at a superficial level, came to be preferred for such serious public purposes. Rhyming verse, and later in the sixteenth century, blank verse, tended to concentrate in their turn, as had been traditional when aiming at literary effects, on personal relationships and the expression of personal feelings, especially love, which had never been a significant topic for much alliterative verse. Rhyming verse, developed in lyrics from the twelfth century, also favoured a more direct line of narrative. The five-stress lines of rhyming couplets had to wait for Chaucer. Blank verse was not developed until the sixteenth century. They are the more modern forms, and favoured more modern, specialised treatments of feeling, though there are naturally exceptions. The late short alliterative poem just referred to in its very failure illustrates the situation. Its first line clearly derives from *Piers Plowman*, reading

> In soumer sesoun, as soune as the sonne

Yet it appears in the Blage manuscript, now D.2.7 in Trinity College, Dublin, most of which comprises poems by Wyatt and his circle, lyrics of a quite 'modern' kind for all their medieval roots. The poem refers to Kent, and is quite free from regional associations. It is an obscure personal expression of jealousy in love. Subject matter and context both show the pull of what had now become, following Chaucer, the main tradition of English poetry, and the poems's own lack of success demonstrates the unsuitability of the alliterative form to such content. Many of the poems in the Dublin manuscript appear in what is now called Tottel's Miscellany, the anthology *Songes and Sonettes* (1557) which includes, unacknowledged, two poems by Chaucer, but mainly poems by Wyatt, Surrey and other early sixteenth-century poets. The Dublin alliterative poem is not in Tottel. A line of development from medieval lyrics to Wyatt and beyond is not in doubt, but the alliterative style generally represents something even more ancient, and such modernistic elements as it has are absorbed in the main stream of English poetry. The four-stress line never dies. It can be clearly heard as a powerful inner rhythm, and occasionally as a clearer music, in Shakespeare, Milton, Wordsworth, Morris, and many others. In modern times W. H. Auden, a master with something in common with Dunbar, has made effective use of it. But its supreme achievement lies in that century of so many cross-currents and tensions, the fourteenth.

A note on allegory and typology

Allegory relates to the generally symbolic nature of language and literature, and has been very variously regarded. Homer has a few characters in the *Iliad* who are neither human nor divine but are personifications of feelings, and may thus be called allegorical. But allegory is generally more of a critical than a creative habit of mind in that it has been mostly used as a device for interpreting and systematising the meanings of stories already written, which were not necessarily intended to be allegorical. Allegory evolved in the centuries before Christ with Greek critics of Homer, and among the Jews with interpreters of what Christians call the Old Testament. St Paul uses the method to interpret Old Testament story (Galatians iv. 24). These traditions were carried on and developed in the Middle Ages, becoming of extreme elaboration among biblical scholars. Biblical interpretation, called exegesis, distinguished the literal sense from sometimes as many as three other senses, given various names, but broadly representing the physical, moral and heavenly. Another kind of Biblical interpretation is known as typology, or sometimes *figura*. Certain events in the Old Testament came to be regarded as pre-figurations of events in the life of Christ, without thereby losing their own reality. Noah and the ark, Abraham ready to sacrifice Isaac, the story of Jonah, were thus interpreted. Jonah's sojourn in the belly of the whale, for example, represented Christ's descent into Hell after his death. Allegory and typology were crucial in biblical interpretation, and they had some effect on the interpretation and eventually in the creation of secular vernacular literature. Dante certainly knew about allegory and in the letter to Can Grande usually attributed to him claims to use it as a principle of construction in *The Divine Comedy*. Both four-fold allegory and typology have been used to interpret *Piers Plowman*, but without justification. Although Langland knew such biblical interpretations, uses allegorical figures, and accepts some commonplace biblical identifications and associations, he is not in general so systematic a thinker. While allegory and typology are important in the general intellectual history of the Middle Ages and especially in biblical exegesis, typology, except as an occasional echo, has little significance for secular literature. Allegory is used in secular literature to some extent but it varies according to the text and usually needs to be interpreted within terms set by the text itself.

11
Drama

The nature of drama

MANY social human pleasures and needs, such as religious and secular rituals, vivid story-telling, charades, dances, mimicry, organised entertainments at feasts, tournaments (the medieval equivalent of modern football) and processions, have something of the drama in them and affect the drama. The drama proper has a narrower definition. First, it is an action 'about' something else than itself, that is, it 'imitates' or symbolises some other action. Secondly, it involves actors as 'characters', that is, it depends on impersonation by one person of someone, or some 'thing', else. Thirdly, it is played to an audience who are to some degree detached, though their sympathies must be involved. Fourthly, it is based on words. (Mime, or dumb-show, therefore, is not truly drama.) In most cases the words, though memorised by actors, will be a written (or, of course, printed) text because that is how we know of them historically, but also because, though the drama is essentially an oral form, it needs to be fixed in the firmness and density of literacy to give it literary value. 'Ad libbing' is possible but by definition transitory.

The beginnings of European and English religious drama

Religious ritual is dramatic but it is not drama, because it is thought of as at least in part 'real', as indicated by the medieval doctrine that the consecrated bread and wine of the eucharist or mass are turned into the real presence of Christ. The congregation in church is not merely an audience because it partakes of the reality. Nevertheless Christian ritual was also obviously symbolical and thus in part fictional, for it had persons dressed up in a special way, who enacted by imitation significant stories from the Bible. These elements were attractive. In the mass for Easter Day at the church of St Martial at Limoges, in the middle of the tenth century, a small addition to the text, called a trope, was made. Priests represented the angels at Christ's tomb and in Latin asked others, who represented the three Maries come to anoint the supposedly dead body, 'Whom do you seek in the tomb, O worshippers of Christ?' ('*Quem quaeritis*', etc.) This *Quem quaeritis* trope is only minimally dramatic in any sense, but its use spread through Europe, and it was moved to the conclusion of the Easter Day Matins, where its symbolic or 'fictional' aspects were more striking. The words were slightly added to, with directions for behaviour, and this text, known as the *Visitatio Sepulchri* ('Visit to the tomb') as found in the *Regularis Concordia,* a code of monastic rules written 965–75, may reasonably be regarded as the first recorded drama text in England. After this there was a gap, while a number of prohibitions against priests taking part in mimes and maskings continued to be promulgated. Liturgical drama however was elaborated on the Continent.

About 1100 a play about Saint Catherine (*ludus de Sancta Katherina)* was put on at Dunstable by the schoolmaster of the abbey of St Albans, Geoffrey le Mans, by origin a Norman. The text does not survive and was probably in either Anglo-Norman or Latin. We know about it because Geoffrey borrowed some splendid copes from the abbey and they were accidentally burnt. In recompense he gave himself to the abbey as a monk, and eventually became Abbot (1119–46), and the spiritual friend of Christina of Markyate (see above, p. 19). St Albans had other liturgical drama, as may be deduced from parts of some of the pictures in the famous *St Albans Psalter,* which was also connected with Christina. The abbey of Malmesbury, in the west, probably had a Latin liturgical play about the journey to Emmaeus (Luke xxiv. 13–35), called *Peregrini* ('wayfarers'), as did several Continental churches.

Early plays in England

About 1150 there suddenly springs forth the brilliant *Mystère d'Adam* in French (either Anglo-Norman or Continental), with Latin stage directions. It survives in only one manuscript. The play tells the story of the Fall and portrays the sequence of the prophets in lively verse, accompanied by music, creating a remarkable range of effects. It was elaborately staged, from flowery Paradise to monstrous Hell-mouth. God wears a dalmatic, a white festal tunic worn by deacons, but also worn by medieval English kings at their coronation. Adam wears a red tunic, Eve a white dress and white silk scarf. Devils scurry and dance around. Formality and realism are subtly mixed. The play was set on scaffolds outside a church and presumably for an audience. Although the links with liturgy are strong and there is a choir, the play is a biblical story rather than liturgy and is fully drama. A little later the Latin life of Thomas à Beckett by William Fitzstephen, written 1170–82, has a reference to the many 'theatres' and saints' plays in London. What he meant by 'theatres' is hard to know, except that they cannot in any way have resembled modern ones. An Anglo-Norman play, *La Seinte Resurecion,* written about 1180, is partially preserved, and from this time there is a tantalising, scattered series of records, or references in non-dramatic works, which suggest a widely dispersed and increasing number of plays. Specific records are inevitably ecclesiastical. In the thirteenth century some great cathedral churches had their liturgical plays – only Salisbury in the south, but in the north and east, Lichfield, York, Lincoln and Norwich. A famous anecdote in the Latin life of St John of Beverley tells how one summer's day, around 1220, a boy climbed into the triforium inside Beverley Minster to look through a window at the play (about the Lord's resurrection) taking place outside in the churchyard. He fell to the floor, but he was unharmed and the accident was recorded as a miracle. Had this not happened we should not have known about the play. It may well have been in Anglo-Norman. No texts survive of such plays except a Latin *Visitatio* and 'Harrowing of Hell' from the Benedictine nuns at Barking. These plays were instituted by the Abbess Katherine of Sutton (1363–76). An Easter play which is part of a processional text from the church of St John the Evangelist in Dublin also survives. Some ecclesiastical authorities were suspicious of the drama, and in the thirteenth century there are ecclesiastical prohibitions (for example in Bishop Grosseteste's decretals of 1236–44), forbidding clerks to take part in various secular festivities and in 'miracles' – presumably miracle plays. The prohibition proves the practice, and in favour of it was the opinion of the greatest of scholastic philosophers, St Thomas Aquinas, who refers about 1270 to actors. He judges that play is a necessary social activity (*Summa Theologica* II ii, Question Cl XVIII, Article iii, Objection i).

The first dramatic texts in English are secular

In the light of this ambivalence towards the drama it is not surprising, though the fact has often been overlooked, that the first dramatic text in *English,* the language of the secular, unofficial culture, and of the great majority, is actually a secular, amusing 'interlude' or little play, about a clerk seducing a girl, *Interludium de Clerico et Puella,* written about 1275. It is unfortunately incomplete but it is clearly the same story, sometimes in the same words, as *Dame Sirith* (see above, p. 78), though here the old woman is called Mome Elwis, 'aunt Elwis'. *Dame Sirith* may well itself have been the text for a minstrel's mimed performance – the 'gleeman with his bitch' in Langland's sarcastic phrase (*Piers Plowman,* B v, 404). There are other semi-dramatic lyrics in the form of a wooing dialogue between a clerk (one might better think of 'clerks' as 'students') and a girl, where the girl is persuaded without too great difficulty. All make a witty use of the clichés of romantic love – the clerks will die, they are so wretched for love, the lady is so bright, let her only have pity. *De Clerico et Puella* is as it were a vaudeville sketch, closely allied to dramatic monologues and popular narrative songs of love and sex.

Such pieces must have been written by wayward clerks and are usually written on the backs or margins of ecclesiastical manuscripts primarily dedicated to loftier or at least more serious purposes, such as religious observance or getting money. The Cambridge Prologue (Cambridge University Library Mm. 1.18.f.62r) is appended to a list of saints' days, and the Rickinghall Fragment (British Library Additional Roll 63481 B) is written on the back of an account roll of the abbey of Bury St Edmunds. The Cambridge Prologue, eleven four-stress couplets long, composed towards the end of the thirteenth century, seems to have preceded a play about an emperor in a ranting style and calls on the audience for silence, not to spoil 'our game'. It exists in two parallel but not exactly similar versions, in Anglo-Norman and English. The Rickinghall Fragment, of two tail-rhyme stanzas in Anglo-Norman and their partly deficient equivalent in English, is by a curious coincidence also an extract of a king's ranting speech. These and a few other fragments and references bear witness to the variety of dramatic activity around 1300. Accident has preserved no masterpiece.

The fourteenth-century growth of drama

From about 1300 onwards references are more frequent and allow us to deduce the existence of both religious and secular plays. The Latin liturgical plays probably included, as on the Continent, the subjects of Herod, the Prophets, the Shepherds and the Wayfarers. There were numerous plays of saints' lives. There were 'miracles', which may have been the same, or may have included religious drama more generally, since, as we have already noticed, descriptive names for types of writing in the vernacular were vague. There was little sense of *genre*. Besides religious plays there were the 'interludes' and probably more serious secular plays.

The Pride of Life

An example of a serious secular play is provided by the second earliest drama text we have in English, *The Pride of Life*. It was composed about 1350 and hastily written out, probably in Dublin, in the early fifteenth century, on the back of an ecclesiastical account roll. *The Pride of Life* is 502 lines long, written in quatrains, and begins with a 'Prolocutor' or spokesman, who describes the King of Life and calls on the audience for quiet. Then the King speaks boastfully to his knights, Strength and Health. His Queen warns him to beware of death and the fate of his soul and calls in the Bishop, but the piece stops, incomplete, with the King still ranting. It is strange that three early pieces (Cambridge, Rickinghall and *The Pride of Life*) all appear to have so similar a topic. The chief point is that a king symbolised 'everyman', as in the familiar portrayals of Fortune's wheel, depicting the ups and downs of a man's life in the form of a king first rising then falling on the wheel. From this point of view all life is tragic, as the Christian message accepts, while at the same time asserting that such acceptance is itself also a release, and that death is the gateway to true life. In this world anything that in a once fashionable phrase 'makes for life' must also make for death, as medieval authors well realised. *The Pride of Life* is therefore in potential a meditation on death, with a mixture of symbolic and 'real' characters, King, Queen, Bishop, with more allegorical ones, the two knights, Strength and Health. The piece is interesting and vigorous, but it has not developed the power of allegory to represent the drama of the inner life as was achieved by the much later *Everyman* (see below, p. 227), though it resembles *Everyman* in its general message. The importance of *The Pride of Life* lies more in marking an early stage in drama than in what it is. The curious mixture of 'real' with allegorical figures and the essentially secular setting recalls the roughly contemporary Langland, but the comparison shows how elementary is *The Pride of Life*, how powerful and rich in meaning is Langland.

Developing biblical dramas

The religious drama was developing at the same period. A partial set of plays in the Shrewsbury Fragment combines the Latin of the liturgical drama with translated passages in English. As in several other cases the manuscript (Shrewsbury School VI) gives one actor's part and only the cues from other parts, but the three subjects of the Shepherds, the Visit to the Tomb, and the Wayfarers to Emmaus, are clear. There is a striking resemblance between parts of the Shrewsbury fragment and the York Shepherds' Play. The mixture of Latin and English in the Shrewsbury Fragment and its relation to the play in the York cycle suggests that it is part of an evolution from liturgical drama to biblical cycle. This evolution in the north Midlands is also suggested by the Cathedral Statutes of Hugh of Nonant, bishop of Lichfield 1188–98, which refer to performances of the same three episodes, a grouping apparently unknown elsewhere in England. The process of the gradual Englishing of groups of biblical dramas arising out of the liturgy suggests how the more extensive cycles of dramatised biblical stories naturally developed. The Shrewsbury Fragment was actually written down early in the fifteenth century, but a mid-fourteenth-century date of composition seems reasonable to suppose. Also about 1350 the Corpus Christi Guild of Cambridge had a *Ludus Filiorum Israelis* ('a play about the Children of Israel'), whose text is lost and could have been in Latin, French or English, but which must have had an Old Testament basis. This may be the earliest example of the secular sponsorship of a religious play, though no doubt the author was a cleric. Thus biblical plays, as well as morality plays, were beginning to build up in English from about the middle of the fourteenth century.

Varieties of dramatic experience

About the same time another strand of drama, less serious, appears in Exeter. Bishop Grandisson in 1348 called on the archdeacon and dean to stop a group of men calling themselves the 'order of Brothelyngham' (a brothel at this date meaning 'good-for-nothing', not a 'bawdy-house') who sported about the streets in monk's habits, captured people and made them pay ransoms, and set up a lunatic fellow as abbot in the 'theatre'. Grandisson wrote 'They call it a *ludus* but it is sheer robbery'. Such sport is as much folk-lore as drama, but in 1352 the Bishop had to write again to prohibit the performance of a harmful play, *ludum noxium,* in the theatre, as it was a satire against the cloth-dressers, and was causing great disturbances. The Bishop speaks strongly if generally about the lubricious play and the culpability of the actors, though it is hard to tell if they were professionals. In the 1340s secular theatrical costumes also appear in manuscript pictures.

There was surely a growing crop of drama from the mid-fourteenth century at least, for in the 1370s, that most vigorous and flourishing period of English literature when poetry and prose burgeon in so many ways, the drama also flowers, if we may judge from the number of references to various forms. The poem *Sir Gawain and the Green Knight* written about this time, refers to 'interludes of Christmas' (1. 472) and these may well have been amusing little secular plays, like those called interludes in the sixteenth century, or even more elaborate set pieces. In Paris there were extremely elaborately staged mini-dramas performed at royal feasts in

1378 and 1389 which Chaucer either knew, or knew of similar examples in England. On 1 May 1371 the town council of King's Lynn paid 3s. 4d. to players *(ludentibus)* as well as to minstrels *(menestrallis)*, which suggests a troupe of travelling actors, and they paid the same fee to *ludentibus* for an interlude on Corpus Christi Day 1385. We do not know what sort of plays they acted.

Meanwhile not only were such semi-dramatic performances as those of minstrels, masked dances and even organised tournaments, developed, but in an age which loved dramatic ceremonial there was an increased use of tableaux and 'street theatre'. An English example is Richard II's entry into London in 1392, where the streets were brilliantly decorated, and painted allegorical figures and tableaux were placed along the route, giving loyal messages. The whole affair was described in a long poem in Latin by Richard Maidstone, Richard's friar-confessor. Such ceremonies and processions were not the less artistic for being ephemeral. They involved great organisation, remarkable artistic direction and huge expense, but alas they are now almost as if they had never been. The written word survives longer; we now find increasing references to performances though we still have to wait for the texts.

In 1378 Wyclif refers to a 'Paternoster Play' at York, in which vices and sins were held up to scorn and virtues praised. It was written in English apparently by a friar, or perhaps sponsored by the friars. It was obviously a morality play, and other examples are known in France and referred to later in England. In the 1370s also now come quite specific references in records to the play-cycles, based on the Bible, generally known as 'miracle plays', which in the fifteenth century come to constitute the great substance of surviving English vernacular medieval drama, at York, Beverley, 'N. town' (unknown; once thought wrongly to be Coventry, the text of whose plays is sometimes referred to, from the name of the manuscript, as the Hegge plays). In the last decades of the fourteenth century there were well-known performances in London at the Skinners' Well where, for example, in 1384 'the clerks of London' staged an extremely elaborate play or plays which lasted five days. They also played in 1390, and 1391 when they were paid £10 by order of Richard II, who may have found that the drama appealed to his own histrionic and extravagant temperament. In 1393 the clerks staged the ever-popular 'play of seynt Katerine', and in 1407 a seven-day cycle covering the history of the world from Creation to Doomsday before an audience of nobility and gentry. This reference brings us fully to the range of the miracle plays preserved only in late manuscripts from more northerly cities. In the late fourteenth century began the upsurge of vernacular drama and from this point the number of references is too great and various to be summarised.

The settings and stagings

The settings in which this great variety of drama was performed varied equally. We need to place ourselves in imagination in various places and with the expectations of varying audiences. The earliest liturgical dramas took place in churches, which were both sacred and practical, stangely splendid, yet familiar and subject to the casual uses of a village hall. We may imagine ourselves in a stone building grander than any other building we know, with echoing space. We are to some extent participants in a stylised but not fictional re-enactment of an actual historical event of supreme importance not only now but for eternity. It would be dark, but beautiful with candlelight, stately, hieratic, calm, hopeful and yet based on suffering. By the thirteenth century, as we know from Beverley, there was a difference. The Resurrection Play was in the churchyard in summer, with crowds of spectators among the graves, children running around inside and outside the church, the play probably on a temporary platform, the actors familiar persons but dressed in fine robes, with Christ perhaps played by a young local parson. If the play was not to be in the churchyard then some relatively clear space easy to get at was needed – the market place, or a field on the edge of a town, perhaps with old earthworks from which the audience could see better. We know from the sketch accompanying the morality play *The Castle of Perseverance*, composed 1405–25, that a large circular area was needed for performance of this play. It required five platforms, partly enclosed like large booths, called 'scaffolds'. In the centre was a representation of a castle. The play was an elaborate affair, needing twenty actors or more, probably travelling professionals. It must have been like a big circus coming to town and must surely have attracted not only a large crowd but all sorts of hangers-on, temporary cook-shops and taverns, pedlars, minstrels, tumblers. Though it is a serious play, with the usual serious message about vice, virtue and death, it has a Gothic admixture of rough knock-about comedy which enhances the sense of festivity, but also promotes greater detachment.

Also in the open air and even more elaborately staged were the Biblical play-cycles rapidly developing from the late-fourteenth century, though scholars are far from agreement about the place and manner of staging. Probably all possibilities were at some time tried. Often the 'pageant wagons' were the basis of performance and the plays were sometimes called pageants. The wagons, which were large farm-carts, were given superstructures of one or occasionally even two storey. At one extreme some have thought a whole line of them moved round the town (particularly York), each wagon carrying a play which was performed at a stopping place, then moving on to be done again at the next stopping place. If this was indeed done it required formidable organisation and at some places the performances seem on some occasions to have taken up to three days. There were thirty-eight guilds which produced 'plays and pageants' at Beverley. At the other extreme plays have also been thought to have taken place in a particular area with stationary scaffolds. Some scholars have thought that the wagons moved but that for the purpose of the plays they were drawn up to and thus extended by other wagons or fixed scaffolds. At times the action spilled over on to the ground and among the audience, as revealed in the Coventry Nativity play stage-direction that Herod shall 'rage' in the pageant and also in the street.

Not all drama was out of doors. The interludes referred to in *Sir Gawain and the Green Knight* were presumably held in hall, as the Parisian ones of 1378 and 1389 (above p. 219) certainly were. When small troupes of wandering actors in the fifteenth century visited great houses, castles or monasteries, it would be natural to play in the hall, but the texts for such plays are rare until the sixteenth century. The earliest seems to be Henry Medwall's *Nature* (*c.* 1495). Some plays might be played in the courtyards of such inns as the fifteenth-century New Inn at Gloucester.

The actors

Who were the actors? There were troupes of professionals. Medieval churchmen knew and mainly condemned a considerable class of medieval 'entertainers', who included actors of some sort, striptease artistes, minstrels, tumblers, jesters, mimics, comics. Envy in *The Ancrene Riwle* (see above, p. 23), may be portrayed as a contemporary semi-professional comic. Some of this interesting riff-raff may well have developed into the small troupes of actors whose existence can be deduced from the fifteenth century onwards, though no names are known: they were the medieval forerunners of Dickens's Crummles family in *Nicholas Nickleby*.

Far and away the vast majority of actors were amateurs. In the early liturgical plays they were clerics, but the great development of the miracle plays depended on lay management and lay actors. The evidence from the Continent is more specific, and in England much of the evidence is from the sixteenth century, but it is clear that many people, often educated and well-to-do, were (as today) very eager to act. Chaucer was a bit of a snob in these matters, and in *The Miller's Tale* it is Absalom, village barber, surgeon and scribe, also parish clerk (another part-time layman's job), who in order to show off sometimes plays Herod 'upon a scaffold high' (*CT* I, 3383–4). The miracle plays really took off when the Church invoked the trade guilds to organise them. An enormous amount has been written on this topic and the records are rich and fascinating, though with serious gaps. By the third quarter of the fourteenth century the guilds were well-organised groups of tradesmen, quite well-to-do citizens, who in the case of London were of vital importance to king and court. They were religious as well as secular in interest, mutual insurance societies both for this world and for the next. They kept accounts and we learn all sorts of interesting details about the costs of wagons, robes, Hell-mouth, Heaven, etc. As far as possible each guild was responsible for the play its craft could best produce; which play would the Waterleaders and Drawers of the River Dee produce in Chester but Noah's Flood? (But elsewhere, for equally obvious reasons, it was the Carpenters.) At Chester the Last Supper was produced by the Bakers, the Harrowing of Hell by the Cooks. Often, of course, there could be no correspondence.

Not only townspeople wished to act. There was a long tradition of 'mummings' and 'disguisings' at courts, and often interludes must have been acted by courtiers, although in the fifteenth century small itinerant groups of professionals seem to have appeared. The youthful Thomas More while a page was notable for his ability to step in amongst the players of an interlude, presumably professionals, and improvise a part within their play, meanwhile illustrating the presence of both amateur and professional actors at court.

The authors

Who wrote the plays? Sir Thomas More was believed to have written comedies in his youth, but if so they have not survived. We may remember that the text of a play, except when written by a genius, is to the total work of art much as the libretto is to an opera (whose stylised conventional form has a good deal in common with medieval drama). The morality plays, being more analytical, are in a limited sense more 'modern', more concerned with the individual than other plays; the text tends to be more original, and it is not surprising that they are the first to have a named author in Henry Medwall. He was chaplain to Cardinal Morton, Archbishop of Canterbury. In the sixteenth century the few morality plays were written by Skelton and Bale, both clerics, and by the Scottish courtier Sir David Lindsay. Presumably their equivalents wrote the earlier plays, but though such a poet as Chaucer had a remarkable dramatic flair the drama did not attract him as a form, nor did it attract the other great writers. The drama only became fully secular in the sixteenth century. It may have been a friar who wrote the York 'Paternoster Play' and such a man, or a local parish priest with talent, must have been the type of those who wrote the texts of the miracle plays. On the margin of the drama Lydgate, the famous Monk of Bury (see above, p. 131), wrote various 'Mummings' for City of London companies. He was an exceptional man, ready to attempt almost any written form, but even he did not try an actual play.

Morality plays

The substantial texts of plays fall into several classes, liturgical and church drama, interludes, moralities, miracles. The liturgical and church drama, being in Latin and rarely written in England, must be left aside here. The secular interludes, having briefly surfaced with *De Clerico et Puella*, do not reappear until the very end of our period, with Medwall's *Fulgens and Lucres* (*c.* 1497) an historical interlude surviving in a single manuscript copy. There are only six medieval morality plays, not all complete. *The Pride of Life* (*c.* 1350), is a fragment. *The Castle of Perseverance* (1405–25), and *Mankind* and *Wisdom* (both *c.* 1460–70) survive only in the Macro MS, though a fragment of *Wisdom* appears in Bodleian MS Digby 133. The fifth morality play is Medwall's *Nature* (*c.* 1495), and the sixth is *Everyman* (*c.* 1500), the first to survive only in printed texts. The influence of the plays extended far into the sixteenth century, for some knowledge of them seems implicit in Marlowe's *Dr. Faustus* with its Good and Bad Angels, and in Shakespeare's recognition of Falstaff's similarity to the comic yet evil Vice, but they are of small bulk compared with the Biblical drama.

The morality plays seem essentially to have been written each by a single author (though drawing heavily on mystical writings in the case of *Wisdom*) and they arise out of the didactic purpose of dramatising the internal moral drama of Everyman at the crisis, or in the light, of death. In *The Pride of Life* man is represented by a king who rejoices in life and challenges death, and the characters speak lengthily and without much dramatic interplay. Much more powerful is *The Castle of Perseverance,* 3,649 lines long, in which the traditional *psychomachia* (the battle in the soul between virtues and vices), and also much didactic and devotional writing, have been thoroughly digested to create a large-scale elaborate action. The manuscript contains a famous plan of how the play should be staged, with five scaffolds and a castle within a large circle. The action covers the spiritual biography of Mankind's life, as he comes under the influence of his Bad Angel and is subject to the three kings, the World, the Flesh and the Devil. The play is carefully patterned with fifteen bad against fifteen good characters, speeches balanced, and the scaffolds symbolically placed, in the East for God, South for Flesh, West for World, North for Belyal (the Devil) and North-east for Covetousness. The North was traditionally the abode of Satan and the bad angels, and in the East lies Jerusalem, the Holy City. The scaffolds were outside the circle which marked the playing area, the spectators were inside, and the Castle of Mankind at the centre, with a bed for Man at the base, under which the character Soul could hide until his time came to rise. So the spectators were closely involved with the action, which has a strong clear story-line and culminates in the attack by the vices on the Castle.

This involvement in common humanity's general predicament is the strength of the play. Without being great poetry the speeches, in fairly regular rhyming stranzas of thirteen lines, express much of the common currency of everyday action which sustains the relatively simple moral points which the allegorical characters convey. Thus Sir Covetyse welcomes the other six Deadly Sins:

> Welcum be ye, bretheryn all,
> And my systyr, swete Lecherye.
> Wytte ye why I gan to call? — Do you know
> For ye must me helpe and that in hy. — quickly
> Mankynde is now com to myn hall.
> [M. Eccles (ed.), *Castle of Perseverance, The Macro Plays* (EETS 262,1969), 1019–22]

There is lively argument at the assault. The bad characters as usual have the more amusing lines, but the good characters are not without dignity and power, and Mankind expresses effectively a range of feelings.

Wisdom, 1163 lines long, in rhyming stanzas, portrays the struggle between Christ (who is Wisdom) and Lucifer for man's soul. The play is lively theatre, with four processions, wild dancing of six men with red beards, a comic-horrible abduction by Lucifer, various maskers. But verbally it is dull, its many borrowings from devotional writings unassimilated.

Mankind, 914 lines long, in a variety of stanza-forms to some extent adapted to speakers, is the first English play where the text mentions the gathering of money from the audience, and was probably played by professionals in inn-yards, or even indoors, in villages near Cambridge and in Norfolk. There are seven parts, five of them wicked and amusing, including the devil Titivillus, all fighting against the rather dull Mercy in order to get Mankind. Surely someCambridge clerk wrote this. After a solemn opening speech by Mercy, Myscheffe bursts out,

> I beseche you hertyly, leve yowr calcacyon, threshing
> Leve yowr chaffe, leve yowr corn, leve yowr dalyacyon. chattering
> Yowr wytt ys lytyll, yowr hede ys mekyll, ye are full
> of predycacyon. preaching
> But ser, I prey this questyon to claryfye:
> Mysse-masche, dryff-draff,
> Sume was corn and sume was chaffe,
> My dame seyde my name was Raffe;
> Onschette yowr lokke and take a halpenye. open your lock
> [M. Eccles (ed.), *Mankind, op. cit.* 45–52]

To this irreverent word-spinning, punning half-nonsense, in which the popular and proverbial is comically mixed with learned 'aureate' words, Mercy later replies stuffily:

> Avoyde, goode brother! Ye ben culpable
> To interrupte thus my talkyng delectable. [64–5]

The popular, sometimes scatological vigour of speech combined with all sorts of tricks, make this amusing play highly successful. Mankind is passive but the vices busy enough. Mankind is saved, but the edification is less memorable than the comedy.

Everyman, 921 lines long (*c.* 1500) in many variously rhyming stanzas, by contrast makes no such appeal to the popular taste for coarseness. It is austere, without wasted words, dramatically effective in the interplay between Everyman and the series of 'characters' who visit him. After God has spoken a prelude Death appears, and then as Everyman enters, hails him with the summons to God to make his reckoning. Everyman's surprise and increasing reluctance and alarm are well conveyed and impossible for the spectator not to share. Everyman seeks help from the good things of this world, Felawship, Kinrede, Goodes, Knowlege, Beaute, etc., but after protestations of loyalty and help, they immediately deny him.

FELAWSHIP: Now in good faith, I will not that waye.
But, and thou will murder, or ony man kill
In that I will help thee with a good will.
[D. Bevington (ed.), *Everyman*, in *Medieval Drama* (Boston: Houghton Mifflin, 1975), 280–2]

The irony is heavy and not particularly naturalistic but makes the point well. Will Cosyn go? No, he has cramp in his toe, and like others, in a more delicate irony, he uses in departing the common phrase commending him to God which has now real meaning for Everyman. The text has many similar felicities. The pressure of inexorable human loneliness and inevitable responsibility for one's own life builds up. Knowlege says:

Everyman, I will go with thee and be thy gide,
In thy moost nede to go by thy side, [522–3]

Who cannot be moved by such powerful simplicity? More moving still is that it is not true. But Knowlege does lead to Confession, who gives absolution from sin after satisfaction that includes self-flagellation, and it is this release that allows Good Dedes to rise. Knowlege, Five Wittes and Discrecion give good advice, and Knowlege gives religious instruction. Even so, none will go with him when it comes to the crunch, except Good Dedes. All else is vanity; but Good Dedes is enough to carry the soul to where angels sing.

This excellent play, proved by many modern performances, well illustrates how analytical and abstract powers can be embodied in an allegory which is totally unrealistic and yet (within the cultural assumptions) completely convincing. The play may be a translation of a Flemish play *Eckerlyc* ('Everyman') first printed in 1495; or the Flemish play may derive from *Everyman*; scholars are divided. In either case it remains a small masterpiece. All the morality plays draw their sharpness from the contemplation of death. Nowadays modern psychology recognises how powerfully the knowledge of death operates even in our modern secular culture, to the extent that one best-selling populariser, Dr E. Berne, remarks that all our lives are preparation for our deathbed scene. However that may be, *Everyman* gains from its sober confrontation with death exclusive of irrelevant comedy, and by the positive creative spirit, and ultimate hope, with which death is met. It is entirely free from the morbidity of much other late-medieval spirituality.

The allegorical figures in *Everyman* may be regarded in one sense as creations of the mind of the protagonist, much as such figures of fairy tales and other traditional stories are in part projections of images in the mind of the protagonist (see Derek Brewer, *Symbolic Stories*). *Everyman* achieves real psychological drama. The inner strength of the morality plays lies in that achievement. The limitations are the rigidity of the allegorical figures (contrast Langland's use) and the unduly simple narrative. A more complex story (as even a fairy-tale is) demands less schematised characters. *Everyman* rises above the limitations of personification allegory and simple narrative by its austere acceptance of them and the vivid verbal realisation of human feeling, but the general form was not itself fruitful. Henry Medwall wrote a long morality play, *Nature*, 2,860 lines long, in two parts, which was designed to be played in a hall, but has no special interest. In the sixteenth century the allegorical form of the morality play was used for mainly historical and political purposes by Skelton, Bale and Sir John Lindsay, continuing the secularising trend, but it never became popular.

The secular play 'Dux Moraud'

A quite different fifteenth-century play, secular, moral, not allegorical, and hard to classify and date (say *c.* 1400), is the strange *Dux Moraud,* written in a fifteenth-century hand on the back of an early fourteenth-century assize-roll from East Anglia. The text is only a fragment of Duk Morawd's own part, but the story is know from several Latin and English versions, the closest to the play being a poem in English, extant in three manuscripts. This popular little story tells of an incestuous daughter who kills first her mother, then her child born of her father, and finally, because he repents, the father, Duk Morawd himself. From the poem we learn that the daughter then goes to another country, lives as a prostitute, repents, dies and is forgiven. This latter part conforms to the pattern of a number of female saints' lives, as for example St Mary of Egypt, and it is interesting to find it grafted on to the former part which is a very clear version of 'the family drama'. The love-hate felt by the protagonist towards the parents is known to everyone, and this story is a particularly violent rendering of such feelings, with an interesting religious solution. What we have left of *Dux Moraud* does not suggest a very sophisticated play, and it has been preserved by the merest accident, but the story is powerful, and how many other simple melodramas based on universal human feelings may not have been played in fourteenth- and fifteenth-century England of which no trace survives? They may well have provided the tilth in which the seeds of such great versions of the family drama as *Hamlet* and many other Shakespearean plays were rooted.

The miracle plays

Popular as the miracle plays were, even the more substantial cycles survive in only a single fifteenth-century manuscript each for York, for the Wakefield plays (known as the Towneley manuscript), and for the N-town plays. Chester alone is rich with eight manuscripts, two late-fifteenth century, six late-sixteenth or early-seventeenth. The Chester plays, though rather more subdued in tone than the rest, attracted great loyalty and only stopped when suppressed by the Government in the late sixteenth century. How great our losses are. There were certainly cycles of miracle plays now lost at Beverley, Coventry, Ipswich, Kendal, Louth, Newcastle-on-Tyne, Norwich, Preston and Worcester, as well as the plays at Skinners' Well in London, and doubtless elsewhere. The spread is well illustrated by the survival of the playing text of a Cornish cycle written in Celtic, though its date is uncertain and other details lacking. However, of the survivors, Towneley borrows some plays from York, and it may be that many sets of plays were interlinked by borrowing or adapting passages or whole plays, much as the many manuscripts of sermons were copied from each other to constitute 'families' of texts with individual variations and original developments. The structure of the play cycles, with from twenty-four to forty-eight short plays each (in the surviving manuscripts), allows both for copying and for local variation.

Terminology

The medieval terminology – *ludus, pagina, pagenda, play, pageant* – is characteristically inclusive and inexact. However the plays began (probably from several causes), they became associated with the Corpus Christi Day procession, that characteristically Gothic form of social artistic celebration. The feast of Corpus Christi had been instituted in 1264 to focus attention on the sacrament of the mass, and depending on the variable date of Easter was celebrated between May 23rd and June 24th. The festival took time to gather popularity but was flourishing by the 1370s, and the combination of religious festivity, procession, summer weather, and the independent growth of interest in plays created the play-cycles. The play-cycles came often to be called Corpus Christi plays because they were played *on* that day, though they were not written *for* that particular feast. They were also traditionally called 'miracles' or 'miracle plays', since they portrayed the miracles of God in history. The word seems to have been in frequent medieval casual use to mean 'religious plays' generally, as when the Wife of Bath tells us she went to 'pleyes of miracles' (*Wife of Bath's Prologue* III, 558). (The term 'mystery plays' arises in the eighteenth century out of confusion with a French usage and has no justification either from medieval usage or as modern clarification.) A number of 'non-cycle plays' and fragments, including one on a biblical story, Abraham and Isaac, might have been played at any time of the year, outdoors or in, and are independent of feast and procession.

Growth and structure

The drama needs stories, and the miracle plays told Bible stories. The stories were selected for their significance in the medieval view of salvation history, not for their literary or dramatic quality. The tremendous saga-like narratives of the Old Testament, surely amongst the greatest stories of the world, secular or spiritual, were almost entirely disregarded. A limited cluster of plays focusing on the Nativity and Resurrection as emphasised by the liturgy has already been described. It seems reasonable to suppose that these plays suggested, perhaps independently to a number of separate people in different places in the second half of the fourteenth century, in both England and Europe, that a further set of scenes should portray the life of Christ. Although the ultimate origin was liturgical the purpose became not liturgical but instructive, and the miracle plays are almost certainly part of the general programme of instruction of the laity by the Church in the later medieval centuries, perhaps connected with the friars, for the miracle plays are written for, but certainly not by, 'the people'. What is remarkable is the alliance of Church with people in terms of the lay organisation of plays with a religious message. The plays themselves are well described by Rosemary Woolf as 'speaking pictures', and she compares them with the many religious pictures portraying episodes from the life of Christ, using well-established symbolism, and expressing an archaic sense of a timeless present, with consequent vivid anachronistic realistic detail.

Plays about Adam and Eve and the procession of the prophets had existed from the twelfth century. Plays on other separate biblical episodes, like that of 'The Children of Israel' produced for the Cambridge religious guild of Corpus Christi, existed elsewhere. When authors wished to add to these and group them together, they used various structural principles. One was typology. Certain Old Testament figures and scenes were regarded as particularly important because they were regarded as 'types' or 'figures' foretelling in their own historical reality the saving work of Christ and the Church (see above, p. 211). Such were Noah and the Ark, and Abraham and Isaac. A second structural principle may have been the desire to illustrate the ages of the world, a concept found in St Augustine, who saw ten ages, though later chronicles saw only seven. The first age is from Adam, the second from Noah, the third from Abraham, fourth from David, fifth from the captivity in Babylon, sixth from Christ, the seventh from Doomsday. This may have been more implicit than conscious for many people, but it expresses that sense of the cosmic story unfolding its significance through the activities of individual human beings from before Creation to Eternity, historical yet also timeless, which is one of the great underlying concepts of the miracle plays. The history does not depend on the clockwork regularity of measured time. Chester has five plays from the Creation to Moses, then moves straight to the Nativity. Towneley has eight Old Testament plays, then begins the Nativity sequence with 'Cæsar Augustus' (another ranting king, reminding us of the popularity of such a figure in the morality plays).

'Speaking pictures'

The artistic sequence of the plays is very Gothic, a series of 'speaking pictures', partly a procession, partly like a series of sculptured or painted scenes, both realistic and symbolic. They indicate a complex intellectual concept of the 'real' world as lying 'behind' appearances, but they also portray the details of normal material reality for their own sake. The connection between the separate plays is not causal; one only leads to the next in a most general way. The connection arises from the intellectual system below the surface. Each scene speaks direct to us – it is both in and out of time – hence the free use of anachronism, Old Testament characters swearing by the Trinity, shepherds referring to contemporary situations, and the use of contemporary realistic detail. Such qualities as the causally connected plot, characterisation in depth, and the general plausibility of the well-made Neoclassical play are not sought. Action dominates, not personality. Characters are stylised, and the main effects depend on the significance of the action in relation to the whole. The scenes are cumulative; meaning is created by correspondence and juxtaposition, not cause and effect. The action is not a completely self-enclosed fiction, for characters may speak to the audience which thus to some extent participates in the drama. Some degree of literalism and dramatic illusion was of course provided, and was responded to by the literalistic criticism of conservative churchmen in earlier centuries, and of Lollards at the end of the fourteenth, who condemned the falsity of representations which were necessarily fictional. But there was an underlying sense (as there must always be in drama) of 'game' which is neither true nor false, having its own self-sufficient reality, allowing symbolism to be real yet not the same as ordinary reality, allowing realism to create a sense of everyday 'reality' yet still to be part of the world of the 'game'. The separate plays of course achieve very varied effects. The astonishingly ambitious representations of

Creation are highly stylised. The representations of the Crucifixion are painfully realistic. There are different degrees of the mixture of symbolism and realism, and different degrees of success.

Multiple authorship

The plays are also very Gothic in that they are the product of multiple authorship. In each cycle several writers must have cobbled up, or replaced, or inserted, additional plays. The clearest example is the so-called Wakefield Master who wrote, as internal evidence reveals, only six of the Towneley plays, including two Shepherds' Plays. Five other Towneley plays are very closely related to York plays, and probably based on them. Other Towneley plays are by less distinctive, different hands. In addition the cycles reveal their traditional character in their use of similar sources, for example of the English poem known as *The Northern Passion*, or in reflection of the influence of the lyrics (in both cases especially in the Crucifixion scenes), of sermons, folk-dramas, popular burlesques, proverbs.

The mixed nature of the tone

The mixed nature, or to put it another way, the lack of decorum, of single tone, in these plays is very Gothic. Dignity is soon followed by coarse comic blasphemy, pathos by grotesque devilish buffoonery, adoration of a child by the absurd yet dangerous rantings of a king. At one extreme is the beginning of the Chester cycle, 'Pagina prima', or first pageant, 'The Tanners' Play', in which God speaks solemnly, stiffly, learnedly, in self-descriptive manner characteristic of the non-naturalistic basis of these plays:

> I ame greate God gracious
> which never had begyninge.
> The wholl foode of parente is sett
> breed of parentage is contained
> in my essention, essence
> I am the tryall of the Trenyte. triple quality
> [R. M. Lumiansky and D. Mills (eds.), *The Chester Mystery Cycle*, vol. I (EETS, 1974), p. 1, 5–10]

This is neither clear not poetic. It makes no concessions to a supposedly ignorant populace, but is uncompromisingly theological and intellectual. Yet it is spoken by an actor playing an old white-bearded man in a long white dress, from the highest point of a scaffold on a cart. At the other extreme is the blasphemous comedy of the Wakefield Master, who is the most lively and dramatic, and by no means the least devout, of all the dramatists, writing about 1420–50. In the play 'Mactacio Abel' (The murder of Abel) Cain is a surly farmer who bullies his cheeky boy Pikharnes (literally 'steal-armour,' i.e. one who strips the dead of their armour; a very abusive name for a thief). The play begins with the boy's instruction to the audience to be quiet, with comic abuse, and here as elsewhere there is no pretence, as there is in Neoclassical drama, that the play takes place without an audience. Caym is angry with Abel and he speaks with brutal coarseness:

> Com kys the dwill right in the ars! devil
>
> [A. C. Cawley (ed.), *The Wakefield Pageants* (Manchester: M.U.P., 1958), I, 287]

God addresses him reproachfully from above, to which Caym replies:

> Whi, who is that hob over the wall?
> We! who was that that piped so small? Hey!
> Com, go we hens, for parels all; perils
> God is out of hys wit!
>
> [297–300]

This is both amusing and horrific.

The Wakefield Master also wrote the play of Noah, which has some delightfully stylised shipbuilding, as well as beginning with a fine extended solemn prayer of Noah to God. The play also includes the rough popular comedy of Noah's shrewish wife, who for long refuses to enter the Ark while both he and she variously address the audience. The Flood is naturally highly stylised in symbolic representation, interesting to contrast with the description of the same event in *Cleanness*. The gamut of mood and style in this one play is astonishing – it has everything except simple naturalism. Moreover behind all this lies the generally available though unexpressed concept of the episode as a 'type' of the Redemption, where the Ark stands for the saving Church.

The Wakefield Master did not write the Towneley Abraham and Isaac, which is incomplete. Though it is without the power and implicit Kierkegaardian irony of the Old Testament original, it has genuine pathos of parental feeling: 'What shall I to his mother say?' says Abraham, on the point of slaughtering his beloved son. This was a favourite scene and there are separate versions of it both in the Brome manuscript and in a manuscript miscellany deriving from Northampton – six versions in all, counting those in the four extant cycles. They merit close comparison with each other and the Old Testament source. Obedience, parental feeling, pathos, joy, all seen in fully human terms, form the characteristically Gothic sequence.

Among the Nativity plays we find the ranting Herod who became proverbial in Hamlet's phrase 'to out-Herod Herod'; a comic scene in which Joseph, an old man, believes that Mary has betrayed him with another; various brutal scenes of the Slaughter of the Innocents (sorrow for death of children must have been one of the commonest medieval emotions, and was one to which religion particularly addressed itself); and above all the Adoration of the Shepherds. Worship of the new-born child is one of the most fundamental and inspiring of human feelings in all times and places: in the miracle plays it is realised with unsentimental tenderness, which worthily releases the cosmic joy and hope given by the Christian Christmas message. The most remarkable versions are by the Wakefield Master, who wrote two Shepherds' Plays, in a style which ranges from high religious meditation, with Latin quotations, through tender diminutives addressed to the Christ-child, to witty and vulgar colloquialism – all in a crisp, complicated, unique rhyming stanza. In the first play, 'Prima Pastorum', the Shepherds are vividly realised in their blunt dramatic interchanges, remarkably evocative of the ordinary life of toil and chat and food and drink. One striking passage is an elaborate traditional jest about imaginary sheep, and another is about a rich meal which is equally imaginary. The power of mind over matter and over the essential physical basis of life (two essentially medieval concepts), are both poetically and strangely conveyed in this popular symbolism. Then the Shepherds sleep, are awakened by the song of angels, and then make their symbolic gifts to the baby that is lord of heaven and earth.

In the Second Shepherds' Play, 'Secunda Pastorum', most famous of all, this forerunner of Shakespeare reveals his deep feeling for popular folk-tale tradition, and a daring constructive power, in the famous preliminary episode of Mak and his wife. The grumbling Shepherds are again most realistically evoked. They visit the shady character Mak, whose wife has a new-born 'child' in the cradle, which turns out to be a stolen lamb. The comic yet not blasphemous parallelism with the Lamb of God, traditional name for Christ, is unmistakable. The dramatic talent for farce is equally delightful, and farce itself, its joy, its partial inversion of worldly values, becomes part of the Christmas message. Mak is tossed in a blanket as a punishment. The shepherds then sleep, and are wakened by the angels' song, to which they respond in a way appropriate to the religious story, rather than as realistic characters. When the first shepherd tries to sing, the second says,

We fynde by the prophecy – let be youre dyn! –	
Of David and Isay and mo then I myn	more than I remember
Thay prophecyed by clergy – that in a vyrgyn	learning
Shuld he lyght and ly, to slokyn oure syn	get rid of
And slake it,	relieve
Oure kynde, from wo;	nature
For Isay sayd so:	Isaiah
Ecce virgo	*Behold a virgin*
Concipiet a chylde that is nakyd	*Shall conceive*

[Cawley, *op. cit.* 674–82]

They offer to the divine child a 'bob of cherries', a bird, a ball for him to play tennis – gifts charming and realistic (up to a point) themselves, but not naturalistic, and with symbolic overtones of fertility (cherries in the depth of winter), of spirituality (the bird), of power (the ball as orb, the image of kingship) and yet also of play, the ball representing an activity purely gratuitous, human and childish.

The Passion Plays the climax

These must serve as representative examples, and we leave aside plays on the earlier life of Christ. The Wakefield Master wrote no Passion Plays, unfortunately, but the Passion Plays are, as in the Gospels, the climax, the whole point of the story as viewed in the paradoxical light of the Resurrection, which gives the Passion significance and hope without depriving it of pain and horror. The narrative in the cycle-plays owes much to contemporary affective devotion in such works as the Franciscan *Meditationes vitae Christi* and the religious lyrics. But the cycles vary in details of treatment. Only the N-town cycle figures Satan extensively, for example, suggesting Continental influence, while Judas, though never merely villainous, is more fully and subtly treated in York than in Chester and Towneley. York and Towneley give Pilate a more extensive part than the other two; in York he is assimilated to the figure of the ranting king; in Towneley he is thoroughly evil. But all plays exploit the buffeting of Christ as a cruel game of blind man's buff, in a way apparently peculiar to the English tradition, while the almost complete silence of Christ throughout his sufferings, though part of the devotional tradition, achieves on the stage its most powerful effect. The late-medieval devotional tradition and many sermons elaborated in an often morbid way the detailed accounts of the actual flogging, and the nailing of Christ to the Cross which the stage-representations make even more vivid and yet actually less morbid. This lack of sentimentality is in part achieved by the inevitable consciousness of fiction, but more profoundly by the callous jesting and chat of the soldiers (*milites*), so representative of ordinary human insensibility. The York crucifixion (by the Pinners and Painters), the work of the so-called York Realist, accompanies harrowing details of the tearing of Christ's body to fit the Cross with cheerfully comic colloquial dialogue. Christ in response finally utters the noble words derived ultimately from the Lamentations of Jeremiah, here of course given new force, combined with words from Luke xxiii. 34.

CHRIST: Forgiffis thes men that dois me pine
What thay wirke wotte they noght. do not know
Therfore, my Fadir, I crave,

Latte nevere ther sinnys be sought
But see ther saules to save.
1 MILES: Er, harke! He jangelis like a jay. *1st soldier; chatters*

[Bevington, *op. cit.* pp. 577–8]

The sharp juxtaposition of nobility and contempt, dignified speech and colloquial proverb, divine and human, horror and jest, realism on a non-naturalistic base, make these Passion Plays the acme of the Gothic style, and though not the greatest works of medieval English literature, give them peculiar power and force. What other style could hope to render even half so effectively the amazing paradoxes and (whatever one's view of the ultimate truth) the unquestionably world-changing power of the Passion story?

The pathos of the burial, the stirring scenes of the Harrowing of Hell, which Langland perhaps remembered, the wonderment of the Resurrection, and the solemnity of Doomsday, lightened by the comic horror of the devils, are variously and dramatically achieved with multiple effect, and effects, of Hell-mouth, and appropriate costumes, which bring a remarkable series to a remarkable conclusion. As Rosemary Woolf points out, the English custom of ending with the Last Judgement, as Continental plays did not, distances the audience. Christ speaks to characters on the stage, not to the audience. The play moves into a different dimension in time. In one sense what was a tragedy is turned to comedy in the medieval meaning of the word, a tale with a happy ending. One of the most characteristic effects of high Gothic literature is the ambivalence which both distances the audience yet forces the reader to take some decision or action in response to the work.

The end of the plays

It is natural for an art-form to reach a climax and then for creative forces in a new age to turn to other related but different channels. The miracle plays remained popular in the sixteenth century. Shakespeare probably saw some. Their basic conventions and Gothic mixed nature characterise much sixteenth-century drama, including Shakespeare's. But religious change and Government hostility ended them. Even if not stopped they must have faded before the great powers of Neoclassical education and thought. Fine as they are, much in them is not only of an older 'archaic' world, but is actually naive and simple, especially at the level of style. Yet seen in their appropriate context, religious and social as well as literary, taking into account other biblical plays, the many saints' plays (of which only two in English survive), the moralities, the interludes, and remembering all the rich effects of staging, costume and music, we may well think that England has never since medieval times achieved so generally rich a drama, so central and enhancing to the national life, except in the plays of Shakespeare, which are themselves in nature so medieval.

12

Later religious prose

The nature of prose

PROSE is the index of civilisation, requiring literacy as verse does not. It both depends on and creates relatively settled conditions, an organised society, an education system, control of the technology required to produce writing materials, and capacity to store and utilise what is written. Prose is particularly concerned with utility, and is closely connected with the beginning of utilitarian documentation about 1200. It would be long before English culture would use prose for entertainment; but utility in a pre-scientific 'archaic' world includes religion and the life to come. Because religion also calls for imagination the most imaginative prose was for long religious, and of this the best is the prose of the mystics.

Richard Rolle

Richard Rolle is the first English mystic to write extensive prose. He was a Yorkshireman born about 1300 at Thornton-le-Dale near Pickering. The language of most copies of his work remains northern, with, for example, distinctive long *a* for southern long *o*, the present participle ending in *-ande* for southern *-ynge*, etc. His father was a small householder. He went to Oxford, became disgusted, borrowed two of his sister's skirts and his father's rainhood, and thus in a makeshift 'habit as a hermit' ran away to an enclosed life in a cell in the house of one John Dalton near Pickering. Here and in other places later he wrote a series of devotional works in Latin and English and eventually became the most influential of English mystics. He may have studied for a while at the Sorbonne in Paris. The early works in ornate Latin prose give a few biographical anecdotes and observations that reveal a passionate, irritable young man, highly sensitive to sexual temptation but determined to live chaste and to devote his whole life to contemplation. He felt very early the mystical and joyous sense of inner warmth, to which later was added the sense of exquisite mystical song, about which he often writes. Sweetness, warmth and song are the subject of his famous Latin work *Incendium Amoris* ('the Fire of Love'). His English works are written for devout women, and he had a considerable following especially in the north, though not only of women, for many works attributed to him appear in Robert Thornton's manuscript now in Lincoln Cathedral. After many moves he came to live near a community of devout women at Hampole in Yorkshire and died in 1349. His works continued to circulate for almost two centuries.

His first English work is a Commentary on the Psalter, translated from Latin authorities, with some interesting remarks about translation (H. E. Allen (ed.), *English Writings,* Oxford: Clarendon Press, 1931, p. 6). His *Meditations on the Passion* and the epistles to individual women, *Ego Dormio* ('I sleep'), *The Commandment of Love,* and his last work, *The Form of Living,* are enthusiastically written with the warmth of personal conviction. He emphasises devotion to the holy name of Jesus and the importance of meditation on the Passion of Christ. Here we have the intense imaginative exploration of biblical event that arises out of *lectio divina* (see above, p. 192) and was widely spread through meditative practices throughout Europe in the fourteenth century. The product of such meditation when written is no 'imitation of life', no historical reconstruction, but an attempt at imaginative creative realisation, comparable with the paintings and drama of the day. Thus, one of a series of paragraphs on the Passion runs:

> Ah, Lord, thi sorwe, why were it not my deth? Now thei lede thee forthe nakyd os a worm, the turmentoures abowtyn thee, & armede knyghtes; the prees [crowd] of the peple was wonderly strong, thei hurled thee and haryed thee so schamefully, thei spurned thee with here [their] feet, os thou hadde ben a dogge. I se in my soule how reufully thou gost. Thi body is so blody, so rowed [raw] and so bledderyd [blistered]. Thi crowne is so kene [sharp] that sytteth on thi hed. Thi heere [hair] mevyth with the wynde, clemyd [clotted] with the blood. Thi lovely face so wan & so bolnyd [swollen] with bofetynge and with betynge, with spyttynge, with spowtynge. The blood ran therewith,

that grysyth in my syght [sickens me to see]. So lothly and so wlatsome [disgusting] the Jues han thee mad that a mysel [leper] art thou lyckere [more like] than a clene man. The cros is so hevy, so hye and so stark that thei hanged on thi bare bac, trossyd [tied] so harde.

[*Meditations on the Passion* in Cambridge University Library MS LI, i 8 (a collection of devotional writings) f. 202v, *cf.*, Allen, *op. cit.* p. 21.]

Rolle was typical of the religious attitude of the time. Contemporary paintings and drama, as well as the lyric, also set out to create the same apparently realistic moving scene. Rolle's style is deliberate, insistent, the vocabulary full, the syntax repetitious, as its purpose requires; alliteration is used for further emphasis. The meaning is clear, the subject matter potent. This exercise in sympathy for the sufferings of another is one of the most important aspects of Gothic Christianity; when that other, who is represented in so pitiable a degree of inferiority, is also believed to be God himself, maker of the whole universe, the paradox is shockingly powerful.

Rolle creates an emotional imaginative world built from, yet transcending, the present world. *The Form of Living* begins as a kind of analysis of temptations, sins and means to overcome them, in the tradition of *The Ancrene Riwle*, though written in a less racy style, but when he comes to the climax of love he evokes an enthusiastic rapture foreign to the wryly perceptive, more wary tone of the *Riwle*. It is remarkable that for all the distrust of sex the essential image for union with God is sexual love, and indeed marital sexual love. The soul is the *bride* of Christ. For ecclesiastical as for secular official medieval literary culture marriage was normally seen as the supreme expression of stable loving personal relationships. Such marriage is warmed and lit by love.

Luf es a byrnand [burning] yernyng in God, with a wonderfull delyte and sykerness. God es lyght & byrning. Lyght clarifies oure skyll [reason]. Byrning kyndels oure covayties [covetousness] that we desyre noght bot hym. Lufe es a lyf [life] copuland togedyr the lufand and the lufed. For mekeness makes us swete to God, purete joynes us tyll [to] God. Luf mase [makes] us ane [one] with God.

[*The Form of Living*, Cambridge University Library, MS Dd. v. 64, iv f. 17v–18r., *cf.* Allen, *op. cit.*, pp. 108–9.]

This work was apparently written originally for a disciple, the recluse Margaret Kyrkby, but was often copied and sometimes adapted to others, or excerpted.

'The Cloud of Unknowing'

Not every devout person in the fourteenth century was so effusive as Rolle. The author of *The Cloud of Unknowing*, written about 1380, is himself unknown, but was probably a recluse or priest in the East Midlands who took a much more austere line, practising and recommending the Negative Way that derived from the works of the pseudo-Dionysius the Areopagite who was probably a Christian Neoplatonist of the early sixth century. His works, including the *De Mystica Theologia*, were translated from Greek to Latin by various translators from the ninth century onwards, and interacted profoundly with later Latin writers. His essential idea was the absolute unknowability of God. In order to reach to an experience of God the mind must be emptied of all images. The author of the *Cloud* translated the Latin text of the *De Mystica Theologia* as *Deonise Hid Divinite*, as well as two other mystical works in the same tradition. He wrote three other original works of the same nature, but the *Cloud* is his great achievement.

Of its dominant image the author writes early in his treatise:

> & wene [think] not, for I clepe [call] it a derknes or a cloude, that it be any cloude congelid of the humours [moistures] that fleen in the ayre, ne yit any derknes soche as is in thin house on nightes, when thi candel is oute. For soche a derknes & soche a cloude maist thou ymagin with coriouste of witte [inquisitiveness of mind] for to bere before thin iyen [eyes] in the lightest day of somer; and also ayenswarde in the derkist night of wynter thou mayst ymagin a clere schinyng light. Lat be soche falsheed; I mene not thus. For when I sey derknes I mene a lackyng of knowyng; as alle that thing that thou knowest not, or elles that thou has foryetyn, it is derk to thee, for thou seest it not with thi goostly iye. & for this skile [reason] is it not clepid a cloude of the eire, bot a cloude of unknowyng, that is bitwix thee and thi God.
> [Harley 674 f. 28b; *cf.* P. Hodgson (ed.), *The Cloud of Unknowing* (EETS, 1944), 218, p. 23.]

The author is cautious about meditation on positive things, as on the Passion:

> Wepe thou never so moche for sorow of thi sinnes or of the Passion of Criste, or have thou never so moche mynde of the joyes of heven, what may it do to thee? Sekirly [Certainly] moche good, moche helpe, moche profite, and moche grace wol it gete thee; bot in comparison of this

> blinde steryng [stirring] of love, it is bot a litil that it doth, or may do, withouten this. This bi itself is the best partye of Mary withouten thees other.
>
> [Harley 674, f. 37b–38a; Hodgson, *op. cit.* p. 39.]

(According to medieval biblical exegesis 'Mary' represented the life of contemplation, Martha that of action; *cf. Luke x. 38–42.*) The author also warns against self-deception in the matter of spiritual warmth. With Rolle it is often difficult to know whether he is speaking literally or metaphorically of sweetness, warmth and song. By contrast, the author of the Cloud emphatically distinguishes several times between the literal and metaphorical or, as he terms it, bodily and spiritual ('gostly') senses. He recognises literalism in order to reject it. Writing of young men and women 'new set to the school of devotion' he remarks that they hear this sorrow and this desire read and spoken of, namely, how a man shall lift up his heart to God,

> & as fast in a curiouste of witte thei conceyve thees wordes not goostly [spiritually], as thei ben ment, bot fleschly and bodily, and travaylen [afflict] theire fleschly hertes outrageously in theire brestes, & what for lackyng of grace, that thei deserven, & pride and curiouste in hemself, thei streyne here veynes & here bodily mightes so beestly & so rudely that withinne schort tyme thei fallen outher into werynes . . . or elles thei conceyve a fals hete, wroght by the feende, theire goostly enmye, causid of theire pride and of theire fleschlines and theire coriouste of wit, and yit, paraventure [perhaps] thei wene [think] it be the fiir of love.
>
> [Harley 674, f. 63b; Hodgson, *op. cit.* pp. 85–6.]

He has rather satirical passages about those who take literalistically the word *up,* for example, as describing the place of God and heaven.

> Thees men willen sumtyme with the coriouste of here ymaginacion peerce the planetes & make an hole in the firmament to loke in thereate. These men wil make God as hem lyst [as pleases them] & clothen hym ful richely in clothes, & set hym in a trone, fer more curiously than ever was he depeynted in this erthe. Thees men wil maken aungelles in bodely licnes, & set hem aboute ich one with diverse minstralsie, fer more corious than ever was any seen or herde in this liif.
>
> [Harley 674, f. 75b; Hodgson, *op. cit.* p. 105]

Such words should be borne in mind when we admire the

glories of medieval and renaissance painting, or respond to the realistic imagery of some devotional writing.

The author of the *Cloud*, as Professor Hodgson shows, follows St Augustine and many others in insisting more than pseudo-Dionysius on the power of love: 'Lift up thin herte unto God with a meek steryng [stirring] of love; & mene himself & none of his goodes' (Harley 674, f. 24b; Hodgson, *op. cit.* p. 16). This is the work most pleasing to God, in which all saints and all his angels rejoice, which maddens devils, and wonderfully helps all men living on earth. The 'naked intent' of the soul towards God is an intent of love 'beating upon the dark cloud of unknowing'. Mystical prayer is itself an act of love, ultimately rewarded, though the ecstasy itself should not be regarded as the aim.

> Than wil [God] sumtyme paraventure seend oute a beme of goostly light, peersyng this cloude of unknowyng that is bitwix thee and hym, & schewe thee sum of his privete [secrets], the whiche man may not, ne kan not, speke. Than schalt thou fele thine affeccion enflaumid with the fiire of his love, fer more than I kan telle thee, or may or wile at this tyme.
>
> [Harley 674, f. 50b–51a; Hodgson, *op. cit.* p. 62]

The prose is strong, flexible, well-controlled, with a full vocabulary entirely adequate to its recondite subject matter. It is paradoxical in that it creates an austere rational world of desire that goes beyond rationality. The author shares the basic commonplaces of contemplation with Rolle, but develops them very differently. He shares with Langland and many other clerics a distrust of the dissecting analytical mind (which he calls *coriouste of ymaginacion* or *witte*) but his injunction to empty the mind of images is the very opposite of Langland's 'incarnational' habit of mind. Yet the *Cloud* too has its appropriate imagery, occasionally realistic and thus satiric and amusing.

Walter Hilton

Lack of space prevents adequate treatment here of another mystical writer, Walter Hilton (d. 1396), whose principal works, *The Scale of Perfection* and *The Mixed Life*, which exist in numerous manuscripts, still await full scholarly editions.

He also wrote *Of Angels' Song* as a warning against incautious mystical dabblings. Hilton was a Cambridge graduate who eventually, after an apparently unsatisfactory period as a recluse, became an Augustinian Canon at Thurgarton near Southwell, in the East Midlands. His writing is sensible, balanced, rich in illustrative imagery, as of the allegory of the pilgrimage to Jerusalem in the second part of *The Scale* and in many brief similes and parables.

Julian of Norwich

Much less popular in her own day, more significant to ours, was Julian of Norwich. On 13 May 1373 in Norwich, when she was thirty-and-a-half years old, she had a series of mystical visions which she called 'showings' or revelations. Probably not long after, she wrote an account of them. When she had them she was probably a nun, but at some later period she became a recluse at St Julian's Church at Conisford near Norwich, which still exists (though her anchorhold is gone) and she died as an old woman of considerable local reputation some time after 1416. She spent much of her religious life contemplating the nature of her revelations and re-wrote them in expanded form perhaps twenty years later, in this respect recalling Langland's life-long brooding over his dream-visions as first recorded in the A-text.

After an editorial paragraph written in 1413 the sole surviving manuscript of the short first text recounts in the first person singular how this devout woman Julian desired three graces from God: to bear in mind his Passion, to have bodily sickness, to have three wounds. We find again the *memoria Christi*, the imaginative act of being present at the Crucifixion and sharing the sorrow of those present. The sickness was desired so that life should not be too attractive and in order to make a good death. The wounds she desired were those of St Cecilia in her neck, but Julian understands them metaphorically as contrition, compassion and longing for God. (That love is suffering is a commonplace of both religious and secular literature.)

On 13 May 1373 Julian had all the symptoms of what would in modern terms be described as a severe heart-attack, and she and everyone thought she was dying. But miraculously she suddenly felt well. She says she thought to have Christ's wounds and desired no bodily vision, yet:

> sodaynlye I sawe the rede blode trekylle downe fro undyr the garlande, alle hate [hot], freschlye, plentefully and lyvelye, ryght as me thought that it was in that tyme that the garlonde of thornys was thyrstede [thrust] on his blessede heede.
> [British Library Additional 37790 f. 98v; E. Colledge and J. Walsh (eds.), *A Book of Showings to the Anchoress Julian of Norwich* (Toronto: Pontifical Institute of Medieval Studies, 1978), I, p. 210]

The sense of confusion, absence of antecedent explanation and refusal to adorn with realistic detail, authenticate the visionary experience. A little later (and again the circumstances are confused, and it is so hard to distinguish between metaphor and literal vision that probably the attempt is anachronistic), Julian proceeds:

> And in this he schewyd me a lytille thynge, the qwantyte of a haselle nutte, lyggande [lying] in the palme of my hande, and to my undyrstandynge that, it was as rownde as any balle. I lokede ther oponn and thought, 'Whate maye this be?' And I was annswerede generaly thus: 'It is alle that ys made'.
> [Additional 37790, f. 99r.; Colledge and Walsh, *op. cit.* pp. 212–13.]

This recalls Blake's 'eternity in a grain of sand' but derives, as the editors show, from the Bible, from Wisdom xi. 23–6. All is sustained by the love of God:

> In this God brought oure ladye to myne undyrstandynge. I sawe hir gastelye [spiritually] in bodily lyekenes, a sympille maydene and a meeke, yonge of age, in the stature that scho [she] was when scho conceyvede. Also God schweyd me in parte the wisdom and the trowthe of hir saule.
> [Additional 37790, f. 99v; Colledge and Walsh, *op. cit.* p. 213.]

Julian comments that at that time she was vouchsafed six showings, comprising bodily sights, as of the bleeding head of Christ; imaginative representations, of spiritual significance in bodily likeness, as Mary; purely spiritual, the Trinity, the lovingness of God (*op. cit.* p. 217). She emphasises that the visions created love in her for her fellow-Christians, and she thought once again she would die. Then she saw again the face of the crucifix that hung before her and she beheld continually part of Christ's Passion, the spitting and buffeting 'and alle his blyssede face a tyme closede in dry blode' (f. 101v; *op. cit.* p. 225). After further sights the word was formed in her soul without voice or opening of lips, 'Herewith is the feende overcommynn' (f. 102v; *op. cit.* p. 227) and seeing God scorn the fiend's malice, but not the fiend, God wishing us to do the same, 'for this syght I lughgh [laughed] myghttelye, and that made thamm to laughgh that were about me, and thare laughynge was lykynge [pleasing] to me . . . Botte I sawe nought Cryste laughgh neverthelesse hym lykes [it pleases him] that we laughgh in comfortyng of us' (f. 102r and v; *op. cit.* p. 228).

Further showings ensued of parts of the Passion, the sorrow of Mary, and then Jesus's own change to a joyous appearance, at which Julian felt joy. Christ's suffering love for man brings joy to both. Yet Julian also felt deep sorrow for sin, though ready to submit herself entirely to Holy Church. 'He answered by this word and said, 'Sin is behovely' (necessary) (*cf. op. cit.* p. 244). The notion derives from the Paschal hymn of Easter night, which refers to Adam's necessary sin, the *felix culpa* or 'happy fault'. This cheering idea is a characteristic vein of Julian's thought, though it has to be seen in context with the suffering. Though sin is inevitable it is purely negative, and pain is purged by God's suffering and ours. 'He comforts readily and sweetly by his words, and says, "But all shall be well, and all manner of thing shall be well"' (*cf. op. cit.* p. 245). Lest we should feel this to be too facile she discusses it further, concluding that we both know and do not know this at the present time, but all shall be made clear at Doomsday. In more showings about the 'necessity' of sin she adds: 'Also God showed me that sin is no shame but worship [honour] to man, for in this sight mine understanding was lifted up to heaven, and then come verily to my mind David, Peter and Paul, Thomas of India and the Magdalen, how they are known in the church of earth with their sins to their worship.' (*Cf. op. cit.* p. 255.)

Julian records further how she distrusted her visions and told a priest that the cross that stood at the foot of her bed had seemed to her to bleed and that she was mad. But he took it seriously, and she was ashamed of her momentary lack of faith.

For the next twenty years she meditated on the showings and then re-wrote them in a longer text, clarifying, deepening, amplifying with theological reflection. The authentic but baffling mixture of visual appearance, spiritual insight and personal response which characterises the 'archaic' nature of the shorter text is rationalised. Sixteen showings are listed in the prefatory table of contents. There is less personal detail, but in some of the showings there is more realism of detail and illustrative comparison, clearer perspective and more analysis, although the basic text is the same and she remains true to the initial experience. Julian was a learned woman, deeply versed in the Bible and in the teachings of the Church, and she brings great power of mind to meditation on the significance of her showings. The progressive elaboration of physical realism in re-writing is a characteristic of most traditional writing. We also see the development of Gothic realism and sentiment and a progressive distinction between material elements and spiritual lessons or metaphorical meanings. Thus Julian adds in the later text to the vision of Christs's bleeding head:

> The grett droppes of blode felle doune fro under the garlande lyke pelottes (pellets), semyng as it had comynn oughte of the veynes. And in the comyng oughte they were browne rede, for the blode was full thycke. And in the spredyng abrode they were bryght rede. And when it camme at the browes, ther they vanysschyd. And not withstanding the bledyng continued tylle many thyngs were sene and understondyd. Nevertheles the feyerhede and the lyvelyhede continued in the same bewty and lyvelynes. The plentuoushede is lyke to the droppes of water that falle of the evesyng [eves] of an howse after a grete shower of reyne, that falle so thycke that no man may nomber them with no bodely wyt. And for the roundnesse they were lyke to the scale of heryng in the spredyng of the forhede.
>
> [Colledge and Walsh, *op. cit.* II, pp. 311–12]

Julian draws various lessons from this, but especially of the 'homely and courteous' – two favourite adjectives – nature of God. The greatest honour that a great king or lord may do his poor servant is to be 'homely' with him.

Among all of Julian's amplifications two in particular are substantial and notable. The first is revelation XIV, chapters 51 ff., which she says she did not understand for twenty years, and thus did not at first record. It is a striking example of medieval mental processes and throws light on *Piers Plowman*. She had a showing of a lord that had a servant. The lord sits solemnly in rest and peace. The servant stands ready to do his will. The lord gives him a command which he eagerly runs to do but falls into a ditch and is hurt and cannot get out. The lord regards him compassionately, and Julian understood that the servant would be highly rewarded without end, more than if he had not fallen. With that the vision vanished.

Eventually she understood the significance of all the details. The lord is God. The servant is Adam. The servant also signifies the Son, Christ, who is one with the Father, yet who fell with Adam. The lord sits on barren earth because he has created man's soul to be his own city and dwelling-place, and man's soul is now barren. The lord's blue clothing denotes steadfastness, its floating expansiveness God's comprehensiveness. Many other details and their significances are cited. Thus the sitting of the father signifies divinity, the standing of the servant, labour. The servant's eager starting signifies divinity; his running, humanity. His falling also signifies Christ's 'falling' into Mary's womb. Each part of the total image is thus capable of multiple significances often suggested by biblical expressions. These significances, though related to each other in the general scheme of thought, and by association, do not conform in themselves to a logically consistent allegory of a naturalistic picture. They are inconsistent with each other. The editors regard these interpretations as particularly the result of *lectio divina*. It is possible to classify the meanings Julian extracts from the showing according to the allegorical senses of scripture (see above, p. 211): the physical (sometimes itself called allegorical or historical): the tropological or moral; the anagogical, or heavenly. Julian does not name these concepts explicitly herself, nor does she take them one after another but in a mixture. In fact her exegesis is very like a modern literary critic's teasing out of multiple significances and implications from a literary text, except that Julian works from a complex image generated without conscious effort from her own mind, as we may suppose Langland's image of Piers and the pardon, or of the Tree of Charity, to have been. To say 'from her own mind' does not deny the influence of her reading, and no doubt of pictures she had seen in Norwich churches, which provided the materials out of which God or the subconscious mind, or both, created a meaningful vision.

Julian begins the following chapter, 52, by saying that thus she saw that, 'God enjoys that he is our father, and God enjoys that he is our mother, and God enjoys that he is our very spouse, and our soul his loved wife'. Here again the imagery is multiple and the elements are in a logical sense mutually incompatible. The Bible offers other examples of such mixed metaphors, as does Shakespeare. So long as we do not seek to rationalise such imagery in the wrong way, measure it against irrelevant naturalistic models, take it literalistically or demand compatibility between different implications, it is perfectly clear. The group of ideas which Julian touches on at the beginning of Chapter 52 leads on ultimately to the remarkable Chapters 59 ff. on 'the motherhood of God', a concept which though it has clear roots in biblical phraseology, in the potent multiplicity of traditional imagery and in some theological teaching, is nevertheless a unique contribution to theology which has had to wait until the late twentieth century to be properly appreciated. These chapters constitute the second substantial amplification of and addition to the shorter text. The evocation of the warmth and steadfastness of mother's love is a characteristically attractive note in Julian, reflecting her psychological health. It restores to the primal image of the fatherhood God a tenderness which it may otherwise lack. The fourteenth century was particularly conscious of the need for tenderness and the emphasis on motherhood, more usually centred on Mary, is an example to be put alongside the constant evocation of feminine tenderness (pity) in secular love poetry.

As with all mystics Julian reinforces the fundamental Christian teaching of love. In the last book she meditates eloquently on her last showing in which God says 'I am ground of thy beseeching'.

> And fro the tyme that it was shewde I desyerde oftyn tymes to wytt in what was oure lord's menyng. And XV yere after and mor I was answeryd in gostly understondyng, seyeng thus: 'What, woldest thou witt thy lords menyng in this thyng? Wytt it wele, love was his menyng. Who shewyth it the? Love. Wherefore shewyth he it the? For love.

Holde thee therein, thou shalt wytt more in the same. But thou schalt nevyr witt therein other, withoutyn ende. Thus was I lernyd that love is oure lordes menyng.

[College and Walsh, *op. cit.* II, pp. 732–3]

This is notably eloquent with all the resources of rhetoric and logical thought. The Aristotelian and scholastic analysis of causes, 'formal', 'efficient', 'material' and 'final', underlies the structure of questions. The presentation of question and answer is a rhetorical device known as *ratiocinatio,* the parallelism is *conversio,* and there is obviously *repetitio.* (There seem to be reminiscences of this eloquence as well as specific quotations from Julian in T. S. Eliot's *Little Gidding.*) Julian's style shows wide reading as well as deep thought. Her vocabulary can accommodate technical concepts. Her syntax is rhetorically polished and ideally adapted to the complex meanings she wishes to convey. Her teaching is both orthodox and personal, and in general she exemplifies some typical movements of the age, but her work seems to have enjoyed only limited circulation in the fifteenth century, mainly in Carthusian circles. After the Reformation it was preserved by English recusants living in the seventeenth century in France and the Low Countries, from whom descend four of the six extant manuscripts.

Margery Kempe

Julian became well known in Norwich as a wise spiritual counsellor and was consulted by another woman of much interest in cultural history, though spiritually rather inferior. This was Margery Kempe, who wrote the first autobiography in English. Almost all we know about her comes from this work, dictated to a scribe first about 1432, revised 1436–8. A single early manuscript of 250 pages, not the original, survives. Religion was to Margery what sex was to Chaucer's Wife of Bath. Margery became in her forties as vigorous and far travelled a pilgrim as the Wife. She was born about 1373, daughter of a burgess of King's Lynn, a port in the north of Norfolk. Her father, John Brunham, was five times Mayor. She married about 1393 John Kempe, by whom she had fourteen children, suffering a period of madness after the birth of the first from which she recovered through a vision of Christ sitting upon her bedside. She became very religious, argued with everyone from bishops downward, scorned Lollards, had mystical experiences, went constantly on pilgrimage. All is recorded in vigorous, lively prose. She gives full details, not least about her religious weeping and crying, which made other people from the Archbishop of Canterbury downwards find her company absolutely intolerable. A reader cannot but be amused by the account she gives of their exasperation. She may have been influenced by the important group of contemporary women mystics on the Continent, especially in Germany where she travelled, but her aggressive humility was all her own. She must have died about 1440. She gives us, with disarming frankness, a vivid picture of many details of early fifteenth-century ordinary life. She knew neither French nor Latin. The only surviving manuscript was later cherished by the Carthusians of Mount Grace in Yorkshire who preserved so much of the contemplative tradition of the fifteenth century.

'The Mirror of the Blessed Life of Jesus Christ'

These same Carthusians had a more direct hand in creating another work of religious devotion, *The Mirror of the Blessed Life of Jesus Christ,* which was translated by Nicholas Love, prior of Mount Grace between 1408 and 1410. The Latin original, *Meditationes Vitae Christi,* was generally though mistakenly attributed to the great Franciscan, Bonaventura, but in fact was written by an Italian, Giovanni de San Gimignano, about 1300. It had widespread influence in Europe in helping to promote the new affective devotion to the person of Christ, imagining the details of his life as a child as well as dwelling on his sufferings in his Passion. Love's translation either amplifies his Latin original or incorporates material from another text. Although most of the material is commonplace edification there are also touches of that reaching out of the imagination, realistic daily detail, emotional sympathy and individual personal response, which characterise so much fourteenth-century European religion. It was extremely popular, forty-seven manuscripts being known besides five sets of extracts, and it clearly met a need of devout lay people, with its intention of offering the milk of light doctrine rather than the solid meat of learning and high contemplation, though passing references show that it is meant for enclosed religious as well. Love's work is well written, sometimes moving, with a wide range of subject matter, granted its primarily devotional aim, and it must stand as representative of a number of mystical and devotional pieces which were produced in the flood of translations of all kinds in the fifteenth century, as well as of such mechanical devotional allegories as *The Abbey of the Holy Ghost* which circulated from about 1350–70.

The Lollard Bible, and sermons and tracts

A somewhat paradoxical aim of Love's *Mirror* was to head off the increasing desire of English people to read the Gospel in their own tongue. This desire had begun to create biblical translations from the end of the fourteenth century by the Lollards, and was spearheaded by the polemical writings of the irascible Oxford don, Wycliffe, who died in 1384. Love's *Mirror* cannot therefore be representative of a significant section of religious prose, biblical translation, which ultimately had great effect. The Church was implacably opposed to Wycliffe and to Lollard views in general, to such an extent that for the first time in England heretics began to be burnt at the stake from the early fifteenth century. Lollardy's literalistic rationalism and its insistence on the Bible in English blew a cold and ultimately refreshing blast through the pious hot-house fantasies of the so-called Lives of Christ. The Lollard attack on the Eucharist, denying that the bread and wine can become in any sense the body and blood of Christ, is an extreme case of literalistic 'modernism' attacking the complex multiplicity (or muddle) attributed to objects by an 'archaic' world-view.

The core of Lollardy was the Latin prose works of Wycliffe in which he developed his beliefs. Out of these arose a substantial body of writings in English and two translations of the Bible. Wycliffe himself wrote nothing in English and most Lollard writings are anonymous, not surprisingly since from 1407 possession even of a Bible in English was *prima facie* evidence of heresy which might well mean death. Wycliffe died in 1384, but his doctrines spread rapdily though the upper classes to the universities and to artisans in towns and villages. A vigorous archbishop crushed the spirit of Oxford university from the 1380s, while persecution killed or cowed the upper classes. Chaucer himself was decidedly sympathetic at least to Lollard attitudes in his middle years, attracted no doubt by Lollard literalism and scepticism. He was friendly with a number of the group called the Lollard Knights. But he finally retreated. By the middle of the fifteenth century it was small clandestine groups of humbler men and women who kept alive the seeking for a fresher religious inspiration, and who in the early sixteenth century, having spread surprisingly, joined up with powerful fresh Protestant influences coming from the Continent, themselves in part an indirect product of Wycliffe's influence.

Persecution was successful in the fifteenth century in preventing new work. All the principal Lollard works and translations were produced in the late fourteenth or very early fifteenth centuries, not later, though they continued to circulate. They have no very high status as independent literature, being analytical, technical, critical. Lollard writing is a vernacular offshoot of Latin scholasticism, critical and specialist analysis of 'the sacred page' (*sacra pagina*) opposite in spirit to the contemplative and descriptive *lectio divina*. But biblical translation and some personal testimonies must be mentioned.

The first Wycliffite translation of the Bible, associated with Nicholas Hereford who recanted in 1391, was made in that great literary decade of the 1380s. It is so close to the Latin as to be virtually incomprehensible apart from it – an extreme example of literalism. In the 1390s revision produced a second more idiomatic version. Many copies were burnt; nevertheless over 240 copies from the fourteenth and fifteenth centuries survive. The Wycliffite translation has not the power and beauty of Tyndale, for which more time and literary genius were needed, but it must have helped to pave the way. Lollard translation of the Bible raised many technical literary problems, such as the authenticity of a text corrupted by careless scribal transcription, the theory of translation, the status of the literal sense. Lollards frequently disparaged *glosing*, that is, interpretative commentary which made use of allegorical senses in the manner of traditional exegesis. Chaucer too prefers the 'naked text' (*The Legend of Good Women*, Prol. G. 86). Nevertheless there were Lollard Glossed Gospels, not always controversial, whose commentary was a valuable development in vernacular literary culture, since however vital the preservation of the literal sense may be as the anchor of meaning, all use of language is inevitably more than literalistic, and the better an ancient text is, the more explanation it needs.

Lollard testimonies burgeoned tragically in the sixteenth century, recorded in Foxe's so-called *Book of Martyrs* (*Actes and Monuments,* 1563) but are scarce in the fifteenth. The most interesting is William Thorpe's account of his bold clash with Archbishop Arundel in 1407, which fortunately he got away with. A woman, Hawisia Moone of Loddon, recanted her Lollard beliefs in 1430 and in so doing gives a useful plain survey of characteristic Lollard beliefs. She abjures her previous rejection of forms and ceremonies from baptism to marriage and the Eucharist; she abjures her belief that immoral priests are no priests, that the church has no worldly dominion nor right to wealth, that oaths, the death-penalty, fasting, pilgrimages, images and prayers to saints are all wrong or futile. These beliefs went far beyond sixteenth-century Anglicanism and they find many echoes today. A modern Quaker would presumably agree with them wholeheartedly. Such a highly internalised, anti-structural attitude, is an aspect of recurrent millenarianism and it was far in advance of its own or any other times.

One of the great Lollard complaints was that the clergy did not preach enough. There are however a few sermons in English surviving from about 1200, and by 1500 the bulk is considerable, though as is the way with traditional literature many are partially copied, then amplified, from earlier versions, so that they constitute complex 'families' of interrelated texts. There is a substantial Lollard sermon-cycle of 294 sermons found in eleven manuscripts, with various derivatives. The Lollard sermons are clear evidence of an organised effort and educated readers. Perhaps all written sermons were intended as much for devout readers of the middle and upper classes as for pulpit delivery, though the effigy in the wall of the church in Tong in Shropshire, showing a late fifteenth-century preacher with a book before him, as in a pulpit, suggests preaching from the book as well. Lollard sermons have little literary interest, but sermons in general are part of English literary culture.

By the end of the fifteenth century, ordinary parishioners could hear sermons read from the pulpit in which that fundamental text of European civilisation, the Bible, was extensively if selectively translated, the views of some great creators of European culture, St Gregory, St Augustine, St Bernard and others, were quoted, and constant exhortations were made to succour the poor, repent of sin, amend one's life. These English sermons have many excellent passages.

Saints' legends

Often as part of the sermon, but increasingly independent, were the ever-accumulating prose legends of the saints. The most influential collection in English was John Mirk's *Festial* of about 1400, giving several sermons for each saint's day. The *Festial* derived from the most influential collection of all, that of Jacobus de Voragine or Varagine of Genoa (and often therefore called 'Januensis'), who compiled in Latin the *Legenda Aurea,* completed by 1267, which became known throughout Europe. It was partially translated into English several times in the fifteenth century, and finally by Caxton in 1483 as *The Golden Legend.* Saints' legends eventually earned themselves a bad name for improbability even among the devout, and they crumpled in England under the impact of devout Reformation literalism. Yet they deserve sympathetic study as a form of traditional religious folk-tale, a counterpart to secular romance, with which they are often closely connected, like the story of Bevis, for example, which is connected with the legends of St Eustace and St George. Variants of their stories were popular well into the seventeenth century. After centuries of Neoclassical neglect modern scholarship and criticism is now rightly paying much more attention to them.

Saints' legends occupy an indeterminate no-man's-land between fact and fiction. They should be understood in the same terms as the secular legends studied by folklorists. There is, or was, in a few saints' legends, a grain of historical fact: there have indeed been martyrs who have suffered horrible torments for the faith. There are indeed wicked men and women who tempt and torture the good. Saints' legends make articulate the ideals of integrity and faithfulness to death, the supremacy of spirit over matter. The extravagance and variety of incident can, as with the romances, in the hands of a good writer create an imaginative world of legitimate excitement. The monsters correspond to real entities in our own minds and experiences. Saints' legends are an essentially archaic non-naturalistic form, and are probably at their best in stark early versions, as in the superb *St Margaret* written around 1200, which is one of the Katherine Group of writings associated with *The Ancrene Riwle*. There is a magnificent conflict between Margaret and the Devil as a monster, in which she forces him to swallow a crucifix which makes him burst. The episode is seen as part of a cosmic conflict. The prose is almost as supple and complex as that of Hooker. The legends met the constant human need for imaginative adventure and excitement and were approved of by the Church. In consequence they were constantly re-told, and as is so often the case with traditional literature, especially at this period, they were amplified with both more sensational event and even greater superficial realism of detail. The effect is to claim more and more historical factuality for more and more improbable happenings. Eventually the clash between the pseudo-historical surface and the fundamentally non-naturalistic base becomes intolerable. Chaucer can get away with this in equivalent stories (for example, of Patient Griselda) but it needs genius to do so. Nevertheless the large number of saint' legends compiled or translated in English especially in the fifteenth century give in bulk a sense of true imaginative life and noble if one-sided ideals. Though they are weakened by pious wish-fulfilment and their facility cheapens suffering, they should not be dismissed entirely by a too thorough-going literalism.

Expository prose

Finally, a brief word must be said of the increasing stream of expository and didactic prose, not least because Chaucer himself did not disdain to contribute to it with his translations of Boethius's *Consolation of Philosophy* and *The Parson's Tale*. Around 1200 were not only the group of writings represented by *The Ancrene Riwle* but other writings from Kent in the south-east, such as *The Vices and Virtues*, which is the earliest piece of prose dialogue in English. The Soul confesses its sins to Reason who expounds the topic of the virtues, including an allegorical section on Mercy. The later thirteenth century offers little and we have to wait until 1340 for a comparable piece, also from Kent, on similar topics, though now translated from the French by Michael of Northgate, a monk of Canterbury, entitled *The Ayenbite of Inwyt* ('Remorse (literally, the return-bite) of Conscience'). The work is important in the history of the language, as giving a datable version of Kentish dialect. The matter does not live up to the memorable title, which so well indicates the developing inwardness of vernacular culture. From now on there is an increasing flow of didactic prose. The effects of the Lateran Council of 1215 very slowly filtered through to England. Archbishop Pecham of Canterbury promulgated in 1281 the Lambeth Canons which ordered that the Creed, the Ten Commandments, the Two Commandments of the New Testament, the Seven Works of Mercy, the Seven Virtues, the Seven Vices and the Seven Sacraments should be expounded to the people in English four times a year. John Thoresby, Archbishop of York, had a Latin catechism composed, based on the Lambeth Canons. This was translated into English and greatly expanded, in 1357, by John Gaytryge, a monk at York, as *John Gaytryge's Sermon*. Some eight copies exist, one of them by Robert Thornton. It was also adapted by a Wycliffite writer. Its obtrusive numerical divisions make it a mechanical piece, but it represents a number of useful writings of the same kind, manuals for parish priests and devout reading for laymen. A variant version of it is called *The Lay Folks' Catechism*. We may recall that Chaucer's *Parson's Tale* is also in part a tract on Vices and Virtues, and its general concern with Penitence represents the feeling of sensitive men and women of the age. Chaucer's exact contemporary, the friar Richard Lavenham who was Richard II's confessor, wrote in English a treatise on the seven deadly sins. All such works testify to a progressively more analytical and self-conscious habit of mind, a capacity for self-examination, a deeper realisation of the self as individual. Chaucer is particularly significant as a layman writing about such matters, and with him we may associate his poetic disciple and presumably friend, the Lollard knight Sir John Clanvowe, whose *Two Ways* is probably the first devotional treatise by a layman in English.

Fifteenth-century consolidation and religious anti-intellectualism

The fifteenth century saw a consolidation of the achievements of the later fourteenth century. The steady expansion of literacy and education in the vernacular, with many translations, began to develop a unified national literary culture. There was one grievous exception, already noted, the rejection of the vernacular Bible, and with it new developments in the vernacular on religious subjects. The anti-intellectualism of the fifteenth century is illustrated by the extraordinary case of Bishop Reginald Pecock (*c.* 1395–*c.* 1460). He wrote a number of books ably defending the *orthodox* position. His best known work in English is *The Repressor of Overmuch Blaming of the Clergy* (*c.* 1450), an intelligent defence against Lollard attacks on such matters as the use of images. Pecock's prose is a strong scrupulous lawyer's prose, not particularly easy to read, but with considerable power. His fate was to be condemned by his own side, and his books burnt. He was too intellectual.

Most people were content with traditional elaborated pieties. Robert Thornton and men like him copied many of the works of Rolle and Hilton, and Caxton and his successor Wynkyn de Worde made available many routine devotional works. Caxton himself translated *The Golden Legend* and published two editions of this enormous book. A reprint of it was the first book that Wynkyn published when he took over at Caxton's death. In religious prose the next new wave, carrying on the literalism, individualism and secularism that had begun to burgeon in the fourteenth century, came in the sixteenth century from the powerful new surge, too long repressed, of reformed religion.

13

Secular prose
Malory and Caxton

Translation and the development of prose for practical purposes

In 1387 John Trevisa (*c.* 1330–1402), Rector of Berkeley and chaplain to Sir Thomas Berkeley in Gloucestershire, prefaced his translation of Higden's *Polychronicon* with a discussion 'between a lord and a clerk'. The lord urges the need of translation from Latin into English, against the clerk's reluctance but obviously with Trevisa's sympathy, and when the lord is asked whether he would prefer a translation in prose or verse he replies, 'In prose, for comynlich prose is more clere than ryme, more esy, and more playn to knowe and understonde'. Such an apparently simple truth already marks a high level of civilisation and literacy, and not everyone agreed with it, for practical works on agriculture, politics, etc. continued to be written in verse until well into the sixteenth century.

The decade of the 1380s was as remarkable for English secular prose as it was for verse. Besides Trevisa's translation of the *Polychronicon* there is Chaucer's translation of *The Consolation of Philosophy* in much more sophisticated prose, and perhaps also his *Tale of Melibee.* Thomas Usk, much inflenced by Chaucer, unfortunate in his political associations, which led to imprisonment and execution, wrote his *Testament of Love* also in 1387, with its autobiographical and self-exculpatory passages inadvertently extending the range of 'confessional' literature. Domestic letters began very uncertainly to disengage themselves from French, as H. S. Bennett shows. More generally in the last two decades of the fourteenth century, and continuing ever stronger in the fifteenth, we find an ever-extending range of prose writing beyond the bounds of religion, though always in a pious framework. The great series of the Paston Letters covering a multitude of topics of interest to a great family in Norfolk extends far into the fifteenth century, not imaginative, but another mirror of England. It should be remembered, though this is not the place to list them, that in the fifteenth century there are works in English prose on medicine, science, hunting, politics; there are histories; for which see H. S. Bennett, *Chaucer and the Fifteenth Century* (Oxford: Clarendon Press, 1947). There are long prose romances, like the *Merlin*, though we have to wait until near the end of the century for Malory's *Morte Darthur* and for the most extensive prose romances which were translated by Caxton and, like the Malory, printed by him.

While Malory's Arthurian achievement is the only example of truly great literature in the fifteenth century it may be set in the context of literary culture by briefly considering two other far more popular prose works. The first is the Latin encyclopædia by Bartholomew the Englishman, a Franciscan trained at Oxford and Paris, who wrote *De Proprietatibus Rerum* ('Concerning the Qualities of Things') at Magdeburg about 1250. It is confessedly a compilation, a huge collection of classical and medieval 'authorities' on topics organised on a descending principle of spirituality from God and the angels to man (half-spiritual) to corporeal things, and then to the attributes of things. Its subdivisions make it easy to consult, and it was extremely popular up to the seventeenth century. It was translated into all the European vernaculars, and besides many manuscripts went into nearly fifty printed editions. Trevisa translated it into English about 1392, and though there are few manuscripts of his translation it was printed three times, the third time slightly revised by Stephen Batman (1582), This, known as 'Batman upon Bartholomew' became a standard late sixteenth-century encyclopædia, known to Shakespeare – a nice example of Gothic continuity. The prose is sometimes laborious, but clear and practical. The book seems to have introduced many new words into the language.

Mandeville's Travels

We move somewhat nearer the fictional imagination with another very popular work that claimed not to be fictional, *Mandeville's Travels*. Its origins are still uncertain. It was probably first written in French on the Continent, perhaps at Liège, about 1357, and has a certain anti-Papal flavour. It immediately became immensely popular and was translated into Latin and all the European vernaculars. In English it was even turned into a rhyming romance, besides four other versions. It was a compilation of earlier travels, but part of its success was due to the Prologue which, after a devout and moralising beginning, claims, in the words of the translation in the Cotton version (Titus C xvi) in the British Library, written early in the fifteenth century, that 'I, John Maundevylle, knyght, alle be it I be not worthi, that was born in England in the town of Seynt Albones', crossed the sea in 1322 in order to go through many lands. He knows that many men desire to hear about the Holy Land, and he will tell how to get there.

> And yee schulle undirstonde that I have put this boke out of Latyn into Frensch and translated it ayen out of Frensch into Englyssch, that every man of my nacoun may understonde it. But lordes and knyghtes and other noble and worthi men that conne not Latyn but litylle and han ben beyonde the see knowen and understonden yif I seye trouthe or non.
>
> [M. C. Seymour (ed.), *Mandeville's Travels* (Oxford: Clarendon Press, 1967)]

Here the English translator has helped the original fantasy on (since the original says it is written in French), which makes one suspect that fewer were taken in by 'Maundeville' than is sometimes thought. Nevertheless the *Travels* is liable to appear in large manuscripts alongside such works as *Piers Plowman*, and was clearly enjoyed by the same sort of reader. Versions could have been current in the 1370s and 1380s. The poet of *Pearl* knew and made use of it for his description of the Dead Sea. It is full of interesting, often extraordinary information, and has some excellent stories. The charm is in the matter: the style of the English versions is at best competent, at worst cramped by too closely following the French.

Malory's 'Le Morte Darthur'

The problem for English prose was that while French, at its best, offered a model of elegance, clarity and sometimes complexity, too close a dependence on a French original destroyed those very virtues in English. To develop a style that should match the French, while remaining idiomatic English, was part of the achievement of Sir Thomas Malory, who produced the unquestionable masterpiece not only of fifteenth-century English literature but of all the vast European corpus of Arthurian tales from Italy to Iceland. His work, *Le Morte Darthur,* is a great gathering together of many forces and topics.

Arthurian subject matter

We may begin with what most interested Malory, the subject matter. He was interested in knighthood, especially at its peak of achievement in English history. The alliterative *Morte Arthure,* dealing with battle and history, (see above p. 150) and the stanzaic *Morte Arthur,* dealing with Lancelot and the tragedy of his love for Guinivere, may have provided initial interest and stimulus, but Malory early sought out the great 'French books' he often refers to as his source. These were the French prose romances of the thirteenth century which had amplified, sometimes in several stages, the romances in French verse which the genius of Chrétien de Troyes had created from the historical vogue intitiated by Geoffrey of Monmouth's *History of the Kings of Britain* (above p. 15). The thirteenth-century French prose versions, known as the Vulgate romances, were thus an amalgam, very characteristic of traditional literature, of elements from Welsh folklore, Classical Latin poetry, chivalric fantasy, Cistercian acetic mysticism and human yearnings for love and significance. They were written in an elaborate, elegant, balanced style, very rational, very realistic. The stories were often 'interlaced'; that is, several narratives were conducted in alternating sections. Malory wanted to bring order into the fascinating welter of ancient motifs of love and doom, of strange sicknesses and healings, of exciting quests and conflicts, contemporary Christian piety and chivalric ideals – all the 'war and wrack and wonder', the 'bliss and blunder' which, as the *Gawain*-poet says, had taken place on the broad hills of Britain with many 'lovely lords' of the Round Table. Malory ordered this superbly imaginative, extremely complicated, romance material according to an historical principle, centring all, as Caxton noted, on:

> the byrth, lyf, and actes of the sayd kyng Arthur, of his noble knyghtes of the Round Table, theyr mervayllous enquestes and adventures, th'achyevyng of the Sangreal, and in th'ende the dolorous deth and departyng out of thys world of them al.

The texts

Malory says he finished the work 1469–70. Caxton published it on 31 July 1485. Caxton's version, or variants of it by later editors, was the only one known, until in 1934 a manuscript of Malory's work was discovered at Winchester College. This is now known as the Winchester manuscript and is in the British Library. It gives a text unedited by Caxton, though a few pages at the beginning and end are missing; and it is quite possible that it was the very text Caxton worked from, since it shows signs of having lain about in his print-shop. Comparison with the Winchester MS shows that Caxton cut out a few of Malory's references to himself as author, halved the account of the Roman Wars, and imposed a pattern of twenty-one books, each with many short chapters, upon an original, broader structure of eight main sections. Malory's modern editor, Eugène Vinaver, considered these eight sections to be entirely separate works, hence the title of his edition, *The Works of Sir Thomas Malory* (2nd rev. edn., Oxford: Clarendon Press, 1973). This extreme view has been generally rejected, while the clarification offered by the structure of main sections, divided by Malory's own personal comments, has been accepted. Caxton also introduced many minor verbal changes, so that the manuscript is closer than Caxton's print to Malory's original text. It is quoted here, except where Caxton's text alone survives.

Who was Sir Thomas Malory?

Malory's own remarks tell us all we know for certain about the author. He names himself and says he is 'a knight prisoner'. Of the two likeliest candidates for authorship among a number of men called Malory in the mid-fifteenth century, one was an obscure Thomas Malory of Papworth St

Agnes, near Cambridge. The other, moderately well-documented especially in legal records, was the extremely turbulent Sir Thomas Malory of Newbold Revel in Warwickshire. There would be a certain piquancy in the certain knowledge, if we had it, that this violent, cattle-raiding, prison-breaking knight, accused of raping the same married woman twice, was the author who so firmly believes in the nobility of knighthood that its inspiration is the theme of his book. But records and accusations may be false or biased. What would we think of Lancelot if all we knew of him were the Public Prosecutor's case during his war with Arthur? Moreover, Malory shows that the honour and glory of chivalry ended in tragedy, and that Lancelot finally exchanged honour for penitence and sanctity.

Summarising a traditional story

Almost everyone in Western Europe and North America for many centuries has heard of Arthur before reading Malory's or any other formal account. We know from childhood that he was a great king, who had many brave and noble knights and who came to a sad end. Malory, too, must have known this before he came to read the French romances seriously, and to adapt and cut them to his own conception. He is a traditional writer telling a traditional story, and he relies to some extent on our previous knowledge and assumptions. We take for granted the excellence, though not the perfection, of Arthur and Lancelot, and the magical power of Merlin, at the very beginning. But Malory in one respect behaves like a minority of traditional storytellers. Unlike his French predecessors, instead of expanding he abbreviates. He summarises, and slashes out great chunks of events and much incidental detail. But he also recreates with some additions in making it all his own. The general effect, especially in the earlier sections of his work, is to make the story seem more primitive, because he cuts out from the French much realistic detail and much plausible cause and effect. He juxtaposes essential episodes without much explanation. Although the stories thereby may appear at first more arbitrary in sequence, they become much more powerful, because the episodes are chosen to illustrate Malory's significant theme of knighthood. They also seem paradoxically more modern because Malory concentrates on relatively few heroes and themes, clarifies the forward movement and creates a superficial (but misleading) similarity with novels. He was helped to concentrate on a main thread of narrative by the example of the *Morte Arthure* and of some other French romances.

The first section: the establishment of Arthur

The story begins (Winchester MS, Section I; Caxton books I–IV) with the familiar mixture of romance, folklore and magic, though already in Malory's laconic 'historical' style. It tells how Merlin enables Arthur's father, by enchantment, secretly to beget Arthur. Arthur is brought up in obscurity, but is able to prove his legitimate claim to the kingdom by the strangely effective symbol of alone being able to draw the sword fixed in the stone. The reader identifies with Arthur. The drawing of the sword, superficially so implausible, is a psychologically effective image of the emerging adult's accession to manhood, physical power, sense of independence ('royalty') and charisma. While Malory could have realised this only subconsciously, if at all, he tells it well, and it is an episode no one ever forgets.

Malory soon begins to drop the more superficial magical tricks, along with Merlin. Such wonders are unrepresentative of the later and best parts of his work. He rapidly develops, even if with some uncertainty at first, the laconic pregnant style which conveys his deep if narrow vision of 'reality'. No words are wasted. King Arthur calls his barons to council, and 'they coude no counceil gyve but said they were bygge ynough'. 'Ye saye wel', said Arthur, 'I thank you for your good courage . . .' (Caxton I x; the Winchester MS begins a little further on.) The wars are more 'historically' conceived and presented than the magic, but Malory gives a foretaste of his supreme genius in narratives of personal chance and destiny, in which larger human issues are involved, in the moving tale of the brothers Balin and Balan. Balin is the 'unhappy' ('unfortunate') man, well intentioned but impetuous and wilful, whose actions all go wrong. He disregards the warnings of a mysterious old man not to go and joust at a certain castle: 'And soo he herd an horne blowe as it had ben the dethe of a best. "That blast" said Balyn, "is blowen for me. For I am the pryse [quarry] and yet am I not dede"'

(Caxton II xvii). A few lines later he says, 'but though my hors be wery, my hert is not wery. I wold be fayne ther my deth shold be'. Then a friendly knight lends him a bigger shield, which will result in Balin being unrecognised when he comes to joust. He in turn will fail to recognise his opponent, who will be his brother Balan, the man he loves best in the world. A damsel laments that Balin has left his own shield. In this kind of story, as in a folk tale, we must accept without asking how really likely are such mysterious offers and warnings. They are images of what is uncertain and inexplicable in our own chance encounters, which yet seem in retrospect to have had an unavoidable fatalism. At the damsel's obscure warning

> Me repenteth, said Balyn, that ever I cam within this countrey. But I maye not turne now ageyne for shame. And what aventure shalle falle to me, be it lyf or dethe, I wille take the adventure that shalle come to me.
>
> [Caxton II xvii]

The concepts of honour and shame drive the heroes to the extremes of nobility, folly and tragedy. The uncomplaining bittersweet pride, regret and bravery of these words sustain much of the splendour of *Le Morte Darthur*. Balin goes on to fight, unknowingly, his brother, and they only recognise each other as they die.

The story is worked into the general pattern of events of Arthur's history, but somewhat clumsily. Its greatness is as a representative episode. Arthur's marriage with Guinivere is then recorded, with a note of doom briefly sounded. Further episodes relate the adventures of other knights, all full of interest, illustrating Malory's concept of knighthood, and showing Arthur established as the pivotal figure of his realm and court. At Arthur's court is established the Round Table of chivalric brotherhood. Every year the knights of the Round Table gather at the High Feast of Pentecost (Whitsun) to renew the oath of noble behaviour which they swear to Arthur.

The second section: Arthur's Roman conquest

The second main Winchester section (Caxton V) is based on the alliterative *Morte Arthure* (see above, p. 150) with some important deliberate differences. The main structure of events, including Arthur's foreboding dream of the Wheel of Fortune, is followed almost to the end. Malory is doing what many French writers had earlier done, turning a verse narrative into prose. He often does little more (though that little could be in effect much) than transcribe alliterative lines, and he found the manner so catching that even his own additional phrases sometimes fall into the alliterative pattern. Malory is deeply sympathetic to the poem. Its patriotic English bias and glorification of Arthur in 'historical' yet epic terms loses nothing in Malory's handling. Arthur's side are 'oure noble knyghtes of mery Ingelonde' (Winchester MS f. 80r; *cf. Works, op. cit.* p. 209). Arthur is the centre, the royal champion, as in his solitary fight with the giant, though made more civilised than in the poem. The excitement of battle in the company of loyal followers and friends is fully realised. Yet Malory also maintains his artistic purpose of summarising, simplifying and uniting the Arthurian history. He concentrates and improves the narrative by cutting speeches, irrelevant actions, bloodthirsty details and descriptions of natural scenery, so that his narrative is half the length of the poem. He also makes positive changes to bring it into the line of history. 'Than leepe in yong sir Launcelot de Laake with a lyght herte . . .' (Winchester MS f. 72v; *cf. Works*, p. 189). The 'young' is Malory's addition. The poem's few references to Lancelot are expanded. He is presented as young and eager to fight for the king, to earn his place in English epic history, being thus established as a worthy soldier before entering the forests of romance. Gawain, too, is presented vividly, though less fully than in the poem, as a brave soldier and leader, following the tradition of English chronicle, not of French amorous courtly romance. Many other Arthurian heroes are also established in a firm context. Malory's sense of place, naming known parts of England, France and Italy, grounds the story with its main heroes in an historical tradition.

At this stage Malory draws on only three-quarters of the poem. He leaves the poem with Arthur crowned emperor by the Pope, for, as Arthur says, 'inowghe is as good as a feste'. Malory causes them to return home to their rejoicing wives, including Guinivere. By contrast, in the poem Arthur is recalled by Mordred's treachery and the Wheel of Fortune begins its rapid fall. Malory, as it were, stays the Wheel with Arthur at its height for the next tales, up to the sixth, that of the Sankgreal, whose partial triumph paradoxically signals the decline to come. Meanwhile we have the chance to relish stories of triumph by Arthurian knights, all of whom reflect their glory on to Arthur, the central unifying figure.

The third section: the story of Lancelot

The first of the knights to be established in his own right is Lancelot, now clearly emerging as Malory's favourite. Malory selects three exciting episodes far apart in his source to construct a single, short unified tale to establish Lancelot as the greatest of Arthur's knights (Winchester MS III, Caxton VI). He is shown as an adventurous knight who is above all the righter of wrongs and the noble rescuer of ladies in distress. He is told of a knight who distresses ladies. '"What!" seyde Sir Launcelot, "is he a theff, and a knyght, and a ravyssher of women? He doth shame unto the order of knyghthode and contrary unto his oth. Hit is pyte that he lyveth"' (Winchester MS f. 104r; Caxton VI x; *Works*, p. 160). He is also asked about marriage and his relationship to Guinivere. Marriage, he replies, would hinder his adventures: adultery would, because it is sin, weaken his prowess. Whether this is an honourable lie, or Lancelot's relationship with Guinivere is still innocent, Malory does not say. He is not moralistic, but Lancelot utters a truth. In the end his adultery will be reluctantly shown to contribute to tragedy.

The fourth section: Sir Gareth

Meanwhile, the time of glory is still present. The unknown, unproven knight Gareth is the hero in the next section of a more traditional type of English romance based on the 'family drama'. He strikes down foes, establishes his identity, wins his lady and is accepted at King Arthur's court, receiving and conferring chivalric prestige. The story is bound into the general history of the court by starting and finishing there, and also by the close relationship established between Gareth (who happens to be one of Gawain's brothers) and Lancelot, who knights Gareth. This will be crucial in the later psychological pattern of events. The tale of Sir Gareth is itself delightful, with many felicitous passages and even a touch of humour, perhaps based on a now lost English source.

The fifth section: Sir Tristram

The next section is based on the tale of Sir Tristram (Winchester MS V, Caxton VIII–XII), with many other adventures interspersed. The story of Tristram is another example of successive re-handlings of a traditional tale which incarnates powerful images. In origin it seems to have been a dark Cornish fantasy about love and death, but the earliest version is by the Anglo-Norman Thomas of the early twelfth century. The story captivated the European courtly imagination. The hero Tristram, bringing home to Cornwall from Ireland his uncle's bride Isolde, inadvertently shares with her a love-potion, and they can never again bear being parted. Their love is adulterous and doomed, but it includes a marvellous episode when they live wild and happy in the forest. In the thirteenth-century German masterpiece *Tristan* by Gottfried von Strassburg, this represents a sacramental and mystical union of secular romantic love. Chrétien de Troyes knew the story but disapproved of it, and his *Cligés* was an 'anti-Tristan' romance. In the thirteenth-century French prose versions the story was expanded and diluted into a more ordinary tale of chivalric romance, incorporating the adventures of many other knights. King Mark, who had originally been more sinned against than sinning, was blackened in character to justify the glorification of Tristram as a chivalric hero. The story was brought within the orbit of Arthurian tales, and the interesting character of Sir Dinadan was introduced; by his much more rationalistic behaviour he satirises the fundamental notions of chivalry. Through him the suffering for love, seeking adventures, in waste forests, fighting against unknown knights, are all mocked. His genuinely modernistic spirit shakes the 'archaic' pieties of knighthood. Malory accepts the chivalric aspects of the story as he found it in the late French prose version. In accord with his generally optimistic temperament he leaves his Tristram and Isode in the equivalence if not the actuality of domestic married bliss in the comfort of Lancelot's castle of Joyous Gard, and he glosses over the adultery. We hear about Mark's treacherous killing of Tristram, which derives from the original story, only later and incidentally (Winchester MS VII, Caxton XX vi). Malory does not like the cynical modernism of Dinadan, for it mocks the knighthood Malory reveres, and he minimises without being able entirely to omit Dinadan's part. At the end of the book of Tristram Malory tells the story of how Lancelot for a while runs mad in the woods for love (a motif also used of Tristram) but is cured and tricked into begetting a son, Galahad, upon Elaine, daughter of Pelles, the Maimed King. This episode locks the otherwise rambling book of Tristram into the sequence of stories centred on Arthur, for Galahad is the Grail hero whose coming has long been forecast.

The sixth section: the Sankgreal

The Book of the Sankgreal comes next (Winchester MS VI, Caxton XIII–XVII). The story of the quest for the Holy Grail has entranced the European imagination. In origin the Grail was an obscure folkloric symbol, or set of symbols, of mystical plenty in paradoxical association with a sexually maimed king. Later stories made it a cup associated with a bleeding spear, the cup being that in which Joseph of Arimathea was fabled to have caught the blood and water from Christ's side, the spear being that which pierced him. The Grail, not yet defined, first appears in Chrétien de Troyes' last, unfinished poem *Perceval*, which was retold in the early thirteenth century in *Parzival* by the great German poet Wolfram von Eschenbach. The basic themes are mystical religion, the education of a wild untutored hero, and the redemptive power of married love. In the later thirteenth century a member of the ascetic order of Cistercian monks captured the story for ecclesiastical purposes in the prose *Queste del Saint Graal*, where it was used as the basis for a treatise on penance and grace, in which the supreme value of virginity in a knight as well as in women, and the wickedness of wanton killing, were emphasised. (Surely the *Gawain*-poet had read the work.) The *Queste del Saint Graal* uses what had become a chivalric myth to condemn earthly chivalry and urge the practice of heavenly chivalry. The Grail appears magically and all knights are impelled to seek it, but the quest destroys or at least frustrates all except the most perfect, that is, the most chaste. Of these Galahad is the supreme example, though he is eventually accompanied by Perceval and Bors. These three attain the vision of the Grail at the castle of Carbonek, where Galahad and Perceval remain to die and enter heavenly bliss. Bors alone returns to tell the tale. In the *Queste* Lancelot is singled out as the most eminent in earthly chivalry, and as having the greatest need, because of his sinful adultery with Guinivere, for repentance; he is granted only a partial, though shattering, potential glimpse of the Grail.

It is Lancelot's fate which interests Malory and allows him to bind the story into his own account of Arthurian chivalry. The Grail story must have seemed to him an essential part of the whole Arthurian story, so he could not leave it out. At the same time it made little appeal to his secular, if conventionally pious, imagination. Although he reorientated its interest to some extent he cut more and changed less of his source than in any other of his Arthurian tales. He accepts the general message, but he minimises Lancelot's failure, and he is ready to see the limited glimpse of the Grail allowed Lancelot as one of his achievements. He accepts that Lancelot's failure is due to his 'instability', that is, his inability to keep his thoughts from his love of Queen Guinivere. The Grail story therefore sharpens our sense, and no doubt sharpened Malory's sense, of the fundamental and tragic instability of the situation between Lancelot, his king whose chief knight and glory he is, and his queen whom he adulterously loves. It is to Malory's credit, as well as to that of the author of the French *Queste*, that enough strikingly romantic scenes remain to delight our imaginations with enigmatic symbols. The bright Grail comes to Arthur's darkened hall, bringing surpassing satisfaction to all, though eventually it leaves the kingdom for ever. We share Lancelot's blinding glimpse. Knights come to ancient chapels in the forest at midnight and have strange visions. Richly decorated ships bearing beautiful beds and jewelled swords sail with mysterious purposiveness. There is nothing else like this in English. If Malory changes and obscures the intellectual content he also humanises and dramatises it, and gives it touches of his own inimitable idiom. His summary may, as in other books, obscure the clear development of the narrative, but the juxtapositions of enigmatically powerful scenes emphasise the poetic mysteries that lie at the heart of this as of so many profound stories.

The seventh and eighth sections: Lancelot and Guinivere and the end of the Round Table

The next main section (Winchester MS VII, Caxton XVIII–XIX) brings us sharply back to the intensely human drama of Malory's more familiar world. The unsuccessful survivors of the Quest of the Grail have returned. Lancelot resorts to the Queen again, forgetting his promise made in the Quest, so that many talk of it. There is a blazing row between Guinivere, the most querulous of all great queens and heroines, and Lancelot. The sombre notes of the coming tragedy begin to mingle with Arthurian glory, yet the glory is even brighter and more moving for the approaching shadow. This seventh section and the eighth and last (Caxton XX–XXI) are closely linked together and frequently refer back to much earler episodes, so binding the whole long accumulating series of adventures together in a history of the glory and the tragedy of Arthur's Britain, of our Britain, symbolically of life itself.

A series of episodes, magnificently related, lead in a poignant mixture of chance and inexorability, nobility and wilfulness, to final disaster and penitence. Each cause of the tragedy is necessary but not in itself sufficient, and not all are connected in the same chain of events. Some causes, like the love of Lancelot and Guinivere, are inherent in the whole structure of medieval Arthurian story; some are serious but incidental, like the malice of Gawain's brothers; others are bitterly arbitrary, like Lancelot's accidental killing of Gareth, who loved Lancelot best of all men and whose death makes Gawain, the elder brother whom Gareth loved less, become Lancelot's fatally inveterate enemy; and some causes are trivial, like the drawing of a sword to kill an adder, which under suspicion of treachery causes two great armies to rush upon each other just as negotiations for peace are in progress.

Malory now turns to the long postponed ending of the alliterative *Morte Arthure* for part of his conclusion, but he is entirely master of the flow of events and far surpasses the original model. He takes up other sources as well; another English poem, the stanzaic *Morte Arthur* (see above, p. 87), and the French *Mort Artu,* using them to enrich a narrative which in clarity and humanity is unequalled in Arthurian narrative before or since. The beauty and pathos of the story of the Fair Maid of Ascolat, the moving humility of Lancelot's healing of Sir Urry, the fight in Guinivere's chamber, the hostility of Gawain set against Lancelot's courtesy, the strangeness of the passing of Arthur, the final parting between Lancelot and Guinivere, are among the great things in English literature.

The king dies, another succeeds. No tragedy is final, and it would be wrong to emphasise doom and dismay as the final note of Malory's work. It has a Gothic inclusiveness. Malory's manuscript was edited and published by Caxton, whose division into many books and chapters obscured its general form, but he added a preface which singularly well sums up the nature of what he rightly calls a 'noble and joyous book':

> Doo after the good and leve the evyl, and it shal brynge you to good fame and renommee. And for to passe the tyme thys book shall be plesaunte to rede in, but for to gyve fayth and byleve that al is trewe that is conteyned herin, ye be at your lyberte. But al is wryton for our doctryne. [etc.]

The implicit theory of literature here, with its internal contradictions that respond to the complexity of experience, is certainly Gothic.

Caxton

Caxton appropriately concludes this chapter on medieval secular prose, while offering a bridge to later literature. He was born about 1422 and had a distinguished career as a leading merchant operating mainly between London and Bruges and living at Bruges. He probably dealt in a variety of goods including manuscripts. No doubt he had always had some taste for books. He tells us he took up translating and how tired he got of copying out versions of his translation for friends – his pen became worn, he says, his hand weary, his eye dimmed. He had noticed on the Continent the spread of new devices for making multiple copies of books. The resources and acumen of a mature and highly successful businessman must have come into play. He 'practised and learnt' at great financial cost, he says, to print; going to Cologne to do so. Whether or not he started it as a rich merchant's hobby, he began to work at it seriously. He acquired a press and two founts of ordinary Continental type and a Continental foreman who became his eventual successor, Wynkyn de Worde. His interests and his sense of a potential market, of a genuine need, brought him to England, which is how England though late, compared with the Continent, acquired printing; why it was a merchant, not a technician (as was normally the case), who introduced printing into the country; why in England, unlike other European countries except Spain, the number of books printed in the vernacular before 1500 outnumbered those in Latin: why Caxton's printing business (if we accept Wynkyn de Worde, who inherited it, as carrying on the same firm) lasted far longer than other early printing houses, which were run by scholars or craftsmen, not businessmen.

Caxton was really a publisher, though as a publisher he had to have his own printing house. It is worth remembering, however, that books as such had existed long before, in manuscript. Printing was revolutionary, but Caxton's conservatism is evident in the form of his printed books. Unlike many Continental colleagues he was extremely slow to accept technological improvement, if he ever did. His printed books closely resemble manuscripts.

In many cases Caxton himself provided the texts of the books he printed. He was still essentially a medieval scribe, who manipulated the text he copied for his own purposes. He was also a medieval translator, more or less accurate, who in the traditional way added his own comments. In the case of Malory's *Le Morte Darthur,* he made considerable changes, most markedly when he halved Malory's account of Arthur's Roman war. When he published Trevisa's old-fashioned English translation of Higden's Latin history, the *Polychronicon,* he modernised the language and added a section of his own. In all this he was treating books as they had been treated before printing. He seems to have made little if any attempt to correct his texts, and his editions of Chaucer, for example, are as full of errors as are the medieval scribal manuscripts.

Caxton has the excuse that he was prodigiously busy as translator and publisher. The total of his translations adds up to more than 4,500 printed pages, and his publishing total to 18,000 pages, mostly folio. It looks as if he could translate at a speed of roughly twenty pages a week, which he no doubt had to fit in to the intervals of chatting with important customers, doing his accounts and consulting with Wynkyn.

Caxton also contributed various prologues and epilogues to his books. These are characteristically composed in part of stock phrases or paragraphs taken from other authors, in a conventional medieval fashion. But Caxton was also in his modest way a great innovator and he introduces a new self-awareness and personal tone. Some of his remarks are personal, as that he was born in Kent, or that he got tired of copying by hand so took to printing. Much is concerned with how good and interesting a book the present one is. Occasionally he discusses his problems. He illustrates the real difficulty of what style of language to use in English with the anecdote of how some English merchants in a sailing ship were delayed at the mouth of the Thames, and so landed to stretch their legs and buy food. One of them, called Sheffield and thus presumably a northerner, asked in his dialect for eggs. 'And the good wife answered', says Caxton, 'that she could speak no French.' Master Sheffield got angry, because he could not speak French either. Then one of his friends intervened and explained what was wanted in the local dialect, where *eggs* were *eyren*. 'Lo', says Caxton, 'what should a man in these days now write, eggs or eyren?' This story is told in the Prologue to the *Eneydos,* published the year before Caxton's death, because some gentlemen had complained that Caxton had sometimes used elaborate language which the common people could not understand. On the other hand, he says, some people want him to write *more* elaborately. Common terms of daily life are easier understood, but which are they? In any case, he says, his present book is not for a 'rude uplandish man to labour therein'. There is much here that reflects the problems of other medieval writers, though Caxton has a more modern consciousness of them.

Caxton agreed with the medieval literary view that instruction was as important as entertainment, if not quite the same thing, but like most medieval writers he had a modest desire to serve his audiences' tastes, as well as a modern publisher's need to find and keep a market. In consequence he published many books of pious instruction, including the saints' lives of the immense *Golden Legend*, which he himself translated. Perhaps his greatest love was for the long late-medieval courtly romances, now virtually unreadable but then highly fashionable. He translated several of these romances from French, besides other works from Dutch, like *Reynard the Fox*. The same taste included Malory's *Le Morte Darthur* and the courtly works of Chaucer, Gower and Lydgate. In so doing he served English literary culture better than if he had had a more scholarly, better educated, more progressive taste, which would have led him to the Latin works of the Renaissance which bankrupted Continental publishers, and which were essentially an intellectual and literary *cul-de-sac*, for all their prestige. But Caxton also did not publish *Piers Plowman*, although it was popular, well established and centrally English, presumably because it was radical and clerical, intellectual and uncourtly.

Caxton represents an interesting stage in the story of English literature. He gathers up so much, if by no means all, of the medieval vernacular achievement. New elements were beginning to surge into English and European literary culture which he did not recognise, and there is something doggedly English in his unintellectual conservatism. In many respects he represents the end of an era. Yet though he appears to have lacked intellectual, creative and mechanical genius, and to have relied on the Continent for expertise, when he became a printer he took up, with simplicity, success and disarming modesty, a radically innovative technology which was the principal instrument in transforming literary and religious culture. He invented in England the new profession of publisher. With vast energy he laid out his money and labour at a time of life when many men are mainly content to conserve both. His spirit of individual enterprise tempered by conservative prudence and a pragmatic response to other people's interests makes a good bridge between the medieval and the later world.

14

The Re-making of English

The demotion of English

WILLIAM the Conqueror tried to learn English at the age of forty-three, but was too busy to persevere. He was crowned in a ceremony that used English as well as Latin. He himself spoke the French of Normandy. From 1066 three languages were in play in England and the vast majority of English people for several centuries laboured under the burden of having most of the precious 'official culture' – religion, law, science, literature – conducted in languages other than their own. There are a number of English statements of resentment against French, and some against the upper classes as being French rather than English through the period, though by the mid fourteenth century such remarks approach the tone of paranoid *cliché*. They nevertheless indicate a serious cultural divide perhaps never completely healed in England.

The continuity of English

Problems arose not from ignorance of English but from the special use of French and Latin. The continuity of English was never in question. The vast majority of the people have always spoken English and most of their conquerors, or at least their children, rapidly learnt English. The story of the historian Ordericus Vitalis is the famous example. He was the son of a Norman knight and of a presumably English mother. He eventually became a great historian, writing in Latin in a monastery in Normandy. Ordericus was born less than a decade after the Conquest, near Shrewsbury, and was taught Latin by a local priest. At the age of ten he was sent to continue his education in a monastery in Normandy where, he later records, he was in exile like Joseph in Egypt, not understanding the language. In other words, he knew no

French. English was his cradle-tongue. Another story, told in one of the Latin biographies of St Thomas à Beckett, concerns the mother of one of the knights who later murdered Archbishop Beckett in 1170. This lady of high rank, whose husband of Norman descent was called Hugh de Morevile, fell in love with a young man of the same social group, called Lithulf (an English name). When he did not respond satisfactorily she determined to have him murdered. When she, her husband and Lithulf were out riding together on some pleasure-jaunt she encouraged the young man to draw his sword in play and gallop forward towards her husband who was out in front. When Lithulf did so she called out, 'Hugh de Morevile, ware! ware! ware! Lithulf heth his swerde adrage [drawn]!' The lady needed to use the most urgent and immediately comprehensible language available, and that was English. If Hugh had understood French, and the English Lithulf had not, it would have been to the lady's advantage to use French, which would have given no warning to Lithulf. As it was Lithulf must either have known French as well as Hugh did or, more likely, Hugh and his lady were not quite at ease in French.

The cradle-tongue tends to be used at times of stress. The saintly Ailred, who died in 1167, was a great writer in Latin, but he prayed on his death-bed in English as had Bede in the eighth century. Edward III (d. 1377) at least swore in English. English was always the basic language in England. French developed greater social and cultural prestige in the thirteenth century. Latin was until the late fourteenth century the unchallenged principal language of religion and learning. French and Latin limited, at first, the use of English, and then, so to speak, yielded their spoils to its progressive advance.

At the time of the Conquest Latin was already accepted as the language of religion and learning, for the good news of Christianity had come in the sixth century from Rome to England in Latin, and Christianity had preserved whatever was known of the learning of antiquity. Christianity had brought literacy in Latin, and the very alphabet of Old English was almost entirely Latin. French had even before the Conquest begun to exert influence on English, and after the Conquest it was soon a powerful and then for a while a successful competitor with English for culturally higher activities, even though French literature was less developed than Old English. Often a French word became current when a perfectly good English word already existed, as for example *peace* came to be used instead of *grith*. The main core of English, naturally enough, remained firm. The structural words, far more intrinsic to a language than items of vocabulary, were unchanged. Prepositions (for example, *by, from, to, with*); relatives (*who, which, what*); most pronouns (*he, him, it*); some adverbs (*very, full*); conjunctions (*and, but*); modal verbs (like *shall* and *will*); such words, the very heart of the language, were and are all English, through occasionally influenced by closely cognate Scandinavian forms from Scandinavian settlers. The words by which we live and die, eat and breed, work, play, love, sleep, choose, go, drive and, ride are all English from the beginning, like all the words but the last in this sentence.

While the continuity of English remained unbroken by the Conquest its rapid reduction in social status and intellectual range, and the loss of the written standard, both revealed and promoted rapid change in sounds, vocabulary and word order. The social situation and the use of mainly Latin and French in the records give us a limited and biased view of English, especially in the twelfth and thirteenth centuries. The vast proportion of the population, speaking English, are unrepresented, and the riches of the spoken language necessarily lost. The improvements in social status for English, its use for records and its more extended intellectual range, in the fourteen and fifteenth centuries, are themselves part of the story of English; by their very nature they allow us to know the language more fully because they led to or are the expression of greater literacy and thus came to be recorded and preserved.

'Old', 'Middle' and 'Modern' English

The linguistic effects of the Conquest were varied. We notice an immediate cessation of new composition in English, except for the steadily dwindling copies of the Chronicle. Only some pre-Conquest religious writings continued to be copied in more or less the old spelling as late as the early twelfth century. The continuous record of the Peterborough Chronicle allows us to see a definite break in the written tradition of English about 1100–20, when presumably the last of the old Anglo-Saxon-trained scribes died. The natives still, as before and as now, called themselves and their language 'English', but it is convenient to call English up to 1100 'Old English' (avoiding the unduly different term 'Anglo-Saxon' for the language, though it is convenient to call the speakers of Old English 'the Anglo-Saxons'.)

The present names of the later stages of the English language are products of the Neoclassical view of European history. In the sixteenth century European Neoclassical scholars, the so-called 'Humanists', invented the concept of the 'middle' ages (middle between them and the Classical period), and thus eventually the term 'Middle English' was devised in the nineteenth century for that period of the language between about 1100 and about 1500. Modern English begins in the early sixteenth century.

The written form of the language

All languages change continuously, especially as spoken. The written form of a language, because of its relative permanence, acts as a brake and makes a generally accepted standard attainable just because it avoids the manifold varieties of the spoken language. There is a continuous but variable relationship between the spoken and written forms of a language. At one period, usually brief and early, the written language will attempt to match, by the use of those conventional signs we call letters, the sounds of words. As soon as an elaborate system of writing develops, its great virtue is its stability, its slowness to change, while the spoken language goes on changing. Thus a stable written standard is created which it is to everyone's advantage to maintain, even because it does not correspond closely to the variability of the spoken word. It may even happen later, as in modern English, that some spoken language tries to match in sound the spellings and patterns of the accepted written standard though that represents pronunciations only current, if at all, centuries ago. In Old English (OE) a written standard had been created from which the spoken language, especially in different regions, was quite considerably different. We can tell this because as Old English scribes died new scribes, trained in Norman-French spelling conventions, transcribed English words with some different letters and to some extent as they heard them, thus revealing changes in spoken Old English which could have taken place up to two hundred years previously. For example OE *c* had originally represented one sound, as represented by modern English *k*. In Old English times this sound had developed when in certain positions to the sound represented by modern English *ch*. Late OE *c* had thus come to represent two sounds, which the new scribes differentiated between, keeping *c* before *a, o, u,* or using *k*, and representing the *ch* sound by the letters *ch*. Paradoxically, therefore, much that we think of as Early Middle English is no more than a record in writing or what had been happening to *spoken* Old English. Another example of change which had begun in Old English is the tendency to reduce all inflexions. In Old English, as in Latin, Greek and modern German, most nouns and adjectives had different endings to the stem of the word according to their function in the sentence. In spoken Old English such inflexions were tending to become simplified to sounds represented by *-e*, or *-es*, which latter became more and more usually the sign of the possessive singular and the plural form of nouns, later often simplified to *-s*. There were many different endings for parts of verbs and these tended to be simplified to forms roughly corresponding to the letters *eth, es, en*. It is impossible even to summarise such changes here but they are important to recognise in reading the texts because major questions of meaning and nuance hang by them. For example, recognition of the use of the subjunctive, with its subtle gradations of possibility, preference and politeness which are almost completely lost in Modern English, may open up new vistas of significance in an apparently simple medieval text.

Development and variation of forms

Another aspect of the change in spelling conventions brought about by the Conquest is the variation of forms implicit in the loss of a written standard. Old English writing is mainly in a standardised form of West Saxon developed from about the tenth century in Wessex, where Winchester was the chief city. The political and economic centre of the country shifted under William to London, whose dialect in combination with the royal court and the courts of law ultimately gave us a new written standard through the development of records in Chancery in the fifteenth century; but in the intervening centuries there was no agreed national standard English. Spelling varied according to the local conventions of scribal habits, and to some extent represented actual local dialects. Since the regional dialects differed amongst themselves in pronunciation, and often in vocabulary, the spelling and diction also varied. The loss of strong written conventions allowed spelling to vary as the language developed in time. In consequence, Middle English spelling varies in a most troublesome way from district to district and from century to century. It is possible to some extent to detect both the date and the place of origin of a piece of writing by comparisons with texts that are dated and which give their place of origin, and by the examination of a large number of variables in spelling. Scholars can describe and analyse the sounds, structures and developments of the language as a whole by examining in detail many small pieces of evidence. An example of what happened to the language in detail is offered by the history of the sound represented by OE *y*. This letter in Old English represented the sound which French scribes wrote as *u*, and it was thus that the Norman-trained scribes represented it when it was pronounced short. OE *mycel* thus became Middle English (ME) *muchel*, giving Modern English *much*. When the sound represented by *y* was a long vowel the Norman scribes represented it by *ui*, as OE *fyr*, Early Middle English *fuir*, modern *fire*. The actual letter *y* thus became spare, and the Norman scribes used it as an alternative to *i* in positions where the letter *i* itself might be ambiguous because of the way letters like *m*, *n*, *u*, were formed. These letters were formed by a succession of small vertical strokes, called minims, one of which made *i*, two of which made *n* or *u* but left them indistinguishable, while *m* written as three minims, was indistinguishable from *in*, *ni*, *iu*, *ui*. The dot over *i* was invented to help with this problem but it was safer to use *y*. Hence the ME spelling *synn* rather than *sinne*, which would have five minims in a row (making possible a wonderful series of meaningless permutations on sequences of the letters, *i, m, n, u*), which hindered rapid comprehension.

To make the matter more complicated, the original vowel sound, whether short or long, represented by OE *y* had a varied development from late Old English times onwards in different parts of the country. In the north and east down to the East Midlands as far as London the short vowel sound became like that represented by Modern English *i* as in *kin*; in Kent and parts of East Anglia it became the sound represented by *e* as in *merry*; in the west and south-westerly parts it became the sound now represented by *oo* as in *mood*, but then represented by *u*. The same word at the same period in Middle English was therefore differently spelt in different parts of the country. OE *cyn*, for example, gave ME *kyn, ken, kun*; OE *brycg* gave ME *brigge, bregge, brugge*, and so forth. Some such dialectal variants can still be heard in England today. Because the dialect of London became dominant and provided the basis for the main development of English in later centuries, modern English retains dominantly East Midland sound and spellings, or their derivatives. Some modern anomalies in sound or spelling may be due to the inevitable mixture of dialects in London. Thus OE *myrge* (also recorded as *merge*) naturally gave ME miri(e) in the East Midlands and London, and this is Chaucer's preferred form. But in Kent it gave *merie*, which Chaucer occasionally uses for a rhyme (and Gower, a Kentish man, always uses), and this pronunciation has surprisingly become standard as *merry*, which is very rare for specifically Kentish forms. In the case of the OE verb *byrgan*, giving rise to the variants *birien, burien, berien*, Modern English has retained the western spelling, *bury*, with the Kentish pronunciation.

This much simplified account of some of the things that happened in connection with OE *y* must serve as an example of the myriad changes in sounds and dialects that were revealed by the change of spelling conventions. They continued because of the disappearance of a standard written language, and are revealed by variations in spelling in different parts of the country at different times in the medieval period. Thus arises the extraordinary variety of spellings which the reader has already encountered.

Scribal habits

Variation of spelling may also occur inconsistently within any single text because it may have been copied by a scribe who spoke and wrote a different dialect from that of the text he was copying. Although there may be a few instances of complete 'translation' by a scribe from one dialect to another, the more usual case is an inconsistent mixture. Rhyme-words, for example, stand a slightly better chance of being copied in their original spelling than words within the line, though even rhyme-words are frequently changed by scribes. In a work copied several times there may be several 'layers' of dialect. The heavy stress in English on the first or second syllable of a word, which led in the spoken language first to the reduction of many inflexions to an obscure final vowel represented by *-e*, and eventually to the loss in sound even of that, also affected spellings. Because the written language is more stable than the spoken, scribes became used to seeing a final *-e* written in words which had no longer any corresponding sound. Scribes in turn began to use final *-e* not to indicate a sound but to mark the previous vowel as long (*cf. ban, bane*) or they even used final *-e* quite arbitrarily. When a poet has used a word which he pronounces with a final inflexion and represents in writing with a final *-e*, and a later scribe fails to recognise the nature of the use of *-e* and writes it arbitrarily or differently, the metre of the poem becomes badly disrupted from the author's original. Chaucer is the obvious sufferer. Robinson's standard text of *The Canterbury Tales* reads in line 8:

> Hath in the Ram his halve cours yronne.

The metre shows that *halve* must clearly be a disyllable, and its final *-e* is justified because *halve* in such a grammatical position would have been a disyllable in Old English. But in several manuscripts the scribe has written *half* or *halff*, which spoils the metre. In mitigation we must add that Chaucer, in whose lifetime the pronunciation of the final *-e* sound was fading, occasionally varied his use of it to help with the scansion of the line. Variations of spelling, with the addition of the many other inaccuracies of scribes and printers, gave Chaucer's verse a quite unwarranted reputation in the sixteenth century as rough so-called 'riding rhyme'. His true music, in which normal speech-rhythms form a counterpoint against basic regular stress, only began to be recovered in the nineteenth century, and there are still a few critics who do not recognise it.

Re-establishment of a standard written form

As the fifteenth century progressed and literacy became widespread a general written standard of English once again evolved, emanating from London, which was the centre of political, social and economic power and influence. The natural effect of more writing and of improved communications is in any case to draw towards a consensus, and the general East Midland dialect as represented in writing in London and the surrounding areas came gradually to be generally accepted as the written standard. When Caxton began to print in 1476 he found considerable problems in the varying dialects and styles available, but being settled in Westminster and needing to appeal to an immediate market, his pragmatic genius led him to reinforce what was already becoming dominant. He disregarded the spoken variants he was aware of and followed the London practice. Later printing-houses, being mostly in London, further reinforced and largely settled in the sixteenth century that spelling which has effectively remained standard up to the twentieth century, subject to some further minor modifications, such as the regularisation of *u* as always a vowel, *v* as always a consonant, a similar rationalisation of *i*, and *j*, and so on. By the late fifteenth century the battle to make English the language of the official culture as well as of the people was largely won. Caxton's own significance is partly due to his perception, not shared by many Continental printers, that what was needed was printed books *in the vernacular*. The books with most prestige were still those in Latin, and the language of the Church was still Latin, but Caxton resolutely stuck to English, making available in print to the English people many religious works and all the great works of later medieval English literary culture except *Piers Plowman*, besides translating and printing huge quantities of French, Latin and Dutch material.

Finally, while considering the conventions of spelling and handwriting, we may note that though Middle English scribes soon abandoned such Old English letters as 'ash' (æ), 'eth' (ð) and 'wynn' (ƿ), they retained into the fifteenth and in some cases even the sixteenth century, the letters 'thorn' (þ) and 'yogh' (ȝ). Thorn has the value now given to *th* and yogh the values of both modern *y*, and of *ch* as in Scottish *loch*. (In this book wherever they occur in the original text they have been transcribed into their modern equivalents.)

Changing styles of handwriting

During the Middle English period the style of handwriting slowly changed from the handsome Old English and twelfth-century scripts to the Gothic scripts, progressively more mannered, sometimes very beautiful, of the fourteenth and fifteenth centuries. A little practice soon enables the patient reader roughly to date any medieval manuscript style of writing. The letters are formed differently at different periods and need to be learnt. The fifteenth century has the most varied and the ugliest, as well as often rather amateurish scripts. Printed books at first closely resembled manuscripts. Fifteenth and sixteenth-century printed letter-forms were designed in the same shape as earlier Gothic scripts, and came to be known from about 1600 as 'blackletter'. In the sixteenth century some Humanist scripts from Italy (hence italic) begin to appear. The 'roman' style of printed letters as nowadays used began to appear first in Europe in the sixteenth century.

Development of the English vocabulary: French words

The clearest index of the development of the status of English is to be found in the vocabulary. The essential basic English vocabulary and structures were never lost. What might be called the superstructure, the words used in the high and official culture, as a result of the Conquest progressively though not completely perished. There were many causes. The actual conquerors were French-speaking, and many English-speakers in high places were displaced, or fled, or in the fullness of time died, to be replaced by French-speakers. French acquired higher social prestige. Hence the replacement of some English words by French equivalents, as well as the introduction of new French words for new ideas and things. This was a long process, and varied in its speed in different parts of the country. *The Ancrene Riwle*, about 1200, is written in a cultured English for ladies whose natural language was English, though they could read French. They did not know Latin, though the English author of the book is thoroughly at home in it. The group of gentry living in Herefordshire who spoke and some of whom wrote this provincial but by no means uneducated English maintained many English words from Old English times. The author of *The Acrene Riwle* uses *bichearren* ('deceive'), *eadmodnesse* ('humility'), *forbisne* ('example'), and many others for which our modern French-derived equivalents were sooner or later substituted. But he also uses very many French words, sometimes for the first time in written records that survive. Up to the mid-thirteenth century some 900 words were drawn from that version of Norman French which is now better called Anglo-Norman. The largest number concern *religion*, itself a borrowing (though in a meaning rather different from the present one, as is so often the case), and others like *baptism, communion, prayer*. The language of *administration* and *government* early *acquired* many words from French – *foreste, tur* (tower), *market, rent, justise* (meaning punishment for wrongdoing). *Political* words like *people*, and *social* and *ethical* words like *courteous, noble, honour* and *glory* were early borrowings. So also the *language* of *war* (though this word itself had originally been borrowed by French from Germanic), and of *peace*. Many legal words, like *tort*, were taken from French, though *law* happens to be Old English of Scandinavian origin).

Anglo-Norman became during the thirteenth century a provincial dialect differing considerably from continental Central French, though it developed a characteristic and impressive literature. A new influx of Central French influence came in during the thirteenth century with a wave of French-speaking Frenchmen (to whom, it was complained, the best jobs went). Central French retained its prestige but, from the beginning of the fourteenth century at the latest Anglo-Norman retreated as an alternative vernacular in England. Froissart tells us that Edward's eldest son, the Black Prince, when governor of Aquitaine in the 1370s, spoke

French to his French barons and English to his English barons. This would suggest that he was bilingual, but they were not, and that he spoke Central French.

The English language adopted and adapted French and to a lesser extent Latin words particularly vigorously in the fourteenth century, and the extensive growth of Anglicised loan words in the medieval period was crucial to the creation of the modern remarkably copious and heterogeneous English vocabulary. The French words are normally of ultimately Latin origin and thus French and Latin may be considered jointly as the Romance element in the English vocabulary, as distinct from the Germanic element represented by Old English, Scandinavian and some other minor elements. The large-scale adoption into English of French words which were originally Latin in turn made it easier to adopt Latin words direct into English. For this reason English has a much larger Romance element than German, Dutch or the Scandinavian languages. This has in turn affected later word-formation and the various registers of style in tone and meaning. An unfortunate effect of such extensive borrowing is a wide potential gap between educated and uneducated speakers which is unusual in European languages. An advantage of the medieval borrowing has been the later ease of adoption of huge numbers of scientific words based on Latin and, later, on Greek in the modern language. While many short and concrete English words are of Romance origin, it remains true that the Romance element in English usually represents the more elaborate, ornate, intellectual, often abstract aspects of English tone and meaning. The obvious examples are the gross English equivalents for physical functions expressed more *decorously* (from Latin) than *forcefully* (from a French stem with an English suffix) or *strongly* (English). We owe to French many of the words we use to name or classify people, their temperaments, rank and status; to manage finance, business, commerce and property; to administer government and the law; to conduct social life; to practise religion, science, art and sport. To sum up the growth of the English vocabulary, consider Chaucer's line, put in the mouth of Criseyde, spoken by her to Troilus:

> Welcome, my knyght, my pees, my suffisance. [III, 1309]

Welcome my knyght are all original English words, though *knyght,* from Old English, *cniht,* 'boy', has developed so as to connote a vast structure of concepts and feelings under French social and military influence (which we usually describe by the French derived word, *chivalry*). *Peace* is one of the earliest words recorded as borrowed from French after the Conquest, displacing English, *grith. Suffisance,* a grand, rather abstract word for 'satisfaction' is (like *satisfaction*) another French word, borrowed in the fourteenth century and rather a favourite of Chaucer's.

The fourteenth-century progress of English against French

In the fourteenth century the English language made progress in education, politics, learning and social status. In the thirteenth century such schools as there were had used French as the language of instruction, and this is commented on by Ranulph Higden in his Latin chronicle, *Polychronicon* (*c.* 1327). He remarks that this is bad for English and also that French has great snob-value. Higden's chronicle was translated into English in about 1385 by John Trevisa, in itself a significant act. Trevisa adds the comment that after the great plague of 1348–9 first John Cornwall then, following him, Richard Pencrich, two schoolmasters, began to teach grammar in English, so that in 1385 all the grammar schools in England were doing the same, to the benefit of learning grammar, and to the detriment of the knowledge of French. This illustrates the dilemma. It is vital to have one's own culture in one's own vernacular. But ignorance of foreign languages deprives one of the knowledge of international culture. In 1362 the Chancellor opened Parliament for the first time in English, though later openings for a time seem to have reverted to French. A statute was passed in the same year ordering that certain law-court proceedings were to be conducted in English, though what became the highly technical and rather quaint dialect of law-French long kept its grip on the law, and the marks are visible to this day, even in the United States.

French thus waned steadily throughout the fourteenth century and even developed a snobbery within the language, whereby speakers of Central Parisian French (like, presumably, the much travelled courtier Chaucer) sneered at those who only spoke home-bred Anglo-Norman, such as Chaucer's would-be courtly, social-climbing Prioress:

> And Frenssh she spak ful faire and fetisly   neatly
> After the scole of Stratford attė Bowe,
> For Frenssh of Parys was to hire unknowe. [*CT* I, 124–6]

That Chaucer wrote his poems in English is enough to establish the fact that by his time it was the natural language not only of the people and of learned men but of the highest social levels in the land, Richard II's own court. Richard was bilingual, like his father, the Black Prince. His successor, Henry IV knew Latin well, besides French, but English was his native tongue. So English had almost fully re-established itself at all levels of society for all purposes where French had encroached, by the end of the fourteenth century, though Chaucer in his *Troilus* (V, 1793–4) complains about the absence of that written standard which would slowly emerge in the fifteenth century.

The direct relation of Latin to English

The *direct* relation of Latin to English (as opposed to its effect through French) is intellectually and socially different from the direct influence of French. Writings in Latin were far more important than those in French, but no social stigma attached to ignorance of them. Ignorance of Latin was at all times common in all classes, and many of the clergy were also grossly ignorant. But Latin was the language of religion. Religion dominated all aspects of life and was not yet fragmented as it is with us today into many separate and specialised spiritual, scientific, political and literary segments. Latin was the storehouse and the implement of all these highly important concerns. It comprised the treasure-house of the achievements of classical antiquity, which were practical as well as literary, including such subjects as the art of war, architecture and agriculture. The most obvious way of advance for civilisation in the Middle Ages was to learn from classical antiquity, and Latin was the vital instrument. Even the Greek works of Aristotle, mediated through Arab sources, were available only in Latin. From the twelfth century onwards Europe (including England) itself added to the resources of Classical Latin its own intellectual and literary achievements, all of them in Latin. The work of the great universities at Paris, Bologna, Salerno, Oxford and elsewhere, was carried out in Latin, and their aim was to make Latin not only the subject and instrument of learning, but also of normal conversation. Even if relatively few scholars achieved the latter, Latin provided an international learned *lingua franca*. Medieval Latin was a developing language that was capable of supporting and extending contemporary knowledge and desires. It produced many new words developed but different from Classical Latin. From scholastic theology and science came, to give only a couple of examples, *quality* and *quantity*, which were still questioned as barbarous neologisms in English in the sixteenth century. Thus Latin developed in itself but also fed the vernaculars. Some European vernaculars were themselves developed from dialects of popular spoken Classical Latin – the Romance languages, French, Italian, Spanish. The very existence of these illustrates the centrifugal pressure on Latin, as on any world-language, such as English today. Diffusion leads to dilution. Variation, which is development and response to new social and intellectual pressures, makes the language differ from its earlier stages, but also fragments the living language itself. Two incompatible tendencies show themselves. From the twelfth century, especially, as education and culture improved, more people were able to learn Latin better and achieve the natural norm of the elaborate language of classical antiquity. But as they achieved it, so the actual living Latin instrument diverged further from the classical norm by natural development, by fragmentation, and by the increasing numbers who used Latin badly, imprecisely and in what seemed a slovenly mixture of various vernaculars. European Latin seemed to be becoming at the same time better and worse.

The consequences of this two-fold development for European and English language, literature and culture were profound; and they affect our whole conception of the Middle Ages. More immediately, in relation especially to the development of the English vocabulary, there was a modest direct inflow of words from Latin in the earlier medieval centuries, difficult to assess because of the influence of French. In Langland and Chaucer appear the first characteristic English jokes about the incapacity of the uneducated to understand words of Latin or French derivation: Langland's Avarice comically misunderstands 'restitution' (B-Text v, 232-9). Avarice says apologetically that he never learned to read a book, and the only French he knows is that of the farthest end of Norfolk. In *The Canterbury Tales* the Shipman, who says he has 'little Latin in his maw', uses the nonsense-word *phislyas* (for Latin *physices*), and the Host, who often swears 'by corpus bones', invents *cardinacle* and *galiones*. In the fifteenth century we note, especially in Lydgate and in Scottish poetry, the phenomenon of 'aureate language', whose polysyllables derive direct from Latin. In each case medieval, normally ecclesiastical, Latin is the source. Medieval Latin style in the fifteenth century developed a florid elaboration, *venustas florida verborum* ('a flowery beauty of words'), and English in certain circumstances follows suit. The style reveals both the imitativeness and the confidence of the vernacular. Signs of it appear in Chaucer; in Lydgate it is often excessive; it runs mad in Dunbar at times out of sheer exuberance.

> Imperiall wall, place palestrall
> Of pierles pulcritud.
> ['Ane Ballat of Our Lady' in Kinsley (ed.), *Poems of Dunbar* (Oxford: Clarendon Press, 1980), p. 6]

Caxton in a prologue can be laced in stiff gold. But some of the words became familiar, like *aureate* itself, which is first recorded as used (not surprisingly) by Lydgate himself about 1420.

Fifteenth-century English: a summary

Once English was established as the dominant language, its progress throughout the fifteenth century, though varied and remarkable in detail, followed a course already set out, and can only be even more summarily suggested. Any historical grammar will demonstrate the mass of detailed change that continued throughout the period, but as far as sounds are concerned two major points may be made. First, the pronunciation of final *-e* representing an earlier full inflexion disappeared. Second, a number of long vowels became diphthongized, that is, vowels in, say Chaucer, which are for the most part 'pure' (single sounds), as in modern French, German and Italian, became as it were doubled by Shakespeare's time, and have remained so. This is why Modern English is a more difficult language in which to sing than modern French, German, Italian and other Continental languages: it is impossible to hold a note for any time on a diphthong. For example the word *time* itself was pronounced by Chaucer like *teem*. However long the central vowel is held it remains the same. In modern English however, if extended, it becomes something like *ah-ee*. Shakespeare's pronunciation was between the two and might have sounded comically rustic to us, but it was closer to us than to Chaucer. Middle English has a 'purer' bell-like clarity of vowel-sound (as has Italian and the other Continental languages) than Modern English. Chaucer's pronunciation sounds more beautiful than Modern English, but the relative absence of diphthongs and the presence of final *-e* put it on the other side of the hill for us, and makes tolerable modernisation, as opposed to translation, almost impossible, in contrast to the more fortunate Shakespeare, whose language and spelling can be modernised with less loss. Besides these fundamental changes developments in vocabulary and syntax are less disruptive though they may be more obvious.

With the rapidly developing written standard the changes in spelling become fewer. It is still possible to find poorly written manuscripts in the late fifteenth century where the same word is spelt four different ways in two lines, and private orthography remained eccentric throughout the sixteenth century, so that even Shakespeare's six signatures are each spelt differently (and none in the modern form). Nevertheless Caxton was able to select an effective London standard, to choose to print *eggs* not *eyren*, and apart from minor variants and the consonantal use of *u* and *i* Modern English spelling may be said to begin about 1500, being essentially a fifteenth-century rationalisation of earlier practice.

The vocabulary continued to develop with the accretion of French and Latin words. Many of these were elaborate and strange, and the poets in particular, but also other writers seeking a 'high' style, embellished their works with 'aureate eloquence'. Examples have been given earlier of such words, known in the sixteenth century as 'inkhorn terms'. As influential and harder to analyse, was the development of subtler aspects of language, of syntax and style. A huge amount of translation took place. Sometimes the very literalness of the translation introduced more elaborate, or more effective, syntax and style, but more often, as with Caxton, it was clumsy. Some French writings now offered a valuable model. Even without models a great deal of workmanlike or even elaborate prose was written, for example in sermons where one can detect, as in the use of 'doublets' (two words where one might do), the development of a style at that time clumsy, but which flowered in Cranmer's prose and Shakespeare's verse. The device of coupling one native English word with one Romance word was often effective and is found in English centuries later. But beside this was also developed a flexible command of colloquial English idiom, in verse in the best of the miracle-plays, and in much prose, most notably in Malory, where the dialogue speaks to us with vivid directness across the centuries. No century which could produce so great a prose as Malory's can be accused of lack of achievement.

Malory's achievement was in a sense translation, but he achieved rather a total transposition of the rhetorically elaborate French into his own more direct and miraculously musical style, which owes something to native chronicle simplicity and something perhaps to pulpit earnestness. He represents the acme of translation in the secular field, and to conclude this chapter we may cast an eye over translation, especially of the Bible, as an index of the development particularly of the literary language.

Translation

Translation had begun in Old English and struggled on through later centuries. One of its oddest manifestations was the work of an Augustinian canon called Orm, who wrote in the north-east Midlands around 1200. He wished to provide a translation of the Gospels as read at Mass, with commentary, and he devised his own spelling system. He addresses his brother Walter, saying he has done the work, as requested, for English folk:

> Nu brotherr Wallterr, brotherr min, affterr the fleshess kinde
> Annd brotherr min i Crisstendom thurrh fulluhht annd thurrh trowwthe. [1–2]

The odd though rational spelling and the intolerable verbosity of the work, called, by the only flash of wit in 20,000 lines, the *Ormulum*, made it unreadable from the first. Only the author's own manuscript survives, or probably ever existed, a lonely paradise for philologists (Bodleian Library Junius MS 32). A considerable flow of other partial translations and paraphrases of the Bible came in the thirteenth century as a result of the educational and missionary initiatives of the Lateran Council of 1215. But education always creates problems. A laity better educated in its own vernacular began to entertain its own opinions which might differ from those of its pastors and masters. The appetite grew by what it fed on. Unfortunately medieval churchmen, with a very few notable exceptions like Wycliffe and his follower, the Czech Hus (who was burnt for his opinions) had come to identify the universal Christian message with the Latin language which had so long been vital to Christianity in Western Europe, and which was almost entirely the prerogative of the clergy and of the learned men in the universities. The ecclesiastical authorities refused to allow the continuation of that process of translation which they themselves had instigated when it came to the full text of scripture, some of the consequences of which have already been explained. In contrast, Lollardy was at the heart of Englishness when it demanded that the Bible, the citadel of the international official culture, should fall to the vernacular. The author of what is known as Henry Knighton's Chronicle wrote, around 1420, in Latin:

> This Master John Wyclif translated from Latin into English – the Angle not the angel speech – the Gospel that Christ gave to the clergy and learned men of the Church . . . so that by his means it has become vulgar and more open to laymen and women who can read than it usually is to quite learned clergy of good intelligence. And so the pearl of the Gospel is scattered abroad and trodden underfoot by swine.
> [Adapted from G. W. H. Lampe (ed.), *The Cambridge History of the Bible* (Cambridge: C.U.P., 1969, p. 388]

The desire for a full literal translation of the Bible, seen most fully in the Wycliffite versions, and the resistance to it, built up through the fourteenth and fifteenth centuries till the dam burst at the Reformation.

Translation both religious and secular had always supplemented and strengthened the mother-tongue which had never been displaced from the centre of the hearts and minds of the English people as a whole, even when its range had been severely contracted. The vernacular was never budged from that central realm of personal relationships where literature is especially at home, and where so much religious feeling is rooted. The simplest but not the least important expressions of religion were always in English for those who knew neither French or Latin. Much oral 'literature' in English, both religious and secular, must have been lost. The vernacular inevitably throughout the medieval period extended its range through the higher levels of literacy and of artistic and intellectual achievement. It borrowed capacity from the Latin and French usurpers until it rivalled and overcame them. General literary culture in English, based on education, made great leaps forward. By the end of the fifteenth century there was still some way to go. Latin, though doomed, retained its grip on the official Bible, on theology and on science, though there was much good translation. Nevertheless, English literary culture was safely and firmly established in England, though still to need its martyrs in the sixteenth. Soon it would fertilise all areas of national life, from the lowest to the highest practical and spiritual levels.

Artistic achievements are only indirectly related to such progress. Around 1200 works of literary art, both religious and secular, of very high quality were produced, but with the exception of Malory's masterpiece in the fifteenth century the height of medieval artistic literary achievement in English was in that remarkable second half of the fourteenth century, whose masterpieces still speak directly to us, if we will listen.

Further reading

General

Books quoted from or referred to in the text are not normally listed again here. No attempt is made to do other than give preliminary suggestions for further reading, which are amplified in the books mentioned. Where no place of publication is noted, it is London.

The major bibliographical guides are G. Watson (ed.), *The New Cambridge Bibliography of English Literature, Volume I 600–1660* (Cambridge: C.U.P., 1974); and *A Manual of the Writings in Middle English 1050–1500*, vol. I (New Haven, Conn.: Connecticut Academy of Arts and Sciences, 1967), and succeeding volumes.

Amongst anthologies to be noted are C. W. Dunn and E. T. Byrnes (eds.), *Middle English Literature* (New York: Harcourt, Brace, Jovanovich, 1973); J. A. W. Bennett, G. V. Smithers and N. Davis (eds.), *Early Middle English Verse and Prose* (Oxford: Clarendon Press, 1966); K. Sisam (ed.), *Fourteenth Century Verse and Prose* (Oxford: Clarendon Press, 1921).

Amongst many surveys of medieval English literature see 'The Sphere History of Literature in the English Language', vol. I, W. F. Bolton (ed.), *The Middle Ages* (Sphere, 1970); J. A. Burrow, *Ricardian Poetry*, (Routledge & Kegan Paul 1971); Derek Pearsall, *Old English and Middle English Poetry* (Routledge & Kegan Paul, 1977); 'The New Pelican Guide to English Literature', vol. I, B. Ford (ed.), *Medieval Literature: Part One: Chaucer and the Alliterative Tradition.* (Harmondsworth: Penguin, 1982).

For Arthurian matters see R. S. Loomis (ed.), *Arthurian Literature in the Middle Ages* (Oxford: Clarendon Press, 1959); *The Arthurian Bibliography:* I *Author Listing;* II *Index;* C. E. Pickford (ed.) and R. W. Last (Arthurian Studies iii and iv Cambridge: D. S. Brewer, 1981, 1982).

For background on literacy and mentality see M. T. Clanchy, *From Memory to Written Record: England 1066–1307* (Edward Arnold, 1979); A. Murray, *Reason and Society in the Middle Ages* (Oxford: Clarendon Press, 1978).

On Layamon's *Brut* see A. Ringbom, *Studies in the Narrative Technique of Beowulf and Lawman's Brut,* Acta Academica Aboensis Humaniore, ser A 36, 1968.

Amongst many books on short poems see Peter Dronke, *The Medieval Lyric* (Hutchinson, 1968); B. H. Bronson, *The Ballad as Song* (Berkeley and Los Angeles: University of California Press, 1969).

For an anthology of romances see A. V. C. Schmidt and N. Jacobs (eds.), *Medieval English Romances*, 2 vols. (Hodder & Stoughton, 1980). See the studies by D. Mehl, *The Middle English Romances of the Thirteenth and Fourteenth Centuries* (Routledge & Kegan Paul, 1968); John Stevens, *Medieval Romance* (Hutchinson 1973); and for some controversial interpretations, Derek Brewer, *Symbolic Stories* (Cambridge: D. S. Brewer, 1980).

Works on Chaucer are legion. For introductions to life, surveys, background and bibliography see Derek Brewer, *Chaucer*, 3rd edn. (Longmans, 1973); Derek Brewer (ed.), *Chaucer: Writers and their Background* (Bell and Hyman, 1974); Derek Brewer, *Chaucer and his World* (Eyre Methuen, 1978); Derek Brewer (ed.), *Chaucer: The Critical Heritage* (Routledge & Kegan Paul, 1978). See also C. Muscatine, *Chaucer and the French Tradition* (Berkeley and Los Angeles: University of California Press, 1957); Jill Mann, *Chaucer and Medieval Estates Satire* (Cambridge: C.U.P., 1973). For text, beside Robinson *Works*, 2nd edn. (O.U.P., 1957), see J. H. Fisher (ed.), *The Complete Poetry and Prose of Geoffrey Chaucer* (New York: Holt, Rinehart, Winston, 1977) with recent bibliography.

For Chaucer's friends and followers see J. H. Fisher, *John Gower* (Methuen, 1965); Derek Pearsall, *John Lydgate* (Routledge & Kegan Paul, 1970); Jerome Mitchell, *Thomas Hoccleve* (Chicago: University of Illinois Press, 1968); V. J. Scattergood (ed.), *The Works of Sir John Clanvowe* (Cambridge: D. S. Brewer, 1975); J. MacQueen, *Robert Henryson* (Oxford: Clarendon Press, 1967); J. W. Baxter, *William Dunbar* (Edinburgh: Oliver & Boyd, 1952).

On alliterative poetry see T. Turville-Petre, *The Alliterative Revival* (Cambridge: D. S. Brewer 1977); K. H. Göller (ed.), *The Alliterative Morte Arthure* (Arthurian Studies ii) (Cambridge: D. S. Brewer 1981).

Among many books on the *Gawain*-poet, see A.C. Spearing, *The Gawain-Poet* (Cambridge: C.U.P., 1970); J. A. Burrow, *A Reading of Sir Gawain and the Green Knight* (Routledge & Kegan Paul, 1965); L. D. Benson, *Art and Tradition in Sir Gawain and the Green Knight* (New Brunswick, N.J.: Rutgers University Press, 1965); W. A. Davenport, *The Art of the Gawain-Poet* (Athlone Press, 1978); P. M. Kean, *The Pearl* (Routledge & Kegan Paul, 1967); I. Bishop, *Pearl in its Setting* (Oxford: Clarendon Press, 1968); C. Morse, *The Pattern of Judgment in the Queste and Cleanness* (Columbia: University of Missouri Press, 1978); E. Brewer (transl.), *From Cuchulain to Gawain: Sources and Analogues of Sir Gawain and the Green Knight* (Cambridge: D. S. Brewer, 1973); on 'cleanness' see Mary Douglas, *Purity and Danger: An Analysis of Concepts of Pollution and Taboo* (Routledge and Kegan Paul, 1966).

For *Piers Plowman*, see E. T. Donaldson, *Piers Plowman; The C-text and its Poet* (New Haven, Conn.: Yale Studies in English 113, 1949); Morton W. Bloomfield, *Piers Plowman as Fourteenth-Century Apocalypse* (New Brunswick, N.J.: Rutgers University Press, (1962)); G. Kane, *Piers Plowman: The Evidence for Authorship* (Athlone Press, 1965); S. S. Hussey (ed.), *Piers Plowman; Critical Approaches* (Methuen, 1969); Elizabeth D. Kirk, *The Dream Thought of Piers Plowman* (New Haven, Conn. Yale U.P., 1972). On allegory see J. MacQueen, *Allegory* (Edward Arnold, 1970); M. W. Bloomfield, *Essays and Explorations* (Cambridge Mass.: Harvard U.P., 1971) (also on many other medieval literary topics); Pamela Gradon, *Form and Style in Early English Literature* (Methuen, 1971) (also on many other topics).

For drama see the now antiquated E. K. Chambers, *The Medieval Stage*, 2 vols (Oxford: Clarendon Press, 1903); Glynne Wickham, *Early English Stages 1300 to 1660,* vol. I (1300 to 1576) (Routledge & Kegan Paul, 1959); V. A. Kolve, *The Play Called Corpus Christi* (Edward Arnold, 1966); Rosemary Woolf, *The English Mystery Plays* (Oxford: Clarendon Press, 1972); S. J. Kahrl, *Traditions of Medieval English Drama* (Hutchinson, 1974); Richard Axton, *European Drama of the Early Middle Ages* (Hutchinson, 1974); W. A. Davenport, *Fifteenth-Century English Drama* (Cambridge: D. S. Brewer, 1982).

On religious prose see the anthologies, W. Matthews, *Later Medieval English Prose* (Peter Owen, 1964); N. F. Blake (ed.), *Middle English Religious Prose* (Edward Arnold, 1972). See studies by P. Hodgson, *Three 14th-Century English Mystics* (Longman, 1967); W. Riehle, *The Middle English Mystics,* transl. B. Stendring (Routledge and Kegan Paul, 1981). For Lollardry see Anne Hudson (ed.), *Selections from English Wycliffite Writings* (Cambridge: C.U.P., 1978); K. B. MacFarlane, *Lancastrian Kings and Lollard Knights* (Oxford: Clarendon Press, 1972); M. Deanesly, *The Lollard Bible and Other Medieval Biblical Versions* (Cambridge: C.U.P., 1920).

Secular prose is also illustrated by W. Matthews, *Later Medieval English Prose* (Peter Owen, 1964); the best survey is in H. S. Bennett, *Chaucer and the Fifteenth Century* (Oxford: Clarendon Press, 1947). For Malory see Derek Brewer (ed.), 'Introduction', *The Morte Darthur Parts Seven and Eight* (Edward Arnold, 1968); Mark Lambert, *Malory: Style and Vision in Le Morte Darthur* (New Haven, Conn.: Yale U.P., 1975); L. D. Benson, *Malory's Morte Darthur* (Cambridge, Mass.: Yale U.P., 1976); T. Takamiya and Derek Brewer (eds.), *Aspects of Malory* (Arthurian Studies i) (Cambridge: D. S. Brewer, 1981); Derek Brewer, 'Malory and the Archaic Mind', *Arthurian Literature I,* Richard Barber (ed.) (Cambridge: D. S. Brewer, 1981), pp. 94–120. For Caxton see N. F. Blake, *Caxton and his World* (Andre Deutsch, 1969); *William Caxton: An Exhibition to Commemorate the Quincentenary of the Introduction of Printing into England* (London: British Museum Publications, 1976).

Amongst many histories of the English language may be noted A. C. Baugh, *A History of the English Language,* rev. edn. (Routledge & Kegan Paul, 1959); B. M. H. Strang, *A History of English* (Edward Arnold, 1970). The story of Lithulf is found in *Materials for the History of Thomas Beckett* (Rolls Series I, 128), noted by G. E. Woodbine, 'The Language of English Law', *Speculum XVIII* (1943), 395–436. For manuscripts and styles of script see A. G. Petti, *English Literary Hands from Chaucer to Dryden* (Edward Arnold, 1977).

Chronological table

DATE	LITERARY EVENTS	OTHER EVENTS
1066		The Norman Conquest
		William I crowned
1087		William (Rufus) II
1100	Play of Saint Catherine at Dunstable	Henry I crowned
c. 1135	Geoffrey of Monmouth's *History of the Kings of Britain* in Latin	
c. 1135		Stephen crowned
c. 1150	*Mystère d'Adam*	
1154		Henry II crowned
c 1157	Final entries in Peterborough Chronicle	
1170		'Young King Henry' crowned in father's lifetime
c. 1175	*The Owl and the Nightingale*	
c. 1180	Play of *La Seinte Resurecion*	
1183		'Young King Henry' (*d.*)
1189		Richard I crowned
1199		John crowned
c. 1200	Layamon's *Brut*	
	The Katherine group of tracts	
	The Ancrene Riwle/Wisse	
	Vices and Virtues	
1215–16		Fourth Lateran Council
1216		Henry III crowned

DATE	LITERARY EVENTS	OTHER EVENTS
1236–44		Grosseteste's *Decretals* (forbidding clergy to take part in plays)
c. 1250	*The Love Rune*	
	King Horn	
1264		Institution of Feast of Corpus Christi
1272		Edward I crowned
c. 1275	*Dame Sirith*	
	Interludium de Clerico et Puella	
	The Fox and the Wolf	
	The Lay of Havelok	
	Floris and Blancheflur	
1281		Archbishop Pecham's Lambeth Canons
c. 1290	*The Cambridge Prologue*	
c. 1300	French poet Machaut (*b.*)	
	Richard Rolle (*b.*)	
	Sir Orfeo	
	Harley Lyrics	
1304	Petrarch (*b.*)	
1307		Edward II crowned
c. 1313	Boccaccio (*b.*)	
c. 1320	Wycliffe (*b.*)	
1321	Dante (*d.*)	
1326	Trevisa (*b.*)	
1327		Edward II deposed and murdered
		Edward III crowned
c. 1330	Gower (*b.*)	
	Guy of Warwick	
	Bevis of Hampton	
1337		Beginning of 'Hundred Years' War'
1340	Ayenbite of Inwit	
c. 1340	Chaucer (*b.*)	

DATE	LITERARY EVENTS	OTHER EVENTS
1342	Julian of Norwich (*b.*)	
1346		Victory of Crecy
1348–9		The Black Death
1348–58	Boccaccio's *Decameron*	
1349	Richard Rolle (*d.*)	
c. 1350	*The Pride of Life*	
	The Shrewsbury Fragment	
	Ludus Filiorum Israelis	
	Wynnere and Wastoure	
	Joseph of Arimathie	
c. 1355	*William of Palerne*	
1356		Victory of Poitiers
1357	John Gaytryge's Sermon	
c. 1360	The *Morte Arthure* (alliterative)	
	The Parlement of the Thre Ages	
	First version (A-text) of *Piers Plowman*	
1360		Treaty of Bretigni
1365–71	'Mandeville's' *Travels* written in French	
1368	Chaucer's *Book of the Duchess*	
1369		War with France renewed
c. 1370	Lydgate (*b.*)	
	Hoccleve (*b.*)	
1373	Julian of Norwich's 'showings'	
c. 1373	Margery Kempe (*b.*)	
1374	Petrarch (*d.*)	
1374–80	Chaucer's *House of Fame*	
1375	Boccaccio (*d.*)	

DATE	LITERARY EVENTS	OTHER EVENTS
1375	Barbour's *Bruce*	
c. 1375	Short text of Julian's *Showings* *Destruction of Troy* *Sir Gawain and the Green Knight* *Pearl, Cleanness, Patience*	
1377	Machaut (*d.*)	Edward III (*d.*) Richard II crowned
c. 1377	Second Version (B-text) of *Piers Plowman*	
1378	Wycliffe refers to *Paternoster Play* at York	Beginning of Great Schism of the Church (two rival popes, one in Avignon, one in Rome)
c. 1380	*The Cloud of Unknowing* Hilton's *The Scale of Perfection* Hilton's *The Mixed Life* Translation of 'Mandeville's' *Travels* Trevisa's translation of Higden's *Polychronicon* Hereford's first Lollard translation of the Bible Sir John Clanvowe's *The Two Ways*	
1381		The Peasants' Revolt
1382	Chaucer's *Parliament of Fowls*	Richard marries Anne of Bohemia Lollardry in Oxford University suppressed
1382–5	Chaucer's *Boece, Troilus and Criseyde, Palamon and Arcite (The Knight's Tale)*	
1385–6	Chaucer's *Legend of Good Women*	
1386–90	Gower's *Confessio Amantis*	

DATE	LITERARY EVENTS	OTHER EVENTS
1469–70	Malory completes *Le Morte Darthur*	
1470		Henry VI reinstated
1471	Malory (*d.*)	Henry VI deposed and murdered Edward IV crowned
1475	Caxton prints and publishes *The Recuyell of the Historyes of Troye* at Bruges	
1476	Caxton sets up his press at Westminster	
1478	Sir Thomas More (*b.*)	
1483	Caxton prints and publishes *The Golden Legend*	Edward V crowned Richard III crowned
1485	Caxton prints and publishes Malory's *Le Morte Darthur*	Henry VII crowned
1491	Caxton (*d.*)	
1492		Columbus discovers West Indies
c. 1495	Medwall's *Nature*	
1497	Medwall's *Fulgens and Lucrece*	Cabot discovers American mainland

Index